ALBERTA LABOUR

Alberta Labour

A HERITAGE UNTOLD

WARREN CARAGATA

James Lorimer & Company, Publishers
Toronto, 1979

ISBN 0-88862-264-3 cloth

Design: Brant Cowie

6   5   4   3   2   1   79   80   81   82   83   84   85

Canadian Cataloguing in Publication Data
Caragata, Warren, 1950-
    Alberta labour

Bibliography: p.
Includes index.
ISBN 0-88862-264-3

1. Trade-unions — Alberta —History. 2. Labor and laboring classes — Alberta — History. I. Title.
HD6529.A5C37   331.88'097123   C79-094479-0

Typeset by Eveready Printers Ltd.
Printed and bound by Hunter Rose

James Lorimer & Company, Publishers
Egerton Ryerson Memorial Building
35 Britain Street,
Toronto M5A 1R7, Ontario

Cover Photo: Public Archives of Canada (C-34438)
Glenbow-Alberta Institute: 7, 10, 14, 16, 25, 26, 27, 35, 38, 43, 44 (top), 46, 47, 50, 54, 57, 61, 62, 67, 75, 79, 80, 82, 84, 87, 90, 94, 96, 98, 99, 101, 103, 104, 106, 107, 113, 117, 118, 120, 122, 123, 125, 129, 134, 142
J. Matthews: 138
McDermid Studios: 72
Priere de Mentionner (National Photography Collection): 3, 8, 12, 21, 41, 42 (bottom), 56, 88, 100, 135
Provincial Archives of Alberta: 11, 22, 29, 30, 31, 34, 36, 48, 59, 66, 78, 91, 95, 109, 111, 115, 121, 131, 133, 137
Provincial Archives of Canada (E. Brown Collection): 17, 19, 23, 24, 28, 37, 39, 40, 42 (top), 44 (bottom), 45, 49, 52, 55, 64, 69, 73, 76, 85
Provincial Archives of Canada (H. Pollard Collection): 127
Public Archives of Canada: 33 (C-56689)
Public Archives of Manitoba: 4

Contents

Acknowledgements

This book could not have been written without the encouragement and support of three people: Maryhelen Vicars; Keith Reynolds and Linda Hughes. Somehow, they were able to enjoy many evenings listening to me talk about conditions in the coal mines at the turn of the century or fights between workers and the CPR. But more importantly, whenever I felt overburdened by the task in front of me, they would again convince me of the need and importance of telling a tale which most people have long forgotten.

That the entire project happened at all is due to large part to one man, Reg Basken, the president of the Alberta Federation of Labour when it was initiated. He had long felt that labour's story had not been told — that the conventional history of the province ignored the men and women — and children — who, in one way or another, gave their lives building it, and instead focused on business leaders and politicians who, in comparison, risked little.

The federation itself deserves considerable credit for undertaking such a project. It would have been all too easy to send someone to the archives for a week and leave it at that. But it decided that if the job was to be done, it should be done thoroughly. The federation, assisted by contributions from the federal Department of Labour and the Lethbridge Labour Club, gave generous financial support to this project and, in effect, did without the services of one staff member for about a year. They have given me a free hand in the writing, ensuring that the story would be told, warts and all.

The new president of the federation, Harry Kostiuk, has been no less a keen supporter than Reg Basken and to him and the other staff officers of the federation who have had to fill in for me — Gene Mitchell, Winston Gereluk and Ernie Clarke — I owe a considerable debt of gratitude. The other federation staff, Karen Mottershead, Felice Young, Linda Dragon, Carol Homes and Kathy Badry, have also had their workload increased because of my almost total involvement with this book and they too have given me the support needed to carry this thing through. My thanks as well to Jean McKinley who transcribed interviews and notes.

The financial burden of travelling across the country researching the book was eased in great measure by the willingness of people to share their homes with me: Keith Reynolds and Sharlene Hertz, Sharon and Gordon Rugg, Steve and Gail Caragata, Vicki Caragata and Liz Hughes.

My thanks to Nancy Stunden and John Smart at the Public Archives of Canada for showing me where to look; Fred Longley at the Department of Labour archives in Hull; George Brandak at the University of British Columbia Special Collections Library and Jean Dryden and Alan Ridge at the Alberta Archives in Edmonton; and to Irving Abella and Allen Seager in Toronto and David Bercuson in Calgary for discussing the project with me and offering me their kind advice.

The staff at James Lorimer and Company were a great help, in particular, Mark Czarnecki who managed, I think, to retain his sanity as he struggled to teach me how to write books.

The list could go on but the most important tribute must be paid to the many pioneers of the movement who willingly gave of their time to describe for me why trade unions were established in this province. Through them I have gained a lot of insight and, I hope, a few friends. This is their story.

As a final note, after the thanks have been offered, I must say that any errors of face or interpretation in the work are mine.

W.C.

Foreword

The absence of a trade union historical record for Alberta is obvious to anyone who has cared to look. It has somehow been expected that because we are a new province, everyone would be able to remember the efforts and struggles in the world of work that gave birth to our labour organizations.

The experiences of workers and their organizations in Alberta have not been unlike those in the rest of North America, but the fact that they were similar at all will be amazing to some. Many people feel Alberta has been an agricultural province and has therefore been without industrial action by workers. This book will help to change that image as it spells out the influence Alberta workers had on the rest of movement in Canada and on the governments that employers have counted on to control their labour forces when their own devices were ineffective.

It was a strike by Alberta coal miners in 1906 that moved the federal government to pass a key piece of labour legis-

lation; and strikes by miners and workers in other sectors of Alberta industry aided the career of William Lyon Mackenzie King. King went from mediating strikes in Alberta, and elsewhere across the country, to helping out John D. Rockefeller and his Standard Oil Empire during the First World War.

The involvement of police, not only in the "Hungry Thirties", but in almost every facet of labour union activity in Alberta, is underscored in the book and should underline the need for commissions like the MacDonald Royal Commission investigating the activities of the RCMP. Inevitably, police were involved on the side of the employer in every significant labour dispute in the history of the province.

For an intelligent viewpoint on where we're going, it is valuable to understand and realize where we've been. That's not to say that history should be viewed as a god but that history must be remembered as a guide. The often-heard and naive comment that "unions were necessary once but have now outlived their usefulness" points clearly to the requirement that we understand the roots of the labour movement and the factors that led to its organization.

We are fortunate that so many of the people mentioned in the book are still alive and have been available for consultation and research. Their opinions and understanding of the circumstances of the times are invaluable when it comes to presenting an accurate view of Alberta over the last hundred years.

Warren Caragata has done an excellent job of putting together what one could view as an unpopular history by today's standards, but to challenge that his history existed would be to deny the truth and rewrite history to make it popular. This cannot and has not been done.

Workers have strived to make their unions strong, aggressive and democratic. The struggle is evidenced primarily by the long and arduous battles of the United Mine Workers to become a strong organization in itself and to free itself of the corruption and lack of democracy that once existed in that union. Unions have multiplied and divided, seeking autonomy and strength in different directions. Still, as we enter the last two decades of this century, we find a continued vigour and determination to build and maintain the strength and democracy of the labour movement in Canada.

One of the struggles outlined in the book is the effort by trade unionists to involve their organizations in politics. Few realize the very political nature of unions, both in the past, and today. The adversary system we have demands political leadership by trade unionists because so many things that are needed to improve the lives of workers are determined by legislation and can't be left to the collective bargaining process. And, as we saw during the time of wage controls, those things that can be won at the bargaining table can always be taken away by legislation. Warren accurately describes the frustrations of people in the labour movement as they tried, and often failed, to use the avenues available under our democracy.

The organization, involvement and influence of the Communist Party will inevitably be viewed in the Eighties as part of the unpopular history of Alberta labour but the decisions of trade unionists to join the Communists were almost certainly the result of the desperate conditions that existed. Pete Youschok's comment: "I'm a communist when I'm broke; you give 90 percent of the men money, they're not going to be Communists are they?'' makes a serious point.

In all of this, there may be a lesson for those who believe in freedom and the brotherhood of man — as well as those who would rape the community in the narrow interest of immediate profit. Freedom is a hard-won thing and it is true, as the song says, that " . . . every generation must win it again." We cannot remain free politically for very long if we remain slaves industrially. This book emphasizes that struggle.

I am honoured to have been asked by the executive council of the Alberta Federation of Labour to write this foreword. I recommend to you that you read the book with a careful eye and a mind directed not only to the difficulties that we've had in the past but to the distance that we still have to go to build and maintain the freedom, equality and brotherhood that will make the world a better place to live.

Reg Basken

ALBERTA LABOUR

Laying track on the prairie. The CPR mainline reached Calgary in 1883.

CHAPTER ONE

The Railway and Early Organization: 1883-1899

The Mainline

Like most things on the Prairies, the labour movement in Alberta owes its birth to the CPR—that group of British-backed Montreal fianciers who, with considerable federal government help, built a railway tying central Canada to the Pacific.

Lord Strathcona and William Van Horne didn't do much of the construction work themselves and few of the dandies in Montreal and London who were backing the project knew how to fire a boiler—they handled the bond issues and the ceremonies and left the work of building and running their railway to others, keeping the expense as low as they could. That is how there came to be a labour movement in Alberta.

The myth of Canadian history is that the railway and Prime Minister John A. Macdonald's economic policies were government instruments to build a dominion "from sea to shining sea." In fact, Canada as a nation was an invention of the Montreal business community. The St. Lawrence capitalists had been fighting for some time to maintain themselves against the encroachment of their American rivals and Confederation and settlement of the West was to be their coup—the creation of a market that only they would be allowed to service. The three elements of Macdonald's National Policy: western settlement, a transcontinental railway and a tariff wall to protect the market, became instruments for survival and expansion of the St. Lawrence business class.

The original survey of the Canadian Pacific Railway was marked out along the traditional water transportation route in the West—up the North Saskatchewan River through the Battlefords and Edmonton—a line that made more sense than a southern route for several reasons. It would service an already existing pattern of settlement; it would pass through better agricultural land and avoid the near desert of the Maple Creek-Medicine Hat region; and it would go through the Yellowhead Pass, an easier passage through the Rockies than southern passes.[1] All the odds were stacked in favour of the northern route, with one important exception—the eastern Canadian merchant class wanted it built closer to the U.S. boundary to block any attempt by American business interests to siphon off trade from their market. The original survey was abandoned in favour of a more southern line.

The CPR was built to provide transport to and from the frontier—to carry in settlers and the manufactured goods they would require to tame the Prairie and to carry out grain and resouces. According to the 1884–1885 census, there were only sixty industrial establishments in the area that later became Alberta. Together they employed only 212 men and 3 women; the annual value of production amounted to less than $500,000. With the coming of the railway, all that changed. New industries, such as coal mining, grew up to service the railway and the incoming settlers needed homes and tools and food. But the vehicle for industrialization—the railway itself—became the first major industry in the Northwest Territories.

The 1881 census showed that in the part of the Northwest Territories which in 1905 became Alberta, there were only eighteen thousand people and most were natives. Railway construction workers had to be imported. Coming from abroad, the United States or eastern Canada and employed by sub-contractors hired by the CPR, the workers, or "navvies" as they were called, built Lord Strathcona a railway.

It was punishing, tough, physical work. With picks and shovels, buckets and horse-drawn scrapers, they levelled and built up the road-bed, then laid the tracks. The financiers who backed the project were handsomely rewarded; not so the navvies, who packed their own blankets or purchased them and other supplies at highly-inflated prices from company stores. They worked long hours for little pay and often lived in boxcars, crude bunkhouses or tents.

In the wilderness that was the Prairie the men were at the mercy of the sub-contractors. Hundreds of miles from anywhere and living in isolation, the navvies were more or less indentured to their employers. The bondage was reinforced by legislation and by the police. Much of working life at the time was regulated by ordinances known as Masters and Servants Acts which made it a crime for a workman to desert his employer. The Northwest Mounted Police, formed by the federal government to bring order to the Territories, scrupulously enforced the act and could always be relied upon to assist the contractors in putting down any disturbances among their employees. "During the building of the CPR mainline," said one historian, "the Mounted Police allowed nothing to interfere with the construction, even if it meant forcing down angry mobs of strikers single-handed."[2] In one phase of construction of the railway in Alberta, a Mountie reported that: "Construction work is going on satisfactorily on the whole, no trouble of any importance having occurred yet. This is true in great measure to good luck and the presence of the police."[3]

Any interruption in the completion of the railway was a blow to the Montreal merchant class and the politicians in Ottawa who had staked their political careers on the project. Both the Liberals and Conservatives were willing allies of the businessmen with their dreams of a new and vast market. Many, in fact, were more than allies. They were part of the merchant community based in Montreal. Sir John A. Macdonald was a founder of an insurance company; his chief lieutenant, Georges-Etienne Cartier, was connected with the Grand Trunk Railway, the transportation bastion of the St. Lawrence capitalists.[4] Construction of the railway was therefore backed by the full power of the new Canadian state. But despite police intervention and legislation binding the workers to the railway contractors, men did risk prosecution and jail terms for desertion as they carried out individual protests against brutal working and living conditions, and failure by their employers to pay them wages due, a frequent cause of dispute along the railway.

Individual rebellions were more common than mass revolt and there was good cause for it. Unskilled workers like the navvies were the forgotten of the North American working class, untouched and generally unwanted by the mainstream of the labour movement organized under the umbrella of the American Federation of Labour and its Canadian counterpart, the Trades and Labour Congress (TLC), both established in 1886. It was a time—and it would continue almost to the Second World War—when unions were formed to look after the interests of skilled workmen. However callous, there was a reason for the policy and it was simply that, at a time when industry in Canada was in its formative stages, even unions of skilled workers had a hard time surviving the constant depressions. With little cushion provided by a tiny industrial sector, depression often meant disaster even for the most solidly-organized and secure workers. The navvies were unskilled, transient and easily replaceable. As they were hit hardest and first when depression struck, they were considered a poor organizing risk by the likes of Samuel Gompers, the cigar maker and former socialist who, in large measure, organized and then ran the American Federation of Labour, and by the TLC. In addition, the conditions faced by the unskilled, and their fears and mistrust of the capitalist economic system which left them in such a precarious position in the labour market, made the navvies and other unskilled workers more receptive to the lure of

*Navvies building the railway. The established unions of the
day left the railway construction workers to their own devices.
Even without unions, spontaneous work stoppages occurred.*

socialism. Because the navvies had no organization behind them and faced the combined power of the country's
leading corporation and the politicians and Mounties who
were determined to see the mainline built at all cost, the
infrequent mass revolts that did occur were brief, spontaneous and easily put down.

In June, 1883, as the mainline neared Medicine Hat,
such a rebellion did take place. The dispute was centred at
a camp near Maple Creek, just inside the Saskatchewan
border, and it assumed more menacing proportions due to
additional unrest at a nearby Indian encampment. "A large
Indian camp near Maple Creek was in a very unsettled
state and about 130 railway workers had gone on strike
threatening a serious disturbance," said one account of the
dispute. More than 25 well-trained Mounted Police were
immediately dispatched from Regina to the scene. They
were commanded by Insp. Sam Steele, who proved his
mettle in this and later disputes as an effective strike-
breaker for the Canadian Pacific Railway. The account con-

tinued: "When the strike-leader assaulted the foreman, he
was arrested and imprisoned while other prompt steps
were taken to suppress revolt by his followers. The trouble
died down and Steele resumed his duties [as a magistrate]
along the railway from Moose Jaw to the end of the line."[5]

In that year, as the mainline was pushed across Alberta,
the Mounties were busy keeping the CPR's workforce
under control. An observer noted that the presence of a
strong police detachment in Calgary was a significant fac-
tor in quelling several "serious strikes on the part of dissatisfied workmen."[6]

One of those disputes involved not the navvies but the
aristrocracy of railway labour, the engineers and firemen,
the highly-skilled workmen who ran the trains. Their
specialized knowledge made it more difficult for the railways to ignore them and their demands and recruit
strike-breakers to take their places, but the CPR was not
above trying. The running trades, as they are called,
were usually backed by well-organized and financially-

A common sight on railway construction — a construction camp and Mounties. Members of the Mounted Police often helped the CPR keep its employees in line.

strong trade unions, but organization of the trades in Alberta and other parts of the Northwest Territories did not take place until 1886. In their 1883 contest with the CPR, the engineers and firemen, acting on their own, fared rather badly and again the Mounties came to the company's rescue.

The trades struck, said the *Calgary Herald,* when the CPR announced that wages would be cut. A posse of constables from the Calgary barracks was recruited by the CPR station agent to protect railway property after the discovery that several engines had been disabled by the "removal of a small piece of machinery by some person or persons unknown."[7] The result was that "Every engine along the line was under guard by the Mounties. . . . Only responsible employees were allowed access to railroad property. . . . What, for a time, threatened to be a general railway strike was completely quelled and the strikers finally returned to work at the rates originally proposed by the company."[8]

Two years after Sam Steele had put down the rising near Maple Creek, he was called on to turn his attention once more to the industrial relations difficulties of the CPR, this time in the mountains near Roger's Pass. There are two descriptions of this Beaver Creek strike, one in the *Calgary*

Herald of April 16, 1885, and the other in a book on the Mounted Police by John Peter Turner. The *Herald* said that accounts of the strike had been "much exaggerated" and that it had ended without violence. Turner, however, reported that during a brawl between the strikers and police and company officials, one of the strike leaders was shot in the shoulder by a policeman and that Steele then grabbed a Winchester rifle and warned that the first person who moved would be shot. The Riot Act was read and, Turner said, a number of the strikers were arrested and fined, or sentenced to six months hard labour.[9] Whatever the differences in the story, the fact remains that about five hundred navvies went on strike at Beaver Creek in early April, demanding that the company pay them the three months back wages owing them and that by mid-April, the paymaster had come up with the money.

The Northwest Mounted Police was a necessary part of the National Policy, making sure that railway workers and Indians did not disturb the dreams of the Montreal business class, but on occasion, even the men of the force became a concern for those who wanted an orderly and peaceful take-over by Montreal of the northern interior of the continent. September of 1883 found C Troop of the Northwest Mounted Police at the Macleod barracks in full revolt over a long list of grievances, including overwork, a ration of bread and beef with no substitutes for six months and meat "unfit for human consumption." At ten o'clock one morning, the troop fell in but refused to march off. Later, when church parade was sounded, the men ignored the call and walked to the chapel individually.

Most of the grievances leading to the refusal to work were resolved and there is no record of any disciplinary action being taken, as there was three years later when Mounties in Alberta again staged a strike over the same issue that later would lead Lethbridge policemen to turn in their uniforms. In February 1886, a young recruit who had enlisted at Edmonton during the Northwest rebellion was promoted over a number of men with longer service. The troop performed its regular duties but refused to take orders from the man who had been unjustly promoted. Headquarters in Regina was informed and a squad of twenty-five men under the assistant commissioner was sent to Edmonton to restore order at the fort. On arrival, the squad found that the promotion was not the only thing troubling the rebellious Mounties. Barracks were poorly constructed, overcrowded and infested with lice and bed bugs. The assistant commissioner persuaded the men to take the horses out of the post for some exercise and while they were away locked up the gun cases. When the ride returned, the troop was disarmed and the six leaders of the strike were dismissed from the force and given jail terms.[10]

The Crowsnest

About seven months after the 1885 Beaver Creek strike, construction on the mainline formally ended and attention turned to the building of branch lines to open up new areas for settlement and exploitation. A spur line was completed from Calgary to Lethbridge in 1885 which gave the CPR access to the coal fields in the area (and ownership of the major mines), but a more lucrative prize in the southwestern corner of the province lay waiting. The large coal fields of the Crowsnest Pass and the metal mining prospects of the adjacent Kootenay region of British Columbia were next to worthless without a transportation system that could bring the coal and lead, zinc and precious metals out of the hinterland. In 1897, aided in large measure by yet another subsidy from the federal government—in return for which the CPR agreed to reduce freight rates on certain articles (the Crow Rates)—and by land grants given out almost as a matter of course by the provincial government in British Columbia, the Canadian Pacific Railway began construction of a line from Lethbridge to Nelson, B.C.[11]

About 4,500 navvies were put to work bringing the Union Jack and the CPR into the Crowsnest and the Kootenays. The bulk of the workforce was made up of men from eastern Canada and conditions endured by the navvies were so brutal that, in some instances, even the Mounted Police, who were again placed at the disposal of the CPR to make sure the work proceeded as planned, were moved to sympathy. In the first year of construction in 1897, one Mounted Police officer reported to his superiors "what, if true, is a disgraceful way of employing men in the East. Some 100 men, chiefly French Canadians and axe men, have recently been employed and sent up by one Landry, from Ottawa, acting as agent for the CPR." The men hired testified that they were told they would not have to pay for their own blankets and that, in some cases, their railway fare to the West would be covered. The report went on: "Not one in 10 can read English and do not know the text of the contract they signed. And it is safe to say that one in five is physically unable to dump a scraper. . . . They naturally get into trouble and in a great many cases refuse to do work they did not engage to do and cannot do and then we are called upon to compel them or send them to jail." But the Mountie was bound to enforce the Masters and Servants Act and the report noted that about six men were in the guard room at Macleod "undergoing sentence for desertion or refusal to work."[12]

About a month later, the police inspector at Macleod, G.E. Saunders, sent a similar report to headquarters in Regina:

There is no doubt that a great number of these men would never have come out here had they known they had to pay their fare, which, from Ottawa here at a cent a mile, is $22.49. These men have families in the East and when they discover that, after working six weeks or two months, there is not a cent coming to them or, more probably, are in debt to the contractors, that they have no money to send their families and that they have nothing themselves, they as a rule leave that particular employer.

Saunders said the men wandered about destitute after leaving the camp:

. . . . without blankets or even boots in some cases. There are numbers of men who are totally unfit for the work and what will become of them during the winter is hard to surmise. . . . No provision has been made by the company for returning these men to their homes, winter is coming on and there is likelihood of much hardship and destitution. Some pressure ought to be brought to bear for fairer treatment of the men.[13]

The brutality of life on the Crowsnest line eventually forced the government to do what governments do best. Not one but two royal commissions were appointed, one in 1898 and another in 1899. Both commissions found that, if anything, police reports reaching Regina were understated. Some contractors, the first commission reported, prohibited their employees from talking on the job. The penalty for violation was dismissal. But the contractors could be even tougher. At one camp, said the Dugas commission in 1898, the men found out that food supplies were running out and that they might not be fed. Upset with this discovery, they stopped work. When Nash, the man in charge of the camp, returned and found his employees idle, he fired fifty-four of them and kicked them out of camp. It was about one hundred thirty miles to Macleod and civilization but Nash refused to give the men any food to sustain them en route. The men, making some unspecified threats, were able to "take what they could lay their hands on in the kitchen and which was sufficient to feed them for three meals." But Nash was not to be thwarted and he either "sent somebody ahead or went himself to give orders at the company's camps not to feed them on their way." Nash admitted to a police officer investigating the incident that his order was given to "teach the other men a lesson."[14]

A frequent cause of dispute was, as it had been on the mainline, the failure of contractors to pay the workers wages owed. In some cases examined by the commission, contractors just abandoned the camps and the men in them. At Wardner, just inside the B.C. border, several complaints were heard from men in a camp that they had not been paid for two months "although a settlement was promised to them every day." In such cases, the options open for the workers were few. The Mounties could come and arrest a navvie for deserting his contractor but there is no reference in the Dugas commission report of any contractor, having deserted a camp full of men and leaving them one hundred miles from Macleod with dwindling food supplies, being arrested and tossed into the guard house.

The only thing the workers could do if persuasion and complaints failed was go to Macleod and sue for back wages. In mid-October of 1897, up to one hundred men did just that. Their case was not a great success: "All or nearly all had to live upon public charity and suffered in many instances through hunger, cold and lack of proper clothing. Discouraged and disheartened they, at the end, consented to a compromise . . . by which they accepted a free pass to return home and five dollars each to buy provisions on the journey." In return the workers agreed to drop their lawsuits against the company.[15] At this point the CPR's construction manager stepped in and offered a slightly more lucrative settlement but one which would require them to continue working on the line. The men refused, several saying they had no further confidence in the company.

It would, in fact, be hard to have confidence in a company that, in mid-winter, housed its employees in unheated tents. The logistics of bringing in construction supplies were worked out, but somehow stoves for the tents didn't arrive until the beginning of January. Making matters worse was that after a long, hard and cold day's work, men would be served a frozen dinner. No stoves, no hot meals.

It happened that men, after quitting their work at six o'clock, would have to pitch their own tents on the frozen earth. The tents not being provided with stoves, the men's suffering was intensified by their clothes being wet, after working amidst snow and snow droppings from the trees and having no means of having them dried. A common result of this was suffering from rheumatism and colds.[16]

As might be expected of employers who didn't provide tents with stoves in December and January, neither were blankets provided. Men either brought their own from Ottawa or Hull or bought them on arrival, in most cases from a company store, for as much as $4.50 a pair with no guarantee they were new. In one case, reported the commission, about one hundred old blankets full of holes were sold, again at a cost of $4.50 a pair. Contractors admitted to the commission that their charges in company stores were from 20 to 40 percent profit. Boots were sold at double their cost and chewing tobacco, which cost the contractors twenty-two cents a plug, was sold to the men at thirty-five cents. Employees bought their own candles at from five to thirty times wholesale cost. Board cost five dollars a week and there were deductions for mail and medical care. For all this, the men laboured mightily for the CPR at wages of $1.50 to $1.75 a day. When weather or other conditions forced a delay in work, the pay stopped.

The Klute commission, established in 1899 to investigate the deaths of two men, Charles McDonald and E. McC. Fraser, found that after twelve days in camp, including sick days, Sundays and days of poor weather when no wages were paid, McDonald was owed $5.35, Fraser $6.35. Depending on the weather and whether a worker's health could stand living in a bunkhouse that one man described as more of a hospital, a worker doing his bit for the National Policy could end up, after nine months, out of pocket about twenty-two dollars, the Dugas commission said. Even when the commission allowed for twenty-six working days a month—a generous estimate—for one year at $1.75 a day, a railway construction worker might be able to clear and bring home to his waiting family in the East all of $115. To the charges for board and blankets, mail and medical service, had to be added transportation costs from Macleod to the camp and full fare back home.

Of all the deductions, the most galling must have been the charge for medical care. At the peak of construction, there were about forty-five hundred workers spread out along about three-hundred miles of near-wilderness and employed by about thirty firms. Five doctors, including the chief of medical staff, had the task of looking after them. The only hospitals were the four general hospitals along the entire line from Nelson to Lethbridge and a private boarding-house in the Crowsnest Pass which passed for a field hospital.

Klute wrote in the commission report in 1899 that:

.... the number of men working upon the road who became ill . . . is, I think, abnormally large. With particularly healthy climate and sufficient good food, how does

it happen that there should be in the neighborhood of 1,500 men requiring treatment in a total aggregate of from 2,000 to 4,000 and all within the space of less than a year?

There must have been an utter disregard for the simplest laws of health somewhere and I think it may be found in the lack of sanitary conditions in the camp. How is it possible that sickness could be avoided where 50 or 60 men occupy a bunkhouse, say 24 by 40 feet, with a seven-foot ceiling and no ventilation provided?[17]

On January 3, 1898, McDonald and Fraser were hired to work at a camp owned by Hugh Mann and James Kennedy eighty miles west of the end of steel (in what is now the Fernie area). They arrived that day and found a

A railway camp bunkhouse of the sort used during construction of the Crowsnest Pass line of the CPR.

camp of two bunkhouses with mud floors, each designed to accommodate sixty men. The diseases common to the navvies in the Crowsnest region were diphtheria, cough, mountain fever and rheumatism—Fraser and McDonald got diphtheria. On January 20, it was decided to send the two men in an open sleigh through to Bullhead and on to Crowsnest, where they could get an ambulance to take them to MacLeod. No attempt had been made to isolate them or send for a doctor. At Crowsnest, they were turned away from the boarding-house field hospital and returned to Bullhead to spend the night. The next night saw them still on their journey. Finally, in the afternoon of January 23, they reached Pincher Creek where they were put in a boxcar.

Four hours later, a doctor arrived to examine them. He was too late.

At one of the hearings held by the commission along the route, a navvy named Louis Fontaine described the camp where McDonald and Fraser had worked. Fontaine said he stayed there only one day. "It was not a healthy place and I left the next morning. I thought I could not stay in that camp because I thought there was too many sick." Asked if he slept in the bunkhouse, Fontaine replied he did, "on some brush. There were beds, there were poles and some brush on top of that. If you have no brush, you sleep on top of the poles."[18]

Not everyone shared Fontaine's criticism of conditions at Mann's camp. S.G. Gallagher, the camp's walking boss, told the commission the bunkhouse was "very comfortable. It is as comfortable a camp as I have seen for railroad men and I have been railroading for twenty years."[19] Gallagher was emphatic that the bunkhouse didn't leak but John Harris, the cook's assistant, told a different story: "It was very unhealthy . . . it was damp, snow on top and leaking through." Harris told the commission there was no ventilation in the building until after Fraser and McDonald died, when two vent holes were built into the roof.[20]

Charlie Griffith, the chore boy, told the commission he had told Dr. Gordon, when he was in camp, that McDonald and Fraser were sick and needed attention. "He asked me what was wrong with them and I told him one of them had a sore throat. Dr. Gordon said he had no time to be bothering with one camp all day." Griffith said the doctor told him the sore throats were due to colds and that he would give him some cough medicine. He then, according to the testimony, put about half a pint of medicine in a baking powder tin, told Griffith to dilute it with water, and left.

Question: "How long had he been in camp?"

"He was there from a quarter of an hour to half an hour."

"And how far would he have had to walk to see these men?"

"About 30 yards."[21]

When asked by the commission what he had done at Mann's camp that particular day, Dr. Gordon responded: "I think I saw everybody that needed attendance."[22]

One of the features of work along the line, not only at Mann's camp, was that men who were sick would be fired. Gallagher told the commission:

"Well, my orders was to fire them out. Of course I did not always do it. Sometimes I would fire them out and sometimes not."

Question: "That is whether they were sick or not?"

"Well, if they were sick and wanted to go to the hospital, we were supposed to send them."

"And if they were sick and did not want to go to the hospital, what then?"

"Well, if they would not go to work I would tell them they would have to go out."[23]

One of the Klute commission's recommendations called for federal legislation that would set health standards and provide for inspection of the camps. With considerable haste, the government passed the Public Works Health Act of 1900 to do just that. Two years later,

an inspector was hired to enforce the act. But even with inspectors, the government was still more interested in encouraging entrepreneurs to build railways and develop the West than it was in the health and well-being of the people doing the work.

The First Unions

Strikes and labour unrest in Alberta preceded the formation of the first unions by several years but they were often spontaneous uprisings, unable to seriously challenge the power of the Canadian Pacific Railway, backed as it was with the full might of the state. The navvies had little choice but to accept their fate. No outside organizations were willing to come to their aid and they had almost no bargaining power. That was not the case with the skilled trades employed by the CPR. The 1883 strike by engineers and firemen had ended in defeat but there did exist organizations within the mainstream of the labour movement that would take them in.

The first union in what later became Alberta was a branch of the Brotherhood of Locomotive Engineers, chartered in September 1886, in Medicine Hat. Several months later, railway firemen followed suit and established a local in that city of the Brotherhood of Locomotive Firemen and Enginemen. Two other locals of the railway running trades were established soon thereafter and until 1900, these four unions, all based in Medicine Hat, were the labour movement in the province.

The brotherhoods did more than act as bargaining agents with the companies on behalf of their members. They acted also as mutual aid societies. In fact, the third union formed in Medicine Hat, a local of the Brotherhood of Railway Trainmen, was named Charity Lodge. Railway work was dangerous, workers' compensation was unheard of and many insurance companies hesitated in taking such high-risk clients. So the workers set up their own insurance and death benefit plans through their unions.

But the most important function of the railway brotherhoods was the policing of the only thing that kept an engineer from sinking to the level of a navvy—his skill. Rigid jurisdictional lines and strong apprenticeship rules kept the railways from flooding the market with poorly-trained workers who would weaken the bargaining strength of the brotherhoods. And, as a rule, the railways depended on the skill of the trained labourers for smooth operation of their lines and were generally unwilling to take the chance of equipment damage that would result from hiring ill-trained strike-breakers. Perhaps more importantly, the railways shrewdly realized that if the brotherhoods were happy, they could be convinced to keep the trains operating, regardless of the actions of other railway

*A banquet in Medicine Hat for CPR engineer Peter Grace in
1895. Railway unions formed in Medicine Hat in 1886 were
the first in the province. Grace is fifth from right in the second
row. On his right is W. Rutherford who, in 1894, was president
of the Medicine Hat local of the Brotherhood of Locomotive
Firemen and Enginemen — the second union to be formed in
Alberta.*

workers. The engineers, firemen, conductors and others
became the "aristocracy" of the labour movement and the
rest of the railway labour force paid the price for their
success, as later events showed.

About three months after the locomotive engineers in
Medicine Hat received a charter for their organization, a
group of workers in Calgary met to found an assembly of
the Knights of Labour. "We have no doubt," said the
Calgary Herald of December 31, 1886, "but this organization will long become an honour to Calgary and an object
of important interest throughout the Territories. Steps are
being taken to organize societies at Donald and Canmore."

The Noble and Holy Order of the Knights of Labour had
been established in 1869 by nine garment workers in
Philadelphia. In the early days of trade unionism in the
mid-1800s, reprisals by employers against union members
came fast and often and to protect themselves, the Knights
started as a secret society with a president who was given
the rather grandiose title of Grand Master Workman. The
order was organized on an industrial basis, as opposed to
the prevailing method of basing unions on craft or skill. In
another departure, women and blacks were encouraged to
join. Strike action was to be avoided if at all possible and,
given the sorry track record of strikes, that was hardly
surprising. It was an attitude shared by many progressive
thinkers of the day. Instead of strikes, the Knights preferred

arbitration and boycotts but their leading edge was education and formation of co-operatives. Education was designed to promote the Knights' aims of making "industrial
and moral worth, not wealth, the true standard of individual and national greatness" and "to secure for the
workers full enjoyment of the wealth they create, sufficient
leisure in which to develop their intellectual, moral and
social faculties."

One event in 1886 had a major impact on the fate of the
Noble Order. In Chicago, about thirty-eight thousand
workers went on strike on May 1 (a date later commemo-
rated as May Day) in support of the eight-hour day movement. On May 4, a mass protest was called in Haymarket
Square to protest the killing of four strikers by police the
day before. As the meeting was drawing to a close, 180
police moved onto the square and ordered the crowd to
disperse. At that point, a bomb was thrown into police
ranks, killing several. In response, the police charged into
the crowd firing pistols and clubbing everyone in their
path. Hundreds of citizens were injured and a number
were killed.

The strike leaders were arrested and charged. No one
ever found out who threw the bomb—the police blamed
anarchists, the protesters figured it was the work of an
agent provocateur—but it didn't matter. The leaders were
convicted of conspiracy to commit murder. They had in-

Ranch-hands before the turn of the century. The Knights of Labour reported in 1887 that "cowboys" in the Calgary area were earning thirty-five to fifty dollars a month.

Bull Whackers Grub Pile.

flamed the populace to wild actions through speeches and pamphlets and that was enough, in an atmosphere of public hysteria, to send four of them to the gallows.[24] The Knights had been active in the eight-hour movement and in the public mind, the order was responsible for the Haymarket bombing.

Calgary Assembly 9787 of the Knights was set up by an organizer from Winnipeg and another from Owen Sound, Ontario. The local was what the order referred to as a "mixed assembly" of workers in various trades and employed by various firms. A letter written in 1887 to the *Journal of United Labour,* the order's newspaper, gives a long summary of wages paid in the Calgary district to workers in various occupations. Stonemasons were receiving $4.00 to $4.50 a day, carpenters $2.50 to $3.00, tailors $1.50 to $2.25, cowboys and stablemen thirty dollars to forty-five dollars a month, clerks twenty-five to sixty dollars a month and sawmill workers forty dollars to seventy-five dollars a month. Good board and room, the Calgary Knights said, could be had for six dollars a week.[25]

In line with the order's policy of education, the Calgary Knights also established their own newspaper, the *Northwest Call,* "intended to be our organ as far as possible." It was probably the first labour newspaper in Alberta. In 1888, the local wrote that it was trying to organize a number of Pennsylvania coal miners who had moved into

the district. Its efforts were without success and soon after, the organization fell apart.[26]

At its peak, the Knights had about twelve thousand members in Canada and they remained a force in the Canadian labour movement until 1902—a date that marked the formal take-over of the movement in Canada by the American Federation of Labour. At a convention in Berlin (now Kitchener), Ontario, the international unions succeeded in amending the constitution of the Trades and Labour Congress barring from membership any Canadian organization unaffiliated with the American Federation of Labour which sought to organize any group of workers that federation unions laid claim to. More than two thousand workers in twenty three unions, including the Knights, were expelled.[27]

Other than the railway brotherhoods, the next union to follow the Knights into Alberta was the United Brotherhood of Carpenters and Joiners. Local 75 was chartered in Calgary in early January 1892 and was actively agitating for a nine-hour day but it suffered the same fate as the Knights' assembly in Calgary and dissolved within the year. Outside of the four running trades locals, Alberta was a wasteland for union organization until the turn of the century, when rapid population increases accompanied by booming conditions gave trade unions a more solid base to build on.

CHAPTER TWO

Foundations of the Movement: 1899-1907

Railway Workers

With the general exception of the running trades, railway workers usually fared rather poorly when fighting the Canadian Pacific Railway for improved working conditions, higher wages and recognition of their unions. It was a contest of power and the CPR had it all.

In 1901, track maintenance workers employed by the railway walked off the job at points across the country, demanding recognition of their union, the Brotherhood of Railway Trackmen. The union, claiming it had the support of 95 percent of the workers, called out its members when the company refused to negotiate. In the CPR's Calgary-area division the strike got off to a late start because of a breakdown in communications between union headquarters and the local. The *Calgary Herald* related a story of how one member had got word that the strike was officially on: "A man . . . came in yesterday. He knew the strike was probable but only became acquainted with the

true situation when, from a passing train, some of the men threw water and small rocks at him. He took the hint and come into town."[1]

In many strikes during this period, there were rumours, often supported by fact, that immigrants were strike-breaking and while that may have been true elsewhere, it wasn't the case in Calgary. The *Herald* twice noted that "Galicians" (Ukrainians) had refused tempting offers to replace the strikers. In Calgary, the trackmen received the full moral support of all other CPR workers and at a meeting on June 28 an offer was made to establish a strike fund to keep the strikers in groceries while they walked the picket lines. Members of the running trades had attended the meeting in Calgary, but from other centres came reports that the trackmen had been sold down the river through the mediation efforts of the running trades leadership. The strike lasted for two months and chalked up yet another defeat for employees of the CPR. The workers received a commitment from the company that they could have their jobs back but the major issue was left unresolved. The union had called the walkout seeking recognition from the company and although almost all the track maintenance workers belonged to it, the CPR would agree only to "partial" recognition.[2]

The *Voice*, the newspaper of the Winnipeg Labour Council, remarked that railway workers suspected that the CPR had "tampered with the heads of the brotherhoods." A senior official of the trackmen's union charged that the brotherhoods' leadership had allowed itself to be used by the company to persuade the workers to return to their jobs at less than favourable terms.[3] The trouble with strikes like the trackmen's fight with the CPR was that the CPR usually won. After all, it had all the odds in its favour—the politicians, the police, the money and the ability to keep operating despite strikes. Also, when the trackmen went out, all other CPR employees stayed on the job—the running trades, the clerks, the shop crafts. Gompers and his colleagues in the American Federation of Labour believed that the way to protect the rights of workers with skill was to organize according to skill or craft. Those with particular skills could defend that which they knew best and so protect themselves from sinking to the level of the common labourer. There were problems with this approach, the major one being that the worst way to fight a corporation as powerful as the CPR was to attack it with various unco-ordinated blows at unco-ordinated times—first machinists, then firemen, then track maintenance workers, then freight handlers. It was obvious—if all CPR employees could get together and take on the company at the same time, they could shut it down. The trains would be silent in the yards and the workers might be able to pull off an unaccustomed victory. After the trackmen's strike and other defeats, CPR employees—and workers in other industries—began to realize they could solve their problems if they organized industrial unions, where all employees in an industry bargained together. It was a fight that would absorb workers in the West for more than fifty years.

The idea, which began to catch the imaginations of workers in the Canadian West after the turn of the century, was not new. Eugene Debs had organized industrially against the Pullman company in the U.S. with a union called the American Railway Union. He had lost but his battle to bring common sense to railway bargaining had made him a popular figure in North America. There was, in addition to the American Federation of Labour, a second trade union centre, the American Labour Union (ALU), which championed the cause of socialism and industrial unionism and the organization of the unskilled. Eugene Debs addressed its founding convention in Denver in 1902. One of the affiliates of the ALU was an organization of railway workers called the United Brotherhood of Railway Employees (UBRE) and when it moved its organizing campaign north of the border in 1902, the millennium was in sight.

In 1903, at the end of February, CPR clerks and other company employees belonging to the UBRE went on strike in Vancouver demanding recognition and an end to the CPR's campaign of intimidation against the union, which took the form of suspensions and dismissal of UBRE activists. Before long, the strike spread along the CPR, hitting Revelstoke, Nelson, Calgary and Winnipeg. The *Calgary Herald* of March 10 reported that the day previous, in the late afternoon, clerks in the CPR's freight department locked up their offices, turned in their keys and walked out. Before long, they were followed by ticket clerks and baggage handlers. In all about forty five CPR employees in the city hit the bricks, claiming their issue was recognition of the UBRE.

Arrayed against the clerks of the Canadian Pacific Railway was the railway itself, its secret police, the railway brotherhoods, the courts and the federal government and its labour expert, William Lyon Mackenzie King, the deputy minister of labour. Even before the strike had begun, the the CPR was preparing for the fight. One company official is reported to have said that the CPR was "ready to spend a million dollars to break the United Brotherhood of Railway Employees."[4] The CPR established an elaborate system of espionage to keep abreast of the plots of the UBRE and was able to plant paid secret agents in practically every brotherhood lodge—one was able to raise high enough in the organization to initiate four new members. But the biggest prize for the railway was Harold Poore, the union's general organizer in Canada. While Poore was travelling across the country on the UBRE payroll, he was secretly working for the CPR, selling his correspondence with union president George Estes for "valuable consideration."[5] When gathering information wasn't enough, the company and its special constables turned to more violent opposition. Frank Rogers, a union organizer and prominent B.C. labour leader, was shot while picketing Canadian Pacific tracks in Vancouver in April. Two men were arrested; one was tried and acquitted in a trial that pro-labour observers said was a farce.[6]

If the strike was a threat to the CPR, it was also a threat to the running trades and other railway brotherhoods. Their carefully built structure of craft and skill, cemented by apprenticeship and seniority regulations and jurisdictional lines, could all be pulled down by the likes of Debs, Estes and the one thousand strikers. The UBRE wasn't just attacking the railway, it was attacking the citadel itself — Sam Gompers and the American Federation of Labour, claiming they were in league with capitalism, which they were, and that they were screwing the workers, which they weren't, at least, not intentionally. Gompers and his colleagues believed that a well-organized labour movement could satisfy the needs of its members within the system and that far-reaching social and economic changes were an unnecessary and divisive dream. The journal of the Brotherhood of Railway Trainmen carried a story on the UBRE which was so devastating in its denunciation of its radical rival that one historian says it was distributed as a pamphlet by the CPR during the strike.[7] The president of the Boilermakers' Union in the United States said none of his members would be allowed to strike in sympathy with the UBRE; if they did, their cards would be pulled.

If all that wasn't enough to break the clerks and freight handlers, there was the federal government and Mackenzie King to deliver the knockout blow. The UBRE strike wasn't the only labour dispute keeping members of the Laurier cabinet awake nights. Other workers in B.C. had struck in sympathy—longshoremen, ships' crews and teamsters were on the picket lines. Adding to the government's fear that its realm was crumbling, at least in B.C, coal miners in the East Kootenay and on Vancouver Island were out and they belonged to, or were trying to join, the Western Federation of Miners (WFM), an affiliate of the ALU and therefore a sister organiztion of the UBRE. The running trades might continue operating trains for the CPR but without coal the locomotives would sit idle. The government smelled a conspiracy hatched by socialists across the border and in April, appointed a royal commission. It was 'headed by the chief justice of the B.C. Supreme Court but the real power behind it was Mackenzie King, the commission secretary.

Evidence submitted to the commission clearly indicated the real reason for the coal strike was recognition of the WFM and the attitude of coal operators such as James Dunsmuir, who fired any miner who belonged to a union. The conspiracy theory had a nice ring to it, however, and the commission would not be done out of it. Stuart Jamieson, in a study for the federal Task Force on Labour Relations in 1968, said the commission members "appeared to have had their own predetermined interpretation of motivations and events leading up to the strikes of 1903, contrary evidence notwithstanding."[8]

The report recommended that unions be incorporated and held liable for damages and that boycotts, "unfair" lists and "scab" lists be outlawed. Not content to stop there, Mackenzie King and the commission proposed jail for anyone not a British subject who led or incited strikes. They also condemned picketing but did not, however, come right out and suggest its abolition. The real sting in the report was saved for the leaders of the WFM, the UBRE and the ALU who were "not trade unionists but socialistic agitators of the most bigoted and ignorant type." Such

organizations, the commission declared, were in favour of tearing down capitalist society and rescuing workers from "famine . . . whoredom . . . and slavery." Said the authors of a biography of King: "Neither the commission nor the secretary sympathized with this enterprise."[9] The commission didn't offer the workers much hope that their lot would improve. "While much good can be accomplished by wise legislation," the report said, "the labour problem, so-called, is incapable of final solution and it will be with us as long as human nature remains what it is and the present civilization endures."

The commission's findings notwithstanding, the *Bond of Brotherhood*, a socialist newspaper published in Calgary which, for a time, carried an endorsement from the Calgary Labour Council, said in its May 30 issue that although the battle was in its thirteenth week and the strike fund was nearly gone, "the men are more determined than ever in their contest with the CPR." Another story in the same issue advised that at its next meeting the Calgary Labour Council would discuss placing the CPR freight department on the unfair list. There was, however, too much for the strikers to handle. Everything was against them and in its June 26 issue, the *Bond* carried a letter from an UBRE official announcing the end of the strike and chalking it up as a victory.

Another letter in the same issue of the paper cast a different light on the strike's end, however. It was a reply from the Calgary general superintendent of the railway to a UBRE striker: "Regarding your standing with the company with a view to re-employment, the position which you vacated has been permanently filled and on that account I cannot offer you employment." The *Bond* need hardly have said more but in a year-end review, it observed that most of the strikers had been blacklisted and "the brotherhood is completely destroyed in Canada with the exception of the division in Winnipeg." For workers employed by the CPR, millennia never lasted very long.

Despite the crushing defeat for the UBRE, the principle behind it—industrial unionism—survived. Victory appeared next to impossible for employees of the Canadian Pacific Railway and the other railway companies but failure after failure did not lessen the railway workers' taste for battle. That taste was kept alive by miserable conditions, low wages and long hours of work. A contract signed in 1905 between the CPR and the Brotherhood of Railway Carmen set the hours of work on the western lines from 7:00 A.M. to 6:00 P.M. with an hour for lunch. Canadian Northern sectionmen, under a 1905 agreement with the Maintenance of Way Employees, also worked ten hour days but the sectionmen could only expect fourteen cents an hour. The carmen, who possessed more skill, could earn anywhere from eighteen to thirty-two cents an hour.[10]

In 1907, an attempted alliance of shopcraft workers with the running trades unions was broken when the company gave the running trades an 8 percent increase. Carmen and other shopcraft groups, who did not receive what they were after, claimed the running trades had been "bought off." Efforts were being made at the time to unite all the shop unions into a federation. They were getting nowhere bargaining on their own and because they were less skilled than the running trades, their brotherhoods were less able to secure reasonable settlements from the company.

In 1907 the company announced it would bring in a large number of Japanese railway workers. The fear of being undercut by immigrant labour pushed the shopcraft federation one step further. Early in 1908, the company said it would reduce wages for boilermakers and other crafts and out of that move came a joint bargaining committee of the carmen and other trades in the railway shops. At its head was a Calgary machinist, R.J. Tallon, who was to play a major role in the Calgary and national labour movements. Tallon was born in 1885 in Belleville, Ontario, and by fifteen was an apprentice in the Grand Trunk Railway

shops there, only natural for a boy whose "playgrounds were chiefly the yards and roundhouse of the Grand Trunk." After living for a time in Revelstoke, Tallon moved to Calgary in 1907 and was soon after elected president of the local machinists' union.

The joint committee's first task was to fight a series of shop layoffs planned by the company. By April 1, 1908 about eight hundred men had lost their jobs. A short time later, the contracts in the shops were cancelled by CPR fiat and wages were cut 7 percent. Tension between the company and its shop employees was building and on August 4 could be contained no longer. The strike was on. The *Calgary Herald* of August 5, 1908, reported that:

> At exactly ten o'clock, a small boy employed in the local machine shop climbed on top of an engine and vigorously rang the bell. Mechanics of all kinds immediately stopped their work, discarded overalls and smocks, cleaned and packed their tools and headed for the time clerk's office where they registered the fact that they had worked two hours today and then left for their homes.

The main issue in the dispute was recognition of the shopcraft federation and across the country, the shops and yards of the Canadian Pacific closed. The trains, operated by the running trades, kept to their schedules. In an interview with the *Herald,* a Calgary shopcraft spokesman said the workers were "all determined to make it a fight to a finish. The trouble has been anticipated for some time . . . and as a consequence the men are well-equipped financially. More important is the fact that we have the moral and financial support of all the great American labour organizations. . . ."[11]

The company, however, was also prepared. Newspaper reports said it was opening employment bureaus in eastern Canada and Britain and by August 8, there were reports of Japanese strike-breakers in the yards at both Lethbridge and Calgary. "Evidently," said a wire story in the August 8 *Herald,* "the company are again availing themselves of Oriental labour to combat organized Occidental labour." In Lethbridge, reported the Calgary *Herald* of August 19, one of the strike-breakers said he and others "had been hired last April to hold themselves in readiness and had been drawing $120 a month ever since. They had been hired by the Thiel detective agency of Chicago and until they got to Winnipeg did not know where they were going to work."

By September 11 the company had recruited about three hundred strike-breakers to work in the Calgary shops where they lived "in boarding cars . . . all other supplies needful being brought to them by the company and the place guarded by special constables."[12] The CPR's action in bringing strike-breakers from the United States

Asian immigrants in southern Alberta, 1908–1910. In 1908, the CPR brought in Japanese workers as strike-breakers to defeat a strike by shopcraft employees.

brought complaints to the federal government that the company was flouting the Alien Labour Law, which prohibited such practices. The government response was to suggest that a private prosecution be launched against the railway.

By early October, it was all over; the CPR had chalked up another win. There would be no discrimination against the strikers but they would have to reapply for their jobs, and they lost their pensions and seniority. Competent strike-breakers would not be fired. Negotiations with the company had taken place in the east and the men were ordered back before anyone was sure of the exact terms of settlement and there were charges that they had been sold out by workers in the East who had less stomach for the strike. One of the strikers said in a *Calgary Herald* interview:

So far as the Calgary men are concerned, they are as game today as they ever were. There must have been something wrong down east . . . of course they may have been in very straitened circumstances, we do not know much about that. There is one thing sure though and that is that we men were prepared to stick it out to the finish, had it taken years. Of course, there are always some quitters in every rank and some of these fellows down East must have got cold feet.''[13]

The Coal Miners

Coal was discovered in southern Alberta in 1792 but not until the coming of the railway did its exploitation become commercially attractive. The industry, which grew up to service the needs of the railway and the settlers and other industry it had brought, had a profound effect on the nature of the labour movement in the province. Coal mining was marked by frequent injury and death, low pay, brutal treatment, child labour, miserable living conditions and disease which found easy prey among poorly-nourished and overworked men and women living in bunkhouses and crude shacks with virtually no sanitary facilities.

The mines in the province, many of them small and marginal operations, had an unenviable safety record. One provincial historian estimated that one man was killed for every hundred thousand tons of coal mined in Alberta.[14] Many accidents could have been prevented by proper safety procedures but safety often cost money whereas men were cheap and easily replaceable. Miners complained that the ponies the coal operators used to haul coal from the face to the mine mouth were treated better than the men. Retired Drumheller miner Art Roberts recalled one fire in a mine that killed about eighty horses. "The coal

ENTRANCE TO COAL MINE
EDMONTON.

operator didn't say this but it was an understood thing that maybe eighty men would have been cheaper."[15]

If men were cheap, children were cheaper. Children twelve and thirteen years old were commonly employed in the mines before the First World War. It was, of course, too dangerous to have them actually mining so they got jobs at the tipple, or on the screening table where dust and small pieces of coal were filtered out. Miners were paid at most mines only for the lumps too large to fall through the screens.

Alexander McLeod, a Crowsnest Pass miner, told a 1907 Alberta commission studying the coal industry that, as far as he was concerned, there shouldn't be any children in the mines under fifteen years old.

That work is pretty hard on a boy. I have seen them spitting up coal dust from one end of the week to the other. They hardly ever get a breath of air during the whole 10 hours they are there and I don't care if he's made of iron, it will tell on him in after years. They cannot speak English . . . and instead of those boys working there 10 and 11 hours in the coal dust, they ought to be in school.[16]

It wasn't that the boys preferred working in the mines to going to school. Their families couldn't afford to have them not working. Miners at the time were earning only about thirty cents an hour. For many coal mining families, the $1.25 a day that a boy could bring home meant more food on the table.[17]

In one coal camp, miners lived in two-room houses made of "odd and ends of boards and coal doors generally used in boxcars. Houses are one-ply of lumber in most cases with building paper on the inside and are infested with bugs." The houses were so close together that "anybody can hear what is said in the next house."[18] Some miners in other camps lived in houses made of old railway ties covered with mud.

In the Coal Branch area south of Edson and a few other places, the coal companies ran the camps and often only married miners were eligible for company houses. Single men lived in bunkhouses reminisent of those on railway construction. In a camp at Cadomin it was sarcastically reported that:

> . . . . conditions are not ideal. There are about 100 men lying around, some of them in filthy and verminous bunkhouses and others sleeping in the bush, preferring to be eaten by ants than by bugs. Management seem anxious to keep the bunkhouses in this undesirable state to make sure of full patronage for the revenue-producing rooming houses where the beds are, in some instances, double-shifted [men on different shifts sharing one bed]. Many families are living in single rooms.[19]

In conditions such as these, it wasn't only industrial diseases that hit the miners—there were typhoid and scarlet fever and flu as well. Pat Conroy, a Drumheller miner who later became secretary-treasurer of the Canadian Congress of Labour, reported that within one nine-month period in the Drumheller valley, about one hundred ten cases of typhoid were diagnosed. "Scarlet fever," Conroy said, "don't come up quite to that amount. I think there is only about 30 percent of that amount scarlet fever cases. The sanitary conditions around here are very primitive, merely outside sanitation, especially in the summer. Inside the town, there is modern facilities for sanitation but in a very large number of cases, owing to lack of finances, the people cannot afford it."[20]

It was little wonder that the miners of Alberta fought back. Crowsnest miner Pete Youschok said that the operators:

> . . . . forced them into the union then. Because if they treated us good, I'd have never been involved in a union because there'd be no damn reason to be involved.

> I worked in a place where you were soaking wet [some places in the mines were always wet because of leaking underground water—in later years, miners got extra pay for working in "wet places"] and you couldn't go home. You had to stay there until your shift ended. . . .

> I've seen in the wintertime where the airways froze— the mines weren't heated like now. You had to go in there and chop ice in an airway—can you imagine, about twenty, thirty below. You'd go numb in there— you couldn't even eat your bucket. You come out to get warm and they're ready to fire you.

> That's the kind of conditions I'm talking about.

Mining began in Lethbridge in 1886; the completion of the CPR's Crowsnest line in 1899 opened the fields in the Crowsnest.[21] The miners' unions followed soon after. The first union interested in helping the miners fight their battles against the operators was the Western Federation of Miners, a tough and militant organization that, in the constant wars it fought with metal mining corporations in the United States Pacific Northwest, often responded with gunfire of its own to the violence of the militia called out to help the owners. Mining was a tough job, the operators were a determined lot and there was no time in the coal fields or booming metal camps of the East and West Kootenay for unions that talked of co-operation with the employer and the ability of the capitalist system to eventually meet workers' needs. In the isolated camps, with the miners living in their little shacks and the bosses in their houses on the hill and the absence of the moderating influence of a "middle class" of skilled workmen and small businessmen, Marx was a better bet than Sam Gompers.

Such were the conditions that gave rise to the WFM. For years, it led a long struggle in the American labour movement for socialism and industrial unionism, first through the American Labour Union and then as a founding organization of the Industrial Workers of the World. The move into the coal mines of Alberta and the border areas of B.C. came naturally for the federation, which had its base in the metal camps of Montana, Utah and the Spokane area of Washington. Its first Canadian local was established in Rossland, B.C. in 1895 and within several years the union moved to Alberta. By 1898, about two hundred Lethbridge miners had signed up and miners from the local began playing an important role in the affairs of the federation. In that year, a Lethbridge member was on the committee that drew up the new constitution for the Western Labour Union, a rival confederation established by the WFM to challenge the American Federation of Labour. A year later, Henry Noble represented the Lethbridge local at a meeting called to set up a Canadian district of the WFM.[22]

Needless to say, the coal operators weren't happy when their miners decided to organize. What was probably the first coal strike in the province occurred in Lethbridge in 1897 when Alberta Railway and Coal cut wages by 17 percent. The miners found their employer had learned some of the tricks employed by the CPR to keep its workers in their place. In September, the president of the company wrote Prime Minister Laurier asking that the number of Mounted Police at Lethbridge be maintained: "Several hundred coal miners of mixed nationalities are employed at Lethbridge who were recently on strike and whose good behaviour was largely the result of the presence of a considerable force of police which acts as a deterrent upon

The entrance to an Edmonton coal mine before the First World War. Most mines in the Edmonton area were in the east end of the city and many were dug into the river-valley bank.

such disturbing influences."[23] At the mine in Anthracite, west of Calgary, the coal company found the police so useful in keeping the camp "orderly [and] life and property safe" that it supplied the Mounties barracks at no charge.[24]

But when they had to, the coal operators were capable of dealing with unions and union activists without the help of the federal government's police force. David Miller, a miner who had worked in mines in Africa, Australia and the United States, told the 1907 commission that he was nervous about appearing before the commissioners. "For this evidence, I may be thrown out of work. They have another law they use, they do not discharge you right away, they starve you out." That sort of pressure had its desired effect on the Western Federation of Miners. Lethbridge miners allowed their WFM charter to lapse in the fall of 1902 and then established what was probably a company union, an independent organization under the control of the company.[25]

In November, some miners began to fight back against what was becoming a management offensive against their union. When the operators of the mine at Michel, on the B.C. side of the Crowsnest Pass, fired the union president,

the workers walked out and stayed out for several weeks before caving in. In February of 1903, the owner of three mines in the B.C. section of the Pass withdrew recognition of the federation, gambling that many of the East European miners would not back a retaliatory strike. The gamble failed and the men walked out.[26] As this was happening, the UBRE strike against the CPR was raging and Mackenzie King was drawing up the report of the Royal Commission on Industrial Disputes. King came down hard on both the UBRE and the WFM, threatening to declare them illegal. This threat, compounded by major battles on its home front in the American metal mines, and the fact that it had landed in such difficulty by organizing coal miners when metal miners were its major constituency, caused the WFM to pull out of the coal camps and invite the United Mine Workers of America (UMW) to replace it.[27]

By the end of 1905, the UMW, one of the few industrial unions affiliated to the American Federation of Labour, had organized many of the mines in Alberta and membership in District 18, which covered the entire province and the mines just inside the B.C. border stood at about twenty-two hundred.[28] Lethbridge was the hold-out, but the miners there eventually tired of their company union and on a Sunday night in February, 1906, 363 men met at Oliver's Hall to found Local 574 of the United Mine Workers of America.

However, the major coal operator in Lethbridge, the Alberta Railway and Irrigation Company, preferred the company union and told the men it would have nothing to do with their new organization. On March 9, the 500 employees of the company walked off the job in a dispute which would have national implications for the labour movement. The company decided it could do without both the union and its members and reopened the mine. Ten days after the strike began, a detachment of Mounted Police was brought in to guard mine property and protect strike-breaking miners.[29] The April 5 Lethbridge Herald reported two incidents that had kept the Mounties busy.

> On Tuesday one of the miners who was working in the mine and had moved near the colliery went to his old home to get his chickens. A howling crowd gathered around him and he got some beautiful bruises before the police were able to disperse the assemblage, the women figuring as active as the men. Last night, the biggest row of all occurred around eight o'clock. The police had occasion to arrest one of the miners. Some of his friends informed the village and in a flash, a crowd of several hundred congregated carrying, it is said, sticks and stones. They marched in a body forward toward the colliery but the police, after a hand-to-hand fight, stopped them before they crossed the [picket] lines. In the midst of this excitement, two houses which had been occupied by two working miners were dynamited. Mounted Police patrolled the village all night. It is learned that an attempt to burn a house in the miners' village was detected in time by the police.

The paper condemned the riot and warned strikers that if such activities continued, they would lose what public support they had. Its real concern, however, seemed to be the effect on the town's reputation: "Lethbridge does not want to be the scene of riots that will give it an unenviable reputation, especially at the present time when hundreds of people are seeking homes here."[30]

The miners didn't accept the Herald's advice and as they saw other workers replacing them and the mine keeping up at least a semblance of production, tempers got rawer, especially after a union proposal to submit the dispute to an arbitration board was rejected out of hand by the company. In August, yet another strike-breaker returned home to find his house not as he left it.

The union charged that the dynamite explosion, in which no one was injured, was the work of the Thiel Detective Agency of Chicago, the same firm that was to recruit strike-breakers for the CPR in the 1908 shopcraft strike.[31]

As the strike continued into the fall, the federal government began to receive letters warning of impending peril due to fuel shortages if the strike lasted into the winter. The government turned to King, one of the few men in Ottawa who had even a rudimentary knowledge of the "labour question", and dispatched him to the scene. Despite the company's objections to arbitration, it agreed to meet King and the workers' committee. King reported in the Labour Gazette that the operator made "certain important concessions [and] the representatives of the men withdrew altogether certain of their demands." The company agreed to allow the workers to join the UMW but the agreement was made with "representatives of its employees," not with the United Mine Workers. There was also no mention in the contract of a check-off, which was a major demand. (With a check-off clause in a collective agreement, the company undertakes to deduct union dues from the pay cheque if the employee approves in writing.) But the Lethbridge workers received a 10 percent pay hike, bringing the rate for a miner doing company work to thirty cents an hour. And they received a promise in writing that they would be given preference in hiring, "provided they make application within a reasonable period."[32]

As in other agreements of the day, the workers were forced to accept a "non-discrimination" clause, saying that management would not object to "its employees being or not being members of any organization," but that all employees would be treated the same, regardless of union membership. Such agreements made membership in a trade union akin to membership in the Kiwanis Club. The two major grievances of the workers—union recognition and the check-off, had been lost and the strikers would have to reapply for their jobs. The compromise was accepted and the strike ended December 2, 1906.

Whether the workers went back happy is unrecorded, however, union officials were as pleased as they could be with the settlement worked out by the young deputy minister, and told him so. John Mitchell, the UMW's international president, wrote to King, saying: "I have written the secretary of our local union at Lethbridge expressing my approval of the contract and I am confidently hopeful that the time is not too far distant when an agreement will be negotiated directly between the United Mine Workers and the operators at Lethbridge."[33] Frank Sherman, president of District 18, told King he hoped "in the near future, with the help of men like yourself, that we will be able to devise a plan whereby we shall not have to call upon you to assist us in settling strikes"[34] To which King replied that he shared those hopes and felt after the Lethbridge strike

Four Ukrainian miners in Lethbridge, 1905. Ukrainians played a leading role in the coal miners' unions.

that legislation was essential to compel arbitration.[35] That was to Sherman. To a woman in Nanaimo, B.C., King went one step further and said it was "a pity" that there were strikes at all. "Perhaps some day we'll find some means which will prevent them altogether."[36]

King went home to Ottawa to ponder the dispute and it soon became apparent that what he and Sherman hoped for were two different things. In the minds of the men at Lethbridge was a system which could equalize the power between them and the company. What King proposed, through the Industrial Disputes Investigation Act, given royal assent in April of 1907, was something else entirely. The act provided for compulsory intervention by the federal government in labour disputes in public utilities, mining and railways, on application by either party, and the appointment of a three-person board to investigate the dispute and recommend terms of settlement. The catch came in that until the board had completed its report, no strikes or lockouts were allowed and no time limit was set on how long the board could deliberate. During that period, King and the government took away the only power workers had to press their case on intransigent employers—the withdrawal of labour.

The Building Trades and Labour Councils

The CPR left more than coal camps in its wake. Cities also sprang up along the route of the railway and pre-eminent among them was Calgary.

While the navvies were pushing the CPR mainline across Alberta, Calgary, with a population of about three hundred, was "a little village of log buildings, including the Hudson's Bay Company, the diminutive churches of the Roman Catholics and Methodists and two not very plausible hotels."[37] Edmonton, on the other hand, was a case of arrested development. With a population of

A group of workers at an Edmonton brickyard in 1903.

seven hundred, it had been prepared to become the major centre in the province when political and economic considerations in Montreal and Ottawa dictated that the CPR would be built through Calgary instead. On completion of the mainline, Calgary's population boomed and received a further boost with construction of the Crowsnest line. It became a major centre of trade and by 1901, with more than four thousand residents, was almost twice the size of Edmonton which was then about the same size as Lethbridge. In the same year about seventy-one thousand people lived in Alberta, a fourfold increase in twenty years.[38]

In Edmonton and Calgary, most of the workers were employed by the CPR, by construction companies and in service industries such as printing and publishing, retail trade, restaurants and hotels. With a few exceptions, like restaurant workers, most union members in the cities before the Second World War were skilled or at least semi-skilled. The cities had a moderating influence on the labour movement. They weren't, first of all, single industry towns like those in the Crowsnest, where a grievance with a single employer affected everyone. In Edmonton and Calgary, where thousands of residents were employed by many different employers and organized into many different unions, it was difficult for a worker employed by the city to share a personal sense of injustice with someone working for the CPR who was fired or laid off. In the Pass, the Drumheller Valley or the Coal Branch, the union played an important role in the life of the community. The union hall was a centre of community activity and the unions organized sports days, picnics and other social events. In the cities, there were more non-union diversions and other than the traditional Labour Day parade and picnic and meetings of the Trades and Labour Council, there was little to bind the workers together.

All of these factors combined to make the urban work-

Sports such as soccer and rugby were popular pastimes for Alberta workers.

force more moderate than its coal mining brethren but that didn't mean, as employers would learn to their sorrow, that the working men and women of the cities would meekly accept typhoid, three-room shacks and poor wages as their lot. And when pushed, as they were during the First World War, city workers could be as tough and militant as anyone.

In Calgary, the first unions to be established on a more permanent basis than the Knights or Carpenters Local 75 were organizations of railway employees. The CPR was, after all, the city's main industry. Local 42 of the Brotherhood of Railway Carmen, which played a leading role in the 1908 shopcraft strike, was formed in March of 1900. A month later, another group of shopcraft workers, the machinists, set up Local 357 of the International Association of Machinists. Apart from the railway workers, the base of trade unionism in the cities of Alberta was formed by construction workers. At the top of the heap, holding the same kind of position among the building trades as the engineers and firemen held on the railways, were the stonemasons. A union of stonemasons was established in Calgary early in 1903 and in Edmonton in May of that year.

The construction union which probably played the largest role in the labour movement in Alberta was the United Brotherhood of Carpenters and Joiners. The carpenters union in Alberta was established first at Frank, in the Crowsnest Pass, a bustling and booming community before a good chunk of Turtle Mountain fell on it in 1903. On a cold night in February 1902, every carpenter in Frank gathered in the saloon to form Local 1002 of the brotherhood. They then hired an organizer, Robert Robinson to spread the word. Robinson first stopped at Calgary where he told a meeting that organized carpenters in Nelson, B.C., were earning $3.50 for an eight-hour day, compared to the Calgary rate of between $1.50 and $2.75 for ten hours. It was an effective message and twenty-nine men signed up. He then moved to Edmonton and spent the later part of October and the first two weeks of November in his organizing efforts and by the 11th had finished his work in the capital. On that date, Local 1325 was set up. Of all the unions established in this period, Local 1325 is one of the few to have survived to the present day under the same charter. With the Calgary local established, the carpenters submitted a proposed schedule of wages and hours to their employers. The *Bond of Brotherhood* reported that the contractors resisted and the union called a strike against thirteen companies employing about ninety men. After two weeks, the "most belligerent" employer weakened and the men succeeded in reducing their hours of work to nine with a daily wage of $2.50.

On May 15 of the following year, according to the first issue of the *Bond* on May 30, the province's first major construction strike started when Calgary carpenters downed tools because their employers were using non-union employees, in violation of the 1902 agreement. The dispute was settled by the end of May and the carpenters had just signed a new contract when the newly-organized teamsters of the city called a strike. Working eleven to thirteen hours a day, they had been making from thirty-five to forty-five dollars a month and wanted a raise to fifty dollars. To give the teamsters a hand, the carpenters decided on June 1 to stop handling lumber delivered by

*Edmonton stonecutters at work on a new building on 100th Ave.
at the turn of the century. Stonecutters at the time were among
the most highly-paid groups of construction workers.*

strike-breakers. Before they had a chance to act on their decision, they were locked out. The major lumber merchants had told the building contractors that if they continued to employ union members they wouldn't get any lumber. The union representing construction labourers then stepped in and said their members would not use or handle lime or sandstone brought to building sites by non-union teamsters.

With a general shutdown of construction in the city, tempers were frayed and not all battles were fought with employers. At the Calgary Labour Council's June 4 meeting, the president of the stonemasons union denounced the carpenters for their sympathy strike and informed the council his members would not support it. The *Bond* on June 5 reported that following complaints that masons were using material delivered by non-union teamsters, the stonemasons were suspended from the council. Bowing to such pressure, the masons agreed to support the strike but by June 12 they were back at work. Of the eighty to one

hundred carpenters who went on strike, about thirty broke rank and returned to work. But still the strike continued; attempts by the carpenters and the labour council to end the dispute by arbitration were unsuccessful.

On July 15, fresh from the royal commission investigating the UBRE and WFM dispute, in which sympathy strikes were roundly condemned, Mackenzie King arrived in the city to straighten things out, which he did, in his own fashion. "Ever since he arrived in the city yesterday morning," said the *Calgary Herald* of July 16, "W.L. Mackenzie King has been on the hustle. Yesterday he interviewed the locked-out men, the various contractors and Messrs. Cushing and Van Wart [the lumber merchants]. His efforts bringing about a settlement were exceedingly successful." King's settlement allowed the carpenters to maintain wages and hours of work won in 1902 but in place of the union shop won in their first agreement, there was now a non-discrimination clause. "By the terms of the new agreement effected by Mr. King," reported the *To-*

ronto *Globe* of July 20 in a dispatch from Calgary, "the contractors can employ whom they like, there is no discrimination between the union and non-union men. The contractors refused to recognize the union and all men must sign the new agreement as individuals." The strike and King's settlement broke the back of the union, which was in serious financial difficulty. The charter was withdrawn and the union was not reorganized until April of 1904.

The carpenters, thoroughly beaten in the strike, laid considerable blame for the defeat on the bricklayers and stonemasons local for its action in breaking the sympathetic strike, a role similar to that played by the railway running trades in strikes on the CPR. In construction, the stonemasons were the most highly-skilled labourers. Their craft was buttressed with the same sort of seniority and apprenticeship regulations the running trades used to keep their trade from being diluted by less-skilled workmen. At a time when most buildings were made of cut

stone or brick, they were essential to the contractors and before the First World War, there were about three hundred in Calgary, the largest industry in the city, second only to the CPR.[40] Although carpenters too were skilled workmen, theirs was not a craft practised by only a select group. Contractors could always recruit homesteaders and others who could handle a hammer and saw to replace unionized carpenters on strike; few farmers knew how to cut stone. Compared to carpenters' wages of $2.50 a day, stonemasons were earning more than $4.00 and journeymen stonecutters were being paid $4.50. In 1890, a stonecutter was making $1.00 a day more than carpenters were earning a decade later.[31]

The seasonal influx of people from farms who competed with carpenters for jobs in the cities, undercutting their organization and making it easier for the employers to hold down wages, was just one of the problems encountered by carpenters as they were organizing their craft in the first years of the new century. Another, shared by all workers in

construction, was the seasonal nature of the work itself. The carpenters may have been getting $2.50 a day but there was no guarantee of year-round employment.

Plumbers were another important construction trade to organize early. In 1903, Edmonton plumbers decided to form a local of the Plumbers and Pipefitters and sent off a letter to the international applying for a charter. The union turned them down — there were only three of them in the entire city. Things had picked up by the next year and Local 488 received its charter with seven men on the roll. In 1905, Edmonton plumbers signed their first agreement with the masters establishing an eight hour day at a rate of sixty-four cents an hour, an immense improvement over conditions in 1904 when they worked nine hours a day Monday to Friday and eight hours on Saturday for between thirty-five and fifty cents. Perhaps to celebrate their first agreement, a gala banquet was held January 23, 1906 at the Pendennis Hotel. After a dinner of soup, salmon, "baked spuds", lobster salad, turkey, "murphies" (more potatoes), corn and peas, plum pudding, fruit and nuts, the celebrants raised their glasses in toasts to the King, the city, the master plumbers and the craft.[42] If such feasts were a

common event for Edmonton plumbers, it is little wonder that by 1912, they had more than two hundred members.

Most construction workers in the various trades were organized in Calgary by 1905 and in 1906, a council of building trades unions was established in the city. Three years later, a similar body was set up in Edmonton.[43]

Aside from the construction and railways unions the most important urban union in the formative years of the movement was the International Typographical Union (ITU). Like the carpenters, its members played a major role in the province's labour movement. M.C. Costello, an early president of the Calgary typos, was elected Calgary mayor and in later years, the mayor's office in both major centres was held by a typographer. A Calgary printer, Fred White, served as leader of a sizeable labour caucus in the provincial legislature from 1921 to 1935. The Calgary local of the ITU, one of the oldest unions in North America, was formed June 6, 1902; the Edmonton local a year later in April 1903. The Edmonton local, however, disbanded in 1906 after losing a strike and did not reform until 1907.

As the movement grew and workers in more and more trades joined unions, some co-ordination and communica-

Calgary painters, all dressed up for the 1912 Labour Day cele-brations.

tion between them was necessary and in addition to the building trades councils, general labour councils representing all unions in local areas were established. The councils were unable to do much in the way of co-ordination of strike activity—unions in Canada jealously guard that job for themselves—and their major role was acting as labour's mouthpiece in the community, making sure that the interests of working people were heard in municipal councils that were then made up almost completely of businessmen. In 1902, R.A. Brockelbank, president of the Calgary carpenters union, became the first labour representative to hold elected office at any level of government in Alberta when he won an aldermanic seat on Calgary city council in 1902. He ran again the following year on a platform endorsed by the labour council but was unsuccessful. The programme called for retention by the city of the ownership of all public utilities, reduction of property qualifications for people elected to public office and extension of voting rights to all tenants and those paying taxes of at least four dollars. He tried again in 1904 and got back on council, where he stayed until 1910.[44]

The original drive to organize a labour council in Cal-

gary came in 1900 when the machinists, organized for only two months, called a meeting on July 12 of representatives of the few unions then in existence to discuss plans for a Labour Day Parade. A formal trades council was formed February 19, 1901. Edmonton followed with the establishment of a labour council on January 16, 1903.

Neither the Edmonton nor the Calgary council was in a hurry to formalize its organization with a charter from the American Federation of Labour. The Calgary council received a charter on May 25, 1905, while the Edmonton charter was granted in 1906. Edmonton's decision to apply for a charter was made at a meeting December 2, 1905 at the Unity Hall, with representatives of the plumbers, typographers, lathers, bricklayers and carpenters in attendance. The carpenters played a large role in the council; the chairman of the meeting and the first president of the chartered council was J.A. Kinney, president of the Edmonton carpenters (who in 1914 became the city's first labour alderman). The secretary of the meeting was another carpenter.

A labour council was formed in Medicine Hat in 1905 and in Lethbridge a year later. Lethbridge unionists held

Labour Day parade in Edmonton, 1906.

their first Labour Day celebration in 1904. Both councils, once established, seemed to have some difficulty staying alive. The Medicine Hat council fell apart and was not reorganized until 1910 while its Lethbridge counterpart struggled along but failed in 1908 to pay its membership fee to the Trades and Labour Congress.

Despite problems in the smaller centres, the labour movement had, by 1907-08, been firmly established in Alberta. It was, however, a beachhead that employers would continue to battle against, hoping to drive the infant movement back into the sea.

Hillcrest in June of 1914 was the scene of one of the worst coal-mining disasters in Canadian history. One hundred eighty-nine men were killed. Below, a rescue team.

CHAPTER THREE

Early Expansion: 1907-1914

Mining Safety

On June 19, 1914, Emile Blas got out of school early. It was not a typical day in the Crowsnest Pass.

Early that morning Thomas Corkle walked to the mine, talking and joking with his friends as he drew his lamp and his tin check. He was getting out. It was his last shift—once more into the mine to get his tools and then off to Nelson where he had some metal mining prospects laid out.

At about 9:30 A.M., William Grafton was standing on the steps of the Southern Hotel in Bellevue, taking in the morning, when he noticed thick smoke coming from the mine mouth at Hillcrest. He rang the Hillcrest exchange but was told everything at the mine was okay.

About ten minutes later, Grafton and the rest of the Crowsnest Pass within earshot of the three blasts on the mine whistle found out that everything was not okay at the Hillcrest mine, not okay at all.

Those three blasts on a mine whistle have special meaning for the people living in a coal camp. For Mrs. Petrie, working in the small restaurant she owned, cleaning up after the morning rush and preparing for the noon meal, it meant that her son Alex, seventeen, and his two older brothers, James and Robert, would not be coming home that evening. For Charlie Kane it meant his dad would never become a fire-boss and that Charlie would be quitting school and going to work in a mine, like the one where his father had died. And for Thomas Corkle, it meant the end of his dream of going to Nelson and greener pastures.

There were 189 such tales in Hillcrest that morning: the three blasts on the whistle signalled the worst mining disaster in Alberta history and one of the worst in the country.

Upon looking across the mine nestling in the hillside, huge volumes of smoke were . . . belching from the dirt. The roads to Hillcrest immediately became alive with

people. . . . On arrival of rescue men from east and west, the men from nearby camps were formed into shifts to relieve each other every three hours in restoring ventilation and recovering the dead. The washing of bodies and preparing for burial was anything but a pleasant task owing to the mutilated condition of the bodies.[1]

A special issue of the miners' paper, the *District Ledger*, published that day, reported:

> The scene at the pit mouth beggars description. Hundreds of tear-stained, anxious-faced women and children are awaiting some news of their loved ones who so recently left them. 220 men entered the mine this morning but so far only 20 have been brought out alive, most of whom were unconscious and were revived and 23 lifeless bodies have been brought out up to the present time, leaving 182 men who are still entombed.

The following day, the *Ledger* remarked: "As in evidence of the great force of the explosion, the engine house at the south entry is simply a pile of debris and the end wall facing the pit mouth, eight inches thick and 16 feet high, was entirely demolished."

There were so many bodies requiring burial they had to dig the graves with a scraper and team, said Emile Blas. That's all he could remember of the explosion, except that when the blasts came on the whistle, the teacher dismissed school. Reporting on the mass funeral, the *District Ledger* said: "Slowly, but surely, the village of Hillcrest is returning to a natural condition of affairs. The widows, braving their loss and realizing that their children will need every attention, are bearing up with the stoicism peculiar to a mining community to whom sudden and violent death is not unknown."

Death had come before to the mining camps of the Crowsnest, usually taking the men by ones and twos. Occasionally, however, these disasters provided massive and dramatic confirmation of the hazards of the industry, as the *District Ledger* commented after Hillcrest:

> It would seem as though the Grim Reaper were somewhere ensconced in the shadow of Turtle Mountain. The toll of death in so sparse a population as is found within a radius of three miles has probably been the greatest in the annals of history. First there was the terrific disaster now popularly known as the great Frank slide, then on Dec. 9, 1910 came the first great accident in Alberta's history in the nearby camp of Bellevue when 31 paid the price incident to winning coal.

The official inquiry established to look into the Hillcrest disaster did not attach any blame for the explosion and the miners complained bitterly that the task of studying the accident was left to a judge instead of someone who under-

stood mining. Following the Bellevue explosion, however, the miners were officially vindicated in their contention that so great a loss of life did not have to be accepted meekly as the price of fueling the nation. A coroner's jury investigating the cave-in and explosion at Bellevue determined that the company had been negligent in ensuring that the provincial mines act was properly enforced. After the jury had released its findings, the miners at Bellevue walked off the job, refusing to return until mine management found a way to prevent cave-ins of the sort that killed thirty-one of their fellow workers. The *Edmonton Capital* of January 17, 1911 reported that other Crowsnest Pass miners were considering similar action. A company official was quoted as saying the operators would try to comply with the miners' demand but noted that compliance would be expensive.[2]

The Hillcrest and Bellevue explosions stand out only because of the numbers involved. Death in Alberta's coal mines usually came less dramatically but it was a reality that miners and their families lived with always. More than 1,200 miners lost their lives in Alberta mines from 1904 to 1963, 134 of them from 1904 through 1910.[3] Not that the miners though of the hazards as they left the wash-house and walked to the mine mouth, picking up the numbered pieces of tin which showed the mine officials that they were underground. "If you have that in mind you

wouldn't have no one to go into the mine," Emile Blas said. "You're brought up that way so you go about your work. Because, if you start to think, today I'm going to get hurt . . . well, there'd be no one going."

Not all the deaths and injuries were due to negligence on the part of mine operators. Many took place just because of the nature of the industry. The presence of methane gas (a particular problem in the Crowsnest), and coal dust, when combined with the blasting necessary to get to the coal seam and then break the coal free from the rock, often resulted in explosions. At the same time, however, many accidents did take place because coal operators really couldn't care less. Their unconcern was shared by the provincial government in Edmonton. It wasn't until 1927 that coal mining became a recognized trade requiring a test of proficiency. Company officials were all too happy to flood the mines with men who were inexperienced and unable to speak English. There were also complaints that the fire-bosses, the men who were supposed to ensure enforcement of the mines act and proper safety procedures, acted instead as agents of the companies in pushing up production.

Mine owners, many of them running marginal operations found that expenses for safety cut into profits. As the mines were dug, heavy timbers were supposed to be placed to prevent the ceilings from falling in. Art Roberts, a retired Drumheller miner, claimed operators were content to see miners scrimp a little in putting up the timbers.

> Timber cost money to the operator. The less of them you put in, the better he liked it. And the fight used to go on all the time—too many goddamn timbers. The guy that came in a couple of days before pay day to measure how much your coal was, how many timbers and so forth—"too many timbers." "You go to hell," some would say. Some, a little afraid of the boss, would lengthen them out and this is where the bloody top would come down.[5]

Retired Pass miner Pete Youschok recalled that when an accident did occur in the mines, the management officials asked first if any horses had been hurt. "They never asked how the goddamn man was. It took time to train a horse. You could replace a man anytime them days."[6]

Cave-ins and explosions were by no means the only killers in the mines. The leading culprit, in fact, was the coal dust which, in a coal town, provides a uniform cover of blackness for everything. Black snow may contain an element of poetry, coal-blackened lungs do not. The tipple where the coal is screened and cleaned has one of the highest dust concentrations but work there is physically less demanding than at the face. The tipple was where the children laboured and where a miner crippled in an underground accident could find work. Harry Gate started working in the McGillivray mine in the Crowsnest in 1925 and soon after was hurt in an accident. He was able to transfer to a job on the tipple where he worked until retirement. Gate said that the coal dust didn't do him much good. When he started on the tipple, there was no equipment to filter out the dust and it "was pretty dusty in there. You damaged your lungs and there's no such thing as compensation for it no how."[7]

It wasn't that the Provincial Mines Act was lax in its regulations, but like the Public Works Health Act that was supposed to guarantee the navvies some measure of dignity in their living accommodations, the problem came with enforcement. Almost without exception, mine inspectors joined the government service after holding management jobs in the mines or went to management jobs in the mines after working as inspectors. The miners constantly pushed for election of inspectors from among their ranks but such requests were greeted with dead silence from Edmonton. Inspectors were supposed to arrive unannounced but operators often had an uncanny sense that an inspection was coming, miners say. To give some credit to inspectors, their lot was not an easy one. Even by the 1920s, when the mining industry was well-established in the province, there were only seven inspectors. The man in Lethbridge looked after 112 mines; the Crowsnest inspector was responsible for 22 and they were among the most dangerous in Alberta.[8]

Workers and the Law

The fight for a decent workers' compensation act that would provide financial security for injured workers and their families was a major battle for Alberta's labour movement in the first two decades of the twentieth century. The 1907 coal commission, as it toured the province taking testimony from miners, heard time and again of the pressing need for compensation. At that time, the only recourse a miner had was to sue his employer. Private insurance was available but miners were hard pressed to feed their families on three dollars a day let alone handle the expense of premiums on accident insurance. The commission reported to the government:

> The evidence taken demonstrates that the provisions of the present law [allowing surviving dependents to sue], while they may be fair in theory, are in practice useless, that the expense necessary to conduct litigation under the present system of trial by jury and with the consequent appeals and long delays has in the past rendered it impossible in almost every case for any compensation to be recovered.[9]

William Graham, employed at a mine in Coleman for about four years and with fifteen years prior experience in England, was one of those who stated the case for a compensation act to the commission.

> Question: "How many fatal accidents at this mine since you have been here?"
> "I think six, including the three men killed in the explosion recently."
> "Any compensation paid in those cases?"
> "I am very sorry to say only what the men have deemed fit to give themselves. As the working class produces all wealth, I think there should be legislation providing compensation for them. I think it is only just. All the fatal accidents that have happened here, it has been the working men that have supported the widows. I don't think it is right. . . ."

Another miner, asked what things would improve the lot of Alberta miners, replied: "A compensation act for us poor workmen. That is what we have been wanting for a long time and it would help a lot."[10]

The commission report gave the miners what they wanted; the Alberta legislature did not. A compensation act was drafted and passed in the 1908 session but it had

The funeral for five miners killed in a mine fire in the river valley in Edmonton, June, 1907.

serious drawbacks, the major one being the continued involvement of the courts in assessing liability and a host of other matters. The act didn't establish a compensation board and it allowed companies to maintain private insurance schemes as long as they provided benefits at least as generous as those set in the act. It did, however, establish a scale of benefits.

From the early days of the 1900s, when the labour movement in Alberta found its feet, workers began to realize that unity of their numbers would bring not only improvements in wages and working conditions through negotiation but would give them considerable clout at the ballot box as well. Workers faced many problems that could best be dealt with through political activity. Compensation was one of those problems and was a major spur to politi-

cal involvement by working people. On January 8, 1909, Lethbridge miner and socialist Donald McNabb became the first labour member elected to the Alberta legislature when he won the Lethbridge riding by acclamation in a by-election. Workers found, however, that unity around political objectives was harder to achieve than union solidarity on the picket line. A general election was called for March of that year and this time, McNabb couldn't even save his deposit. He came in last.

Labour continued to have a voice in Edmonton, however, and a colourful voice at that. Charlie O'Brien ran in the 1909 general election as a socialist in the Rocky Mountain constituency, which included the Crowsnest, and won by a narrow thirty-five-vote margin over the second-place Liberal. O'Brien was an organizer for the Socialist Party of Canada and, according to his biography in the

Employees of an Edmonton brickyard, about 1910.

Parliamentary Guide, "picked up his education in logging, mining and railroad camps." A fellow socialist described him as "a very genial chap"[12] but the authorities and establishment politicians had a different view of Alberta's first revolutionary MLA. In 1910, the legislature was preparing what, in O'Brien's absence, would have been a routine resolution of sympathy after the death of King Edward VII. But O'Brien decided that death was death and since his fellow legislators were in a mourning mood, moved an amendment to send condolences to the wives and families of three hundred miners killed in a British mine disaster. The old-line politicians were so upset that anyone would dare link the death of royalty with the deaths of coal miners that they threw books and inkwells at their socialist colleague.[13]

In 1912, the year before O'Brien lost his Rocky Mountain seat by eight-one votes (three other socialist candidates came in last), Alberta workers tried a different tack to make themselves heard in the councils of government in Edmonton. Their vehicle was a provincial federation of unions which could lobby the government for such legislative improvements as a new compensation act to abolish judicial involvement and raise benefits. Donald McNabb, the former Lethbridge MLA and a socialist of moderate views, chaired the founding convention of the Alberta Federation of Labour (AFL) and told the forty delegates gathered in the Lethbridge Trades Hall on June 14 that more education would be required before the federation could take a "definite line of political action" and that the federation would "aim at obtaining legislation of a reform character."

Not all of the delegates saw it that way, particularly those from the mining camps, where the Socialist Party of Canada had built up an impressive base. The president of District 18, Clem Stubbs, said the miners had been fighting for some time to "remove or alleviate the oppression to which they were subjected as wage workers and after running into numerous blind alleys and continually driving their heads against stone walls, they had finally arrived at the conclusion that the only solution to the problem was the abolishing of the wage system altogether. "If that's what the federation would do, the mine workers were all for it," Stubbs said.

An unusual feature of the founding convention was the presence of thirteen representatives of the United Farmers of Alberta (UFA). Said McNabb: "The interests of the farmers and the city toilers are identical. . . . If organized . . . they would be in a position to go to the legislative halls as a

Settlers arriving in Wetaskiwin, south of Edmonton.

united band and co-operate in demanding legislation for the farmer, the city toiler and the miner." In a province where the majority of the population lived in rural areas, co-operation with farmers was vital to labour's success. Labour had earlier co-operated with the Society of Equity, an early farm organization, but after the 1912 convention had ended, the UFA decided against any close relationship with the labour movement, despite assiduous wooing by federation officers. The UFA had been granted two vice-presidencies in the federation's first constitution; both posts were filled in 1912 but never again and in 1918, all mention of the UFA was dropped from the constitution.[14]

By 1913, the federation represented more than four thousand workers, the bulk of them members of the United Mine Workers, which contributed not only the organization's first president, Hillcrest miner J.O. Jones, but more than 60 percent of membership dues in the first year.[15] The 1913 convention of the federation confirmed its role as a lobbying organization; the political factions within it were too numerous to permit it becoming a political body. The federation committed itself to press for the repeal of the 1908 compensation act and replace it with a more modern piece of compensation legislation. It also decided to urge a fair wage clause for all government work, (requiring that employers receiving government contracts pay union wages), and a better way to collect unpaid wages than by court action.

In 1914, the federation decided to appoint someone to keep an eye on sessions of the legislature. Its legislative programme in that year gave compensation major billing but added to it were demands that the province set standards for sanitation and ventilation of workshops, prohibit labour by children under sixteen, and bar employment of "white girls" in Chinese restaurants and laundries, which were considered unfit places to work. (Such overt racism was not uncommon in the early days of the labour movement, and stemmed in large part from the fact that employers were often instrumental in bringing very poor immigrants into the country so that they could be employed at low wages with poor working conditions.) Some of the things then on the federation's agenda are still on, namely the provision of free dental care for children and elimination of private employment agencies.[17]

Of all the legislation that affected the labour movement in this period, probably the most important was Mackenzie King's Industrial Disputes Investigations Act (IDIA) passed after the 1906 Lethbridge coal strike. Until it was declared *ultra vires* twenty years later, it was the nation's premier piece of labour legislation. King had thought it would bring in a new era of industrial peace. He was wrong. The act did nothing to remove the causes of unrest in the coal fields; it only made it more difficult for miners to press their demands for better wages and working conditions and their right to have a union.

In 1906, for example, seeking to challenge the power the United Mine Workers had built up, with the bulk of Alberta and eastern British Columbia miners in its ranks, the coal operators decided to band together and meet District 18 head on. They formed the Western Canada Coal Operators Association and in March of 1907 met with

union officials to negotiate a district-wide agreement to replace the individual contracts previously signed between the UMW and the employers; these contracts expired April 1, 1907. Bargaining broke down and the union locals applied for boards of conciliation and investigation under the IDIA. Boards were established but the companies objected on the grounds that applications under the act had been made by the union, not by committees of their employees. The miners walked out and by mid-April, nearly all the mines represented by the association were shut down.

The miners were now faced with a new curve—the strike was illegal. A board had been applied for and no strike could take place until the board had released its report. Mackenzie King arrived at the coal fields and informed the miners their walkout was against the law. Illegal or not, the men decided to continue their strike and in early May, an agreement was reached with the operators association providing an immediate wage increase and a mechanism to settle future disputes. The contract allowed for limited recognition of the union but again the miners were saddled with the non-discrimination clause.

About a year later, western delegates to the Trades and Labour Congress, including District 18 chief, Frank Sherman, demanded the repeal of the IDIA. Eastern delegates, however, more moderate than their western brethren, were unconvinced and it was not until 1916 that the TLC asked for repeal of the act. King may have believed the IDIA was based on a "sympathetic understanding and apprecia-

tion of the working classes in their industrial struggles and on principles of truth and justice, which are the great determining factors of this universe."[18] Victor Clark, who prepared a report on the legislation for American president Teddy Roosevelt, saw it more clearly: The act, he wrote, "has accomplished the main purpose for which it was enacted, the prevention of strikes. . . ."[19] One industrial relations expert has pointed out that while the act act placed limitations on labour's right to strike:

> . . . . there were no effective restrictions on employers to prevent the familiar practices of imposing yellow-dog contracts, blacklisting, discriminatory discharge of union members and employment of non-union members or strike-breakers. [In a yellow-dog contract, the employee, in return for a job, promises not to join a union.] On balance it [the IDIA] appears to have operated adversely to the strength and effectiveness of organized labour in Canada."[20]

Neither King's involvement nor his legislation was effective in bringing a truce in the industrial warfare in the coal camps of Alberta. Miners were still working for pittance, dying in the mines or dying from waves of typhoid or influenza. In 1909, a strike involving about two thousand miners was called. The Hillcrest Coal Company indignantly wrote the federal labour minister demanding that if a "settlement is not reached, the mine owners should be allowed to import men whom the government should protect with soldiers." Several weeks later, with

A railway construction crew west of Lethbridge, 1912.

the strike still on, the company again wrote Ottawa, this time proposing that strikes should be declared illegal. "The whole trouble," said the Hillcrest official, "was caused by Mr. Sherman. . . . The men are all anxious to go to work so far as I could learn, but are afraid to do so owing to the union miners preventing them." When the strike was settled after three months, the miners had won the right to buy goods wherever they wanted, freeing them from the necessity of shopping at company-owned stores which were more expensive than independent merchants.[21]

In negotiations for a new contract in 1911, the principal demand of the miners was again a closed shop and again the operators would have nothing to do with it. Despite government suggestions that the dispute be referred to a board established under the Industrial Disputes Investigation Act, seven thousand miners in District 18 walked off the job April 1 in what would be one of the largest strikes of the pre-war period. There were some reports of violence early in the strike as miners in the Crowsnest tried to stop production at several mines where pump and fan men (usually left on the job by the union to prevent the mines from flooding) had been ordered to dig coal to fill railway orders. By April 10, District 18's objections to a conciliation board under the IDIA had been overcome and a board was applied for. The strike, however, was not called off and Alberta miners were again afoul of Mackenzie King's legislation. This time, there was also a question of whether the international would support the miners in an illegal strike, however, it eventually did.

Even with the board sitting, trouble continued in the fields as the operators fought back. At Frank, Canadian Consolidated Coal secured warrants to evict miners from their homes and seize their furniture. Other mines tried to reopen with strike-breakers and by August, there were from three hundred to four hundred men working at four mines. As the strike dragged on into the fall, there were again, as there had been during the 1906 Lethbridge strike, warnings of an impending fuel shortage on the Prairies. In late October, the federal minister of the interior arrived and pushed through a settlement modelled on the majority report of the IDIA board. The miners had been out for eight months and although they won a 10 percent wage increase, they came away empty-handed in their major demand. The non-discrimination clause and an open shop would continue in the Alberta fields at least until 1915, when the contract expired.[22]

Building the Northern Transcontinental

Following the deaths of Fraser and McDonald on the Crowsnest Pass railway construction project and the reports of the two royal commissions appointed to examine the deaths and the navvies' complaints, the federal government passed the Public Works Health Act of 1900. Unfortunately, the legislation brought little change to the lives of those who laboured on railway construction. Not until two years after the act was passed, were inspectors appointed to enforce it, and even that made little difference.[23]

From 1905 through 1912, the boom that had hit Calgary with the building of the mainline and Crowsnest Pass line moved north to Edmonton as two more transcontinental

Camp life during mainline construction west of Edmonton before the First World War.

routes and their branch lines were pushed through. Edmonton became a city of transients. Tents and shacks housed thousands of men who flocked to the city to seek their fortunes and there found poverty, misery and hard work. The *Edmonton Capital*, one of three daily papers in the city at the time, reported in 1912 that Edmonton had gained almost twenty-three thousand residents in one year, including twenty-five hundred transients.[24] Many of the transients, on their way to or from the railway camps west of the city, lived in a shantytown of shacks and tents in the east end, north of the railway tracks. A story in the July 20, 1912 *Capital* described one such group of about sixty-five tents and shacks surrounding pools of open and stagnant water. Reports of diphtheria in the area were not uncommon.

If such were the living conditions in the booming metropolis, little wonder that hundreds of miles to the west, in the bush and muskeg, things were considerably worse. One navvie wrote to a union newspaper from a camp along the construction line of one of the railways saying that there had been "several government inspectors along this line during the last year which has not amounted to as much as the wind blowing from the south." Speaking of one inspector in particular, the navvie wrote:

The first thing done when arriving at the end of steel was to make arrangements for a team to convey him over the road with F.W.&S. [Foley, Welch and Stewart, a contractor] officials, which I followed to Mile 148. He did not enter one bunkhouse but slept in the offices, with fine accommodation, eating with the foreman and time-keeper, not witht the men; and all these so-called inspections are the same. What have they amounted to? Nothing. Conditions are worse than ever.[25]

By the early 1900s, contractors were no longer relying on labour from eastern Canada as eastern and southern European immigrants began to make up the bulk of their labour force. By the early 1920's, Alberta's workforce was 13 percent Ukrainian; Czechs, Yugoslavs and Italians comprised another 22.5 percent.[26] One of the reasons for this change was that non-immigrants were increasingly less willing to put up with what the contractors had to offer. Immigrants had less choice and there were lots of them available for work. Between 1905 and 1912 new immigrants to Alberta numbered close to 250,000.[27]

A 1908 letter to the Winnipeg labour newspaper, the *Voice,* said that the boxcars where the navvies slept were:

.... not fit for dogs to sleep in, let alone humans. These cars have been used for sleeping purposes for years until they are infested with vermin and it would be almost impossible to cleanse them. Another trouble with the cars is the overcrowding. Anywhere from 20 to 35 men are crowded into an ordinary 35-foot length boxcar and I can assure you that the stench that protrudes from those cars about 11 o'clock at night and 4 A.M. is enough to knock a man down.[28]

Such conditions, the letter said, were some of the reasons "white" men would not work on the railways. Pay was also a complaint but "$15 or $20 is more to a Galician [Ukrainian] than a Canadian."

As in Mann's camp in the Crowsnest, the overcrowding and unsanitary conditions in the bunkhouses or boxcars took their toll. Mounted Police Inspector R.E. Tucker of the Entwhistle detachment west of Edmonton reported on November 18, 1909, the death of a Swedish navvie. Olaf

Anderson, of typhoid fever. "Hospital authorities notified his relatives. He had no effects except blankets and some clothing. These were all burned at the hospital."[29]

If it wasn't typhoid or diphtheria, it was industrial accidents. According to one estimate, about thirty-seven hundred railway construction workers in Canada lost their lives in accidents between 1901 and 1918.[30] One of those killed was Joseph Johnstone, a structural iron worker from Buffalo, New York, who fell to his death when working on a high level trestle over the Pembina River in 1912. The *Edmonton Capital* of October 9 said Johnstone, a riveter, was changing his footing on the top tier of the span when he "accidently touched the trigger of the pneumatic riveter which rebounded." Johnstone was hit in the forehead and thrown into the air. The Pembina River was 170 feet below. With the proper precautions, such as lifeline, Johnstone probably would have lived to finish the bridge.

Injury and death were no strangers in the camps along the rail lines, this time being built by the Grand Trunk syndicate and the two promoters of the Canadian Northern, Sir William Mackenzie and Sir Donald Mann. And, as was the case with McDonald and Fraser, sick men received little sympathy from contractors.

A man got his fingers crushed at Mile 148 and laid off work several days. When his funds were exhausted he was told to get out by the foreman and had to go to Mile 114 to the hospital. The hospital would not take him in. Leaving 114, he walked to 152, during which time he had only one meal to eat, which he begged. At Mile 152 he laid his case before the officials of the company for whom he worked. They turned him down. He then went

to Foley, Welch and Stewart's office and they gave him a line to take to his original camp so that he could get a soft job. The job was to take care of a sick mule. Oh, the irony of it.[31]

If the inspectors and police were lax in enforcing the sanitation sections of the act, there was one piece of legislation that received their undivided attention—that dealing with the liquor traffic. It was against the law to have liquor within a certain distance of railway construction. During the period of construction, Edson achieved a certain notoriety for its illegal drinking establishments known as blind pigs because liquor was often smuggled inside pork bellies.

Ladies do not care to walk on parts of the main street on account of the drunken men. . . . Since the licences have been granted here there has been an extraordinary amount of drunkenness in Edson. Hundreds of men are coming through every day, a great many from the west. Labourers paid off after several months work have considerable money and of course they proceed to get drunk.[32]

Other reports, however, like one written by a navvie to the *Industrial Worker*, the newspaper of the Industrial Workers of the World, told of conditions in the area that seemed to escape the notice of the police officer.

On July 7, I went to the Logan employment office in Edmonton and after giving them a hard luck story they booked me for a job gratis. A bunch of slaves booked in that office the same day I did and each dug up a $1 piece.

Construction of railway bridge across the Oldman River valley at Lethbridge, 1909. The bridge, 5,327 feet long and 314 feet high, is still the highest railway bridge in Canada.

After several days, we got a train. There were about 100 in the bunch and we were told that when we arrived at Wolf Creek [near Edson] the cook would be waiting for us with a good supper. We arrived at Wolf Creek about 3 A. M. and it was raining hard. We were all lined up after leaving the train and marched through the woods about three miles, wading through the mud and soaked by the rain. Before getting to the camp, we had to cross the McLeod River in a scow. When we arrived in camp we were wet to the skin and hungry as bears but there was no sign of anything to eat. We were all so tired that we flopped down any place we could in our wet clothes and slept until breakfast time. The grub in this camp (Head-

quarters No. 1) was something fierce. It was so rotten and so poorly cooked that it made nearly everyone sick, including myself.[33]

The IWW was one of the few labour organizations that ever took on the task of organizing the navvies, but by the time it had moved into Canada, railway construction on a massive scale in Alberta was drawing to a close. The IWW led several strikes along the lines of the Canadian Northern and Grand Trunk Pacific in British Columbia in 1912, and as Edmonton was one of the centres for construction work, it established a base there. But its work in Alberta was to be among the unemployed, not the navvies.

Liquor was smuggled into railway camps in the bellies of pig carcasses. Police spent more time enforcing liquor legislation than laws setting health standards for railway camps.

A man with a scraper, at work on the Canadian Northern Railway near Edson, 1916.

Construction workers building a railway bridge near Red Deer in 1911.

Expansion of the Urban Labour Movement

Booming economic conditions are not just a recent development in Alberta history. The explosion in the province's growth in the first decade of the century more than matches the growth of contemporary times. Between 1901 and 1906, the population more than doubled to 184,000 and by 1911, it almost doubled again. Nearly four hundred thousand people were living in a territory that twenty-five years earlier had been called home by less than twenty-thousand.[34] The 1884-85 census had reported the total value of industrial production in Alberta at only $400,000. By 1906, it had jumped to $5 million and by 1910, it had more than tripled to almost $19 million. The boom of the war years would push the 1920 figure to close to $30 million.[35]

Between 1906 and 1914, the populations of both Edmonton and Calgary increased from 14,000 to more than 72,000, while Lethbridge and Medicine Hat tripled their populations to 9,000. So great was the influx to the capital in 1906 that the existing immigration hall couldn't handle it. Between three hundred and five hundred new residents were arriving in the city every day. New immigrants were bunked in the exhibition grounds and a new hall was built north of the Canadian Northern tracks. By 1912, with the city a base for construction of the northern transcontinentals, about twenty-five hundred residents of the capital were transients.[36]

Real estate speculation became big business in Edmonton. In 1907 almost half of city businesses were real estate agencies and in 1912, Henderson's Directory reported 32 brokers and 336 real estate agents. In the same year, according to a report in the *Edmonton Capital* on July 20, a house "could not be secured for less than forty dollars a month." Even skilled tradesmen such as the plumbers, then earning seventy cents an hour for forty-four hours a week,[37] would find their budgets stretched by such costs, especially at a time when families of six and seven children were not uncommon.

The skilled in Alberta's cities—the construction trades, typesetters and machinists—could afford their own small frame houses, each with a kitchen, living room, several small bedrooms and a dirt cellar. For unskilled labourers laying tracks for the street railways or digging ditches for sewer installation, home was most often a rented, three-room house.[38] Unmarried workers lived with working class families or took rooms in downtown hotels or boarding-houses, sometimes sleeping three or four to a room. Still others put up their own shacks or tents in areas such as Calgary's Hillhurst district, northwest of the city

Immigration hall in Edmonton, 1911–1912. Immigration increased the city's population from 14,000 to 72,000 between 1906 and 1914.

Edmonton Plumbers, Local 488 members, at their annual picnic.

With the large increases in population in Edmonton in the pre-war period, land speculation was big business. In 1907, half of the businesses in the city were real estate agencies. Lots, such as this one near 111th Ave. and 106th St. were sold as "high and dry." They weren't.

Photographer Ernest Brown wrote of this picture: "New arrivals from England solve housing problem." They weren't alone. In June 1912, an Edmonton newspaper found more than 2,500 people living in tents.

Telephone operators in High River, south of Calgary, wear masks during the 1918 flu epidemic. More than 3,000 people died and schools, churches and theatres were closed.

centre, or along the Grand Trunk tracks in Edmonton to avoid "being swindled to pay rent or being at the prey of real estate sharks."[39] In June of 1912, the *Edmonton Bulletin* took one of its occassional looks at the city's housing situation and found more than 2,500 people living in tents in the river valley or on the outskirts, with some being temporarily housed in a curling club.

Some of the labourers building the Calgary waterworks project in 1909 lived in bunkhouses just outside the city and ate meals in a tent used to thaw dynamite. The city's health inspector, accompanied by George Howell, a labour council representative who, later that year, ran and lost as a socialist candidate for the legislature, found as many as forty-four men sleeping in bunks in a tent measuring 630 square feet [half the size of a modern three-bedroom bungalow]. In the dining tent, the inspector found Ukrainian labourers "eating their meal, sitting on boxes of dynamite with one small stove between them." The sleeping tent for the workers was one-third the size of the dining tent used by the foremen. After the inspection, city council allowed as how things at the camp could be improved but then moved on to more pressing issues like cruelty to animals and the necessity of building an animal shelter. The crowded slums, with little or no sanitation, were easy breeding grounds for disease and the workers and their families, weakened by poor food and not enough of it, long hours of work and little recreation, were easy prey. Edmonton city commissioners reported to council in October, 1912 that there were eighty-nine cases of typhoid in the city, but one alderman claimed there were eighty-six cases at the Royal Alexandra Hospital alone and that another fifty cases had been turned away.[40]

The unwholesome living conditions permitted disease to spread with devastating quickness, as it did in the 1918 flu epidemic when more than three thousand Albertans died. In one day during the epidemic, fifty-four people died in Edmonton alone. A labour newspaper in Drumheller reported that workers "literally died like flies."[41] The Alberta Federation of Labour said the high number of deaths and the rapid spread of disease showed "how inadequate are the sanitary arrangements of our towns, villages and camps." The federation's complaint was echoed in the provincial police report for the year, which noted that the death toll was particularly high in those "communities where large families are occupying small houses which, at the best of times, are anything but sanitary. In such cases, whole families were wiped out by this dreaded scourge."[42] Disease was more than the threat of death. With no paid sick leave, it was a potential financial tragedy as well. J.W. Findlay, an Edmonton railway machinist,

told a commission in the spring of 1919 that he "took the
flu here some time ago and was laid off for a couple of
weeks. That meant I went $100 behind. Probably it will be
two or three years before I could catch up."[43]

The growth of Alberta cities, particularly Edmonton,
brought accompanying expansion in trade union numbers. At the turn of the century, there had been only four
local unions in the province; by 1913, that number had
jumped to 171 locals with a combined membership of
about eleven thousand five hundred. In the three years
between 1907 and 1910, 72 locals were added to Alberta's
trade union roster. In 1911, Calgary had forty locals while
Edmonton workers had organized themselves into thirty-
three. Lethbridge had twenty-eight, Medicine Hat fifteen
and there were thirty-three locals, primarily miners'
unions, in twenty-seven other centres.[44]

The years following the coming of the Canadian Northern Railway to Edmonton saw workers in almost all sectors
of industry taking to trade unionism. In 1906, Local 92 of
the Hodcarriers and Builders Protective Union (now the
Labourers Union, still with the same charter number), was
established. A year later, labourers installing underground
telephone lines were earning twenty-five cents an hour for
ten hours work, six days a week. Rooms were $4.50 a week,
meals cost a quarter, and a work shirt the same.[45] Unions of
blacksmiths, journeyman tailors, barbers and teamsters
were all established in Edmonton in 1907, as was Local 55
of the Hotel and Restaurant Employees Union. Reflecting
the growth of the railway industry in the northern part of
the province, unions of railway carmen, machinists and
maintenance of way workers were also formed. The United
Mine Workers, from its established base in the
Lethbridge-Crowsnest region, made an attempt in 1907 to
move into the Edmonton area, setting up two locals within
a month of one another. Several other locals were formed
in 1909 but by 1911, all had dissolved. Of all the mine

fields in the province, Edmonton would prove the toughest to organize and the UMW never did succeed in overcoming the intractable opposition of Edmonton coal operators.

Also caught up in the organizing boom were groups of public sector workers. The Federated Association of Letter Carriers which formed in 1891, moved into Alberta in 1907. The day before Christmas, Calgary letter carriers established Local 14 of the union. Two months later, thirteen Edmonton letter carriers formed Local 15. By the end of 1913, membership in the Edmonton branch stood at sixty-four.[46] Locals in Lethbridge and Medicine Hat were organized in 1912 and 1913. In 1907, Calgary postal clerks wrote the postmaster general complaining that their wages of forty-five to sixty dollars a month couldn't be stretched to cover the costs of room, board (thirty dollars a month) and other necessities. But workers in the public sector

could do more than write letters protesting inadequate wages, as two dramatic strikes in 1912 demonstrated.

In Edmonton, at the end of September 1912, the militia was ordered to the ready in case it was needed to put down disturbances arising from a strike of city labourers working on sewer construction. About two hundred and fifty city workers went on strike September 27 and began picketing other city works sites in an effort to make other workers "come out of the ditch," said the *Capital* in its edition of that date. The men were asking for a five cent an hour increase to bring their wage to thirty-five cents. In turn, the city offered to let the labourers work nine hours a day, instead of eight, at the old rate, with the additional hours to be paid at forty-five cents.

The strike lasted only five days and the men returned to work on the city's terms, but what made the situation ominous enough to warrant alert of the militia was the

A crew in Edmonton, about 1912, digging ditches for sewers. In September of that year, 250 ditch diggers went on strike seeking a wage increase of five cents an hour. The Industrial Workers of the World, then organizing in Edmonton and Calgary, took a hand in the strike. After five days, the workers returned to their jobs on the city's terms.

involvement in the strike of a seven-year-old union that struck fear into the hearts of businessmen, police and politicians alike. The American Federation of Labour may have considered unskilled labour unworthy of organization but the Industrial Workers of the World (IWW), formed in Chicago in 1905, harboured no such qualms. Navvies, ditch-diggers, harvest workers and women in sweat shops, immigrants and native-born, all were welcomed into the IWW.

Big Bill Haywood, a leader of the IWW who had come out of the Western Federation of Miners, said the Wobblies, as they were called, would go "down into the gutter to get at the mass of workers and bring them up to a decent plane of living."[47] Sam Gompers and many of the craft unions of the day had decided they could live with the current economic system but the Wobblies would have none of it. Haywood, speaking at the IWW founding convention in 1905, urged members to "confederate the workers into a working class movement that shall have for its purpose the emancipation of the working class from the slave bondage of capitalism."[48]

"The working class and the employing class," said the preamble of the IWW constitution, "have nothing in common. There can be no peace so long as hunger and want are found among millions of working people and the few who make up the capitalist class have all the good things in life." The IWW had some of the most colourful working class leaders on the continent and some of the best strike strategists the labour movement has ever had. Its long-term interest was the overthrow of capitalism, but in the years from 1905 to 1920 when it was at its peak in North America, it went where the American Federation of Labour feared to tread, and with determination, commitment and imagination brought the ignored underclass of

The Teamsters Union float for a Lethbridge Labour Day parade, about 1912.

immigrants and the unskilled out of the gutter.

It was the Wobblies who organized the navvies on railway construction in British Columbia in 1911 and 1912. They used every imaginable tactic to win the strikes they led and in most, the 1912 Edmonton walkout being an exception, they were successful. The sit-down strike, which was to become a common tactic in the industrial organizing drives of the Thirties, was first conducted by the Wobblies. In a mining town in Nevada, Wobblies organized the entire community, from engineers and miners to newsboys. When city council passed by-laws outlawing IWW soap-box orators and arrested street-corner speakers, as they did in Calgary, Wobblies mobilized transient workers throughout the country to move to that particular city and defy the law. In most cases, municipal councils, their jails filled beyond overflowing, would relent. To organize the highly-mobile harvest workers in the American West, organizers rode the freights, and the red membership card of the IWW became the equivalent of a railway ticket.

The militancy and determination with which Wobblies fought on behalf of those Sam Gompers ignored made the names of many of their leaders well-known in working class North America: Joe Hill, song writer and organizer, executed by an Idaho firing squad; Ralph Chaplin, who wrote Solidarity Forever; Eugene Debs, who later left

because of the IWW's anti-political stance; and Mother Jones, a white-haired, grandmotherly woman and miners' union organizer who once told a group of miners they were losing their strike "because you haven't the guts to go out and fight and win it—why the hell don't you take your high-powered rifles and blow the goddamn scabs out of the mine?"[49] But the best know was Haywood, blind in one eye, stooped, six foot two and 225 pounds—a brawler and a drinker. One man who met him in Calgary described him as a "great, big, rough fellow [whose] belly would shake when he laughed."[50]

During the Edmonton strike, the Wobblies organized marching bands that walked from one work site to another. "A halt would be made and speeches delivered. Likewise, IWW songs would be sung, which are IWW sentiment put to the tune of popular airs. The purpose for doing this," said a story in the September 27 *Capital* "would be to make those at work realize there was a strike on." Such tactics had their desired effect. One gang working in the Norwood district was thus persuaded to put down its tools and "the strike committee found not a great many men at work and all at work being other than Ruthenians and Galicians." The Wobblies became involved in the dispute after the strike was called and such was the reputation of the organization that, at a meeting of the workers, Henry Rosenburg, a painter, urged the men to let the IWW look after things, "declaring that the IWW had never lost a strike." To counter the Wobblies' roving and singing pickets, police were stationed at the work sites and "when the strikers hesitated at one job, two police officers exhibited their revolvers, evidently for the purpose of making an impression," reported the *Capital* of September 28. In another move to take the wind out of the strikers' sails, police arrested the secretary of the IWW Edmonton local, Gus Larsen, and charged him with vagrancy.

A month later, law and order in the province was again under attack, this time more directly. October 1912 was an exciting time in Lethbridge. The *Lethbridge Herald* was expecting a "big influx of visitors to the city" as it prepared to host a convention on dry-land farming. The week of October 21 had been designated Dry Farming Week in the southern city and many distinguished delegates were expected in town for the big event. There would be "crooks and con men" as well. It was not the best time for police in Lethbridge to go on strike. Police Chief Davis, quoted in the *Lethbridge Herald* of October 21, said that "the action of the men in leaving the city in the lurch just when Lethbridge is most in need of police protection [is] a most disgraceful one and not one of these men will ever again serve in the Lethbridge police force as long as I am chief."

The dispute, quite probably the first municipal police strike in Canada, arose when a Toronto policeman was given the post of police inspector over Sergeant Brown, a member of the Lethbridge force considered by the men to be in line for the promotion. The *Herald* reported that:

> Consultations were held amongst the men Saturday afternoon and it was unanimously agreed that they would quit unless Chief Davis agreed to appoint a local man. The new chief absolutely refused and the result was that the entire force, headed by Sgt. Brown, marched out of police headquarters last night. They then immediately went home, took off their uniforms and sent them back to the police station. Last night, the floor of the courtroom in police headquarters was strewn with the uniforms of men and sergeants alike .... Not a single policeman could be seen on the streets .... As soon as Chief Davis saw that the men would remain firm in their intention of going on strike, he communicated with the Mounted Police barracks and several red-coats are doing the duties of the regular force.

Davis said he expected within several days to have an entirely new force made up of men from Calgary and Toronto, and in the meantime, eleven special constables were sworn in. The strike didn't last long. Strike-breakers arrived from Calgary on the afternoon of the first day; several of the strikers reconsidered and went back to pro-

tect Lethbridge during Dry Farming Week. As the *Calgary Herald* of October 21 said, "Chief Davis has the whip hand and is coping with the situation effectively."[51]

By 1914, the labour movement in Alberta was a fact of life. Through painstaking effort, Alberta workers had built the organizations they believed would defend and protect their interests. In the coming years, they would be put to the test.

CHAPTER FOUR

Depression and War: 1914-1918

Pre-War Depression

There must have been times when Robert Laird Borden, the eighth prime minister of Canada, thought his world was falling apart. Everything he believed in was under attack, and from all sides. Across the Atlantic, the heart of the empire itself was threatened by German militarism; peace, order and free enterprise had been tossed aside by Lenin and the Bolsheviks, and there was little solace at home: riots in Quebec; patriotism and the love of country in tatters as Canadians balked at doing their duty for the empire; IWWs everywhere, fomenting revolution; Canadian workers enchanted with the Russian revolutionaries; and general strikes or threats of same across the country.

Before the war, Alberta was plagued by mass unemployment, protest marches and demonstrations as the bubble of perpetual growth finally burst, leaving in its wake thousands without jobs. In 1913 and 1914, the situation in far-off Europe had an immediate and profound effect on the young working class of the province. As war neared, the financial barons of London who had bankrolled much of the pre-war expansion that had turned the Northwest Territories into two provinces decided to withdraw their capital and wait for things to stabilize. That decision, made thousands of miles away, resulted in thousands of Albertans walking the streets of once-bustling cities, looking for work. "Throughout the whole West," reported a federal government official in December 1913, after a tour of western Canada, "the number of unemployed is considerably larger than in former years. Unemployment is not confined to any particular trade or occupation but is general. In the building trades, the outlook for the winter months is not promising. A large number of mechanics connected with the building trades have left the country owing to lack of employment."

Even highly-skilled workers were having trouble keeping their jobs. In September of 1913, the CPR laid off one-quarter of its employees in Calgary's Ogden Shops and many of those still employed were working fewer hours than usual. In Medicine Hat, the carpenters and painters unions surrendered their charters. Even such normally secure workmen as printers and typesetters were hit: about 40 percent of them across the West were out of work. Some seven thousand people in Calgary were unemployed in 1914 and *Labour Gazette* correspondents expected that in Edmonton the number of jobless would jump from about four thousand to seven thousand as winter set in and harvesting and construction jobs ended.[2] Many unemployed, especially in Edmonton, were unskilled workers who had come to the city expecting jobs on railway construction or were coming back through after being laid off. One report said about 40 percent of Edmonton unemployed were railway construction workers.

In the early days of the depression, only family men in Edmonton were given relief work and in Calgary, work on various city public works projects was given out a week at a time to the city's unemployed. To qualify for a bed in Calgary's Associated Charities bunkhouse, unemployed had to work for nothing in the public woodyard. The city then sold the cut firewood to dealers at a dollar a cord.[3] For the authorities, the "menacing feature" of the unemployment problem was not its proportions, but rather that, in both Calgary and Edmonton, the jobless were being organized and were demanding work, and that the group doing the organizing was the Industrial Workers of the World, back again in the gutters of the West fighting for the people it found there.

Organization of the unemployed, especially in Edmonton, came naturally for the Wobblies. They had been active among railway construction workers west of the city and with a good number of the capital's jobless former railway workers, the connections were already there. Two locals of the IWW had been established in the province by 1913: Local 79 in Calgary and Local 82 in Edmonton. The northern unit was large enough to send a delegate to the 1913 convention in Chicago and was entitled to fourteen votes under the IWW's block-voting formula.[4] The Wobblies organized demonstrations, meetings and marches on city hall, but their most flamboyant gesture in bringing to the attention of prosperous Edmontonians that there were men in the city without work, was a march and sit-in at two downtown churches. At McDougall Methodist, several hundred men told the minister they wouldn't leave until they were given places to sleep.[5] The fact that the sit-ins occurred during Sunday services bothered the Wobblies not at all.

"In the bitter-cold weather, intense feeling was created by public demonstrations and marches through the streets of the unemployed, their numbers increasing daily," said T.R. Turnbull, Edmonton's civic relief officer. The Wobblies were having some effect.

To avoid outbreaks of lawlessness [the relief department of the city] gave to the unemployed men 3,697 meals and 709 beds, covering a period of five days. . . . During . . .

December, January and half of February, we have sent 3,489 men to work, the character of this work being entirely emergency: cleaning up lanes, brushing lots and parks and sewer work. Each man had offered to him a 3½ hour day at 30 cents per hour which has removed the acute stage of the situation.[6]

From Calgary, the *Toronto Globe* reported:

. . . . promptness of action has been required on the part of the police on one or two occasions to scatter certain fractious elements of the unemployed. During one protest march, the demonstrators, moving toward City Hall and carrying such banners declaring 'We Want Work' and 'If We Don't Get Work We Will Beg and Steal,' were broken up by police who arrested a man carrying one of the 'dangerous-looking' banners. When searched, it was discovered that the prisoner was one of the IWW speakers who had come into Alberta a few months before to take advantage of the existing economic conditions by stirring up the unemployed classes with pseudo-socialistic doctrines.

The miners were also hit by the depression. Employees of collieries in the Taber field were working an average of one day a week for the whole of 1914. Of all miners in the province, they were the worst off, but miners in all fields were working short-time.[7]

With the "streets black with men crowding around the employment offices looking in vain for work"[8] and unions in disarray as membership dwindled, some employers took the opportunity to cut wages. The Alberta Federation of Labour convention in October 1914 was told that in July, the mayor of Medicine Hat had attempted to pay employees of the city with meal tickets and scrip for groceries. One third of wages owed to municipal workers in the city was held back by the council and paid out in three instalments five, six and seven months later.

Workers in the Canadian West had been unceremoniously dumped from their jobs because of events in Europe. On August 3, 1914, they received a rather back-handed rescue—Britain and Germany were at war and the economic outlook, buoyed by war orders, was again rosy. Many of the unemployed marched right off the streets into the recruiting halls. In Edmonton, new recruits were served a hot meal right after they had taken their medicals. One man told a meeting of the Winnipeg Labour Council that he might just as well fight for his food in Belgium as Winnipeg. By the time the war ended, more than four hundred thousand Canadians had tasted trench warfare. Two-thirds were injured and more than forty-nine thousand never came back.[9]

An Edmonton crowd reading the latest war reports on the bulletin board of the Edmonton Journal, *1914.*

War and Conscription

A nation that had begrudged its unemployed relief had suddenly, when confronted with the needs of war, found the resources to put the country back to work. Arthur Meighen, a member of the Borden cabinet and later prime minister, declared he was ready to bankrupt the country for the empire and her defence. Taxes were immediately imposed on sugar, coffee and tobacco, but borrowed money financed the bulk of expenditures. Including railway loans, the federal debt between 1913 and 1921 increased sixfold.[10]

That fact, and the circumstances surrounding it, was not lost on the unemployed, who had to fight for relief. At a conference to discuss the unemployment problem, called in Calgary in November 1914 and attended by both labour and government officials, a representative of the Calgary Committee of Unemployed, Miss Mushcat, a teacher, told the government representative present it was his duty to

"come to the aid of those who are suffering and the children who are barefooted and are going to school half-fed. The dominion government has a right to levy taxes for war purposes," she said. "If the dominion government has a right to levy taxes for the purposes of war to destroy one another, I think the dominion government can preserve an equal right to levy a certain tax to support one another."[11]

The outbreak of war meant different things to different people. Many workers, particularly the British-born, needed little urging to go off in defence of Britain and British ideals. For some, war meant a chance to eat regularly; for the workers who stayed behind, it meant jobs. The *Labour Gazette* correspondent in Calgary reported that, as of March 1915, there had been some reduction in the number of jobless and that in May, a contract for 5,000 shells was given to Calgary businesses with production spread among four iron works companies and the CPR's Ogden shops. In Medicine Hat in May, it was reported that "employment on war orders is expected to bring

Recruits in Edmonton in the winter of 1914. Many workers marched off bread lines into uniform, but by the end of 1916, enlistments had dropped from a high of 30,000 a month to about 6,000.

improvement in the near future'' and by September, munitions factories in the city were actively turning out the necessities of war.

The war may have put the economy back in gear but there was a prevailing sense that, although jobs were available, workers were getting a bad deal. The obvious fact was that it was primarily the workers and farmers who were dying on the battlefields of Europe. The labour movement, or at least the activists in it, had always exhibited a strong current of anti-militarism, even to the extent that the Calgary Labour Council in 1911 roundly condemned the Boy Scout movement "on the ground that it tends toward infusing the spirit of militarism." Before the war, the Trades

and Labour Congress, meeting in convention in Calgary in 1911, had proposed a general strike to prevent Canadian participation in any war. The TLC view, which was supported by western leaders of the movement, was that capitalists caused the wars and then conned the workers into fighting them, making huge profits in the process.

On the day the war started, the Edmonton Labour Council passed a resolution, proposed by carpenters' delegate Joseph Knight, a leading Edmonton socialist, that "the sympathies of the Edmonton Trades and Labour Council are entirely with the working class, irrespective of nationality, who will, as they always have in the past, bear the burden of misery and privation which will be the in-

Midland Collieries, Drumheller valley, 1916. Drumheller miners staged a brief strike opposing the national labour registration programme.

evitable result of the war being waged at the present in Europe."[12] The 1915 convention of District 18 took a similar line after hearing from David Rees, a Welsh immigrant to Fernie, B.C. who had become the district representative on the union's international executive, that: "the only thing that will cause the cosmopolitan proletariat to go to war is the capitalist holding on to that which does not rightfully belong to him." After a lusty singing of the Red Flag, the convention adjourned.[13]

Despite the rhetoric and resolutions, little could stop the workers from signing up. In Calgary, the entire membership of the painters' union was in uniform and locals suffered declines in membership as men enlisted for a battle their leaders said they were fighting solely for the ruling class. The TLC in 1914 repudiated its policy of a general strike to stop the war by claiming that the war was not of Britain's choosing. The world's socialist parties, grouped together in a body known as the Second International, had taken strong anti-war positions prior to 1914, but leading parties in Germany, Britain and France all backed their respective governments when the crunch came.

At best, labour could hope that all sectors of Canadian society would share equally in the burdens imposed. Early events in Calgary indicated that was not likely. In the initial stages of the war, Calgary businessmen patriotically suggested that the best way to prosecute the war effort was to stop paying cash wages to employees and issue scrip instead. In some cases this policy was effected and labour's dislike of it hardened when it was found that many merchants refused to give change if purchases were not made to the full amount of the scrip.[14] The battle over scrip was finally resolved in labour's favour but the issue had deepened beliefs that employers would take advantage of the war and feelings of patriotism to strip workers of hard-won rights.

In pronouncements opposing the war as a capitalist plot, the main issue was conscription. The basic demand of almost all trade unionists in the West was that all resources of the country should be mobilized for the war effort. If working men were to be conscripted to risk their lives in Europe, they wanted to know that Canada's industrial leaders were making comparable sacrifices. If Borden and his conscription lieutenant, Calgary lawyer R.B. Bennett,

made conscription and salvation of the empire their rallying cry, it was answered by labour demands for conscription of wealth. The *B.C. Federationist,* the official publication of the B.C. Federation of Labour, declared in February, 1916 that conscription was being pushed by "all of those interests that have their fangs of exploitation fastened in the flesh of the workers and that fatten upon the profits sucked from their blood and sweat."

The initial battles were fought, not over conscription, but over its predecessor, a scheme known as registration. It had been advocated by many influential sections of Canadian society, including the recruiting leagues, and called for an inventory of Canadian manpower resources. Ben-

nett was made director general of the National Service Board appointed by an order-in-council in August of 1916. The inventory, Bennett decided, would be carried out by having workers fill out registration cards. Labour correctly viewed registration as a prelude to conscription and refused to have anything to do with it. Miners at one colliery in the Drumheller valley called a strike lasting several days, in part because they objected to filling out the registration cards.[15]

After the first rush of enlistments, the Canadian armed forces began having trouble filling the ranks. By the end of 1916, recruitment was seventy thousand men short of the goal and enlistments had dropped from about thirty thousand a month at the beginning of the year to about six thousand at its close.[16] Registration was only one of the attempts to fulfill Canada's obligations overseas. Patriotic employers also did their part. One of the best-known examples of company pressure was the action of B.C. Electric. It inlcuded in the pay envelopes of its employees a notice: "Your King and country need you, we don't." Such pressure was not confined to British Columbia. In Calgary, the school board cancelled the contracts of all single male teachers and told them to enlist or be fired. Both the Calgary Labour Council and Alberta's coal miners, through District 18, denounced moves by companies to force their employees into uniform but most of labour's energy was expended battling Borden and Bennett.[17] The westerners, however, found themselves fighting without the full backing of the Trades and Labour Congress. As was the case with its position on the war, the TLC found it easier to be opposed to things before they happened. Conventions in 1915 and 1916 had bound the congress to "unchangeable opposition to all that savours of conscription" and there had even been a suggestion from the leadership for a general strike to demonstrate labour's opposition.[18]

The TLC had been shoddily treated by the Borden government in the registration issue. There was little doubt that labour was concerned and that co-operation from the TLC would aid the plan's success but labour was not granted any representatives on the National Service Board and four months after the plan was introduced, the congress had still not been able to get a copy of the order-in-council from the government. After a western tour by Borden later in the year to sell the programme, during which the Calgary Labour Council denounced both the prime minister and "irrational service"[19] Borden and Bennett asked for a meeting in December with the TLC executive. Borden refused to guarantee that conscription was not on his agenda and made clear his opposition to conscription of wealth. Despite Borden's rejection of the congress, the congress decided not to reject him. Shortly after the meeting, workers across the country were urged by the TLC executive to comply with registration and fill out the cards. Another element was now added to the combination of factors that would lead to the final revolt.

There had always been tensions within the congress between the moderate eastern trade unionists and their western brothers, where the resource-oriented economy made industrial unionism and militancy more attractive. Friction had shown up in the debate over the Industrial Disputes Investigation Act—westerners wanted a resolution calling for its repeal but the numerically-larger eastern delegation blocked such a move for almost ten years. The 1911 TLC convention in Calgary, with more western delegates in attendance than usual, had come out in favour of industrial unionism. The following year, with the convention safely back in the East, the 1911 resolution was watered down. East-West tensions in the movement were also on show after the 1908 shopcraft strike, when the Calgary workers, who were prepared to strike to the finish against the CPR, felt they had been let down by workers in the East who got "cold feet." But now, over the issue of conscription and registration, the tensions exploded into a sectional split that would widen as the war continued.

The Alberta Federation of Labour in January, 1917 endorsed a Calgary Labour Council resolution calling for a special national convention to consider the registration question, but that was as far as it was willing to go in opposition to the eastern trade union establishment. Joseph Knight and another Edmonton carpenter had brought a resolution to the convention which called for "severest censure" of members of the TLC executive who had demonstrated, by endorsing registration, "their inability to act in accordance with the interests of the working class." The resolutions committee proposed to drop all mention of censure and instead just ask for a public explanation of the TLC executive's about-face but even that was too much for some of the delegates.

It was not just a question of tackling the eastern establishment—Knight's resolution would have been an open declaration of war against Samuel Gompers, who later in the war made a speech to the Canadian House of Commons supporting conscription, and the leaders of their unions in the United States, who, in most cases, had fervently adopted a "win the war" stance. Alf Farmilo, an Edmonton stonemason and former socialist moved that Knight's resolution be deleted entirely from the proceedings and the convention agreed.[20] There was a mood of rebellion in the West but it was not developing as quickly as Knight judged. The absence from the convention of most of the miners delegates (there were only five present compared to 13 the following year), may have contributed to Knight's failure to push the federation further along the road to open revolt. Events over the next two years would give him all the help he needed, however, even turning Farmilo into a sometime ally.

In June of 1917, suspicions that registration would be followed by conscription were confirmed. A bill was introduced to the House of Commons providing for compulsory military service. Labour councils in Edmonton, Calgary and Medicine Hat and the federation of labour all sent off telegrams to Borden restating their position that workers would support conscription only when industry had been nationalized. Ever more, socialists in the labour movement were finding that opposition to conscription was broadening their constituency. Even the Calgary city council bought the argument about conscription of wealth

Miners at Hillcrest with mine ponies, early 1920s. Miners complained that mine management was more concerned with the welfare of the horses than that of the miners.

and so informed the federal government.

Although the TLC had recommended compliance with registration and had softened its stand against the war and conscription, it was not giving up the fight altogether. At its convention in September, 1917, the congress decided that the best way to oppose Borden and conscription was at the polls. The incoming executive was instructed to "call a convention of representatives of trades unions and Non-Partisan Leagues, locals of the Socialist Party of Canada, the Great War Veterans Association, labour representation leagues and other organizations with a view of forming a working class political party."

The move met with great favour and represented a breakthrough for the TLC which, in previous stabs at political action, had always rejected co-operation with the socialists. Delegates from both East and West were ready to get behind the new venture but western delegates were less than pleased that the convention had decided that politics was the only way to rid the country of conscription and a government considered by most to be firmly anti-working class. The use of a general strike to oppose conscription had received wide support in the initial shock following the announcement that it would be introduced. But now, said TLC officers, the law was the law and "we do not deem it right, patriotic or in the best interests of the labour movement or the Dominion to say anything that might prevent the government from obtaining the result that they anticipate in the raising of reinforcements for the

Canadian Expeditionary Forces by enforcing the law."

The West again found itself at loggerheads with the more conservative eastern leaders of the TLC. Alf Farmilo, who the year previous had put the damper on Knight's attempt to bring the Alberta Federation of Labour into open revolt against the TLC over the registration issue, and Alex Ross, a Calgary stonemason and one of the more cautious and moderate leaders of the movement in the province, proposed an amendment to the TLC's position on conscription calling for conscription of wealth and resistance to the legislation if the government didn't follow labour's advice. The Farmilo-Ross amendment was defeated, as was another calling for repeal of the act. The seeds of a sectional split in the movement had been sown long before; the 1917 convention added a healthy does of fertilizer.[21]

When Borden called a federal election for December 17, there was one issue and one issue only in the campaign — conscription. Arrayed against the prime minister were Sir Wilfred Laurier and the Liberals, who, concerned about the growing rift in the country, especially in Quebec, were promising a referendum. Also in the fight were 38 labour candidates in English Canada, some of them, particularly in Alberta, endorsed by the Laurier Liberals.

On the surface, Borden and his government were facing an uphill battle, but the reality was that it would be no contest.[22] The forces opposing Borden were in disarray. Laurier was left to fight with a rump of his own party, western Liberals, including the premier of Alberta, having joined the government in a unionist coalition October 12, submerging party identity in one great and united effort to win the war. In Alberta, the action proposed by the TLC to establish an all-inclusive labour party came too late and "it was felt," said the federation president and secretary in their report to the 1918 convention, "that the federal elections would be receiving the attention of these organizations, some of whom had candidates in the field, and that it would be wise to defer action to a later date."

Labour in Alberta did contest the election but its ranks were divided between the socialists and the straight labour candidates who received the backing of the Laurier Liberals. In Lethbridge, the remnants of the Liberal party had nominated a candidate but withdrew him in favour of Lambert Pack, a farmer, who had been put forward by the Lethbridge Labour Council. The other labourite who received Laurier's blessing was Bill Irvine in Calgary East. Irvine, who would later become a leading figure in the Co-operative Commonwealth Federation (CCF), was nominated by Calgary's Labour Representation League and shared a platform with the former prime minister when Laurier advised his followers to develop "harmonious relations with organized labour." In constituencies where straight labour candidates were not in the running, the Socialist Party of Canada put up candidates.

Labour's lot in the campaign was not to be a happy one. The *Lethbridge Herald,* six days before the election, said that "Canadian Labour surely does not wish to see Canada following in Russian footsteps but such would be the result if the small, disgruntled section of labour men who have presumed to dictate for the whole in this riding had their ways." Pack received less than half the votes given to the Unionist candidate and Irvine did about as well. The Socialists running in Medicine Hat and Bow River between them only picked up about 700 votes. The *Red Deer News* said of Joe Knight, who was contesting that seat for the Socialist Party of Canada, that he was not just a misguided theorist "but a German soldier doing military work for Ludendorff." It was a message that sank home, especially among members of the armed services who were particularly partial to the unionist cry that only Borden and his coalitionists supported Canadian troops and that Laurier and the labourites would leave the men in the trenches to make do as they could. Irvine, in his Calgary riding, picked up only one hundred six of the more than two thousand military votes cast. About thirteen hundred soldiers voted in the Red Deer riding but only eleven voted for Knight.

Labour's fight on the political front had been an unmitigated disaster. Across the country, not one of the thirty-eight labour candidates won. The appeal to patriotism, combined with the Wartime Elections Act which had disenfranchised persons of alien birth naturalized after 1902 and enfranchised only those women with close relations in the armed forces, had worked. To a point, it proved the Wobblie adage that while workers could unite around trade union demands, forging the unity necessary to win elections was an almost-impossible task. An increasingly influential section of the trade union leadership in western Canada was left with only one device in its arsenal to defeat what it saw as an alliance between Borden and employers — the general strike.

Borden had considerable cause for celebration Christmas Day of 1917 as he contemplated his victory. English Canadians, including the working class, had lined up almost to a man behind his government. Labour leaders threatening general strikes were obviously talking through their hats. It was Borden who had won the hearts of Canadian workers. On December 17, they had repudiated their radical leaders and demonstrated their faith in Borden, the empire and free enterprise.

Profiteering and Inflation

But Borden was soon to learn that the rejection of radical appeals to workers was limited solely to politics. On economic issues, the rank and file of the labour movement became much more willing to let control of their organizations pass into the hands of socialists. Workers at home and soldiers in the trenches in Europe were discovering that while they were making sacrifices, the business community viewed the war as an opportunity to get rich. Boots with paper soles were arriving at the front and horses that had been rejected for the Boer War at the turn of the century were now being sold to the government. Canadian troops were being supplied with the Ross rifle, a weapon with one major drawback—it jammed. Soldiers were reported to be throwing them away and salvaging British-issue Lee-Enfields.[23]

Wartime profiteering at the expense of Canadian soldiers and munitions workers did nothing to increase the confidence of Canadian workers in the patriotism of Canadian business. It was further undermined by complaints of profiteering at home, the main complaint being levelled at Sir Joseph Flavelle, the head of Canada's largest meat-packing company and chairman of the Imperial Munitions Board (IMB) in Canada. The charge was given added heat by a widely-publicized comment from Flavelle himself criticizing business for viewing the war as an exercise in profit-making.[24]

Of all the issues during the war that would lead workers in western Canada to throw in their lot with the radicals and join in the general strikes of 1918–1919, the rapid

Women at work in an Edmonton factory, 1918. War provided an opportunity for women to move into non-traditional occupations.

increases in the cost of living, unmatched by wage increases, was the most important. Between the start of the war and December 1917, the cost of living shot up 65 percent; by June 1920, prices were double their 1914 values.[25] Food costs between 1914 and 1917 increased by almost 55 percent and by 1919 had shot up 86 percent. In 1917, manufacturers were reporting profits of 40 percent on butter, 50 percent on eggs, 107 percent on cheese and 130 percent on beef. Sir Joseph Flavelle's William Davies Company had made profits (as a return on capital) of 43 percent in 1915, 80 percent in 1916 and 57 percent in 1918. Members of the Borden cabinet came quickly to the defense of the profiteering companies, an action which reinforced the socialists' argument that the government was nothing more than a front for big business. In 1916, the minister of railways said munitions could not be made without a profit "because that would interfere with private enterprise." Said a government commission in 1917: "Eliminate the profit and you eliminate the enterprise."[26]

Economic recovery, spurred by war, resulted in a spectacular increase in labour militancy beginning in 1917. In the pre-war depression, when demand for labour was low and trade unions disorganized as membership dropped, few workers dared strike. According to figures kept by the federal labour department, there were nine strikes in the province in 1913, a drop from seventeen the year before. Only five strikes were reported to Ottawa in each of 1915 and 1916. In those two years, only thirteen thousand man days were lost due to strike activity, less than one-fifth the number lost in 1912 alone. In 1917, with the economy again in full swing and labour in demand, workers were once more willing to resort to strikes in an attempt to keep from being swamped by rapidly increasing living costs. The number of strikes in 1917 was triple the number of the year before and had doubled again by 1918. In the two and a half years from 1917 to June 30, 1919, more than six hundred thousand working days were lost because of strikes in Alberta, almost two-thirds of all the man days

Underground in an Edmonton mine, 1915.

lost in the first twenty years of the century.

Most of the strikes were called by coal miners. Between 1914 and 1920, 80 of the 111 strikes reported in Alberta involved miners. Nationally, coal strikers accounted for only about 12 percent of all disputes but amounted to 23 percent of time lost in that period.[27] (Coal miners were active in more than 60 percent of the 602 disputes reported to the federal labour department between 1907 and 1950.) After the eight-month strike in 1911, there were no major disputes in the Alberta fields until 1916. Most miners were working short-time—Taber miners during the peak of the depression worked one day a week. In 1915, the number of men employed in Alberta mines dropped by more than fifteen hundred and stayed below the 1914 figure until

1917. Production of coal from the Crowsnest in 1915 was lower than at any time since 1909 and didn't surpass the 1913 level until 1918. The impact of the depression on the usually militant miners can be seen from the fact that between 1912 and 1915, only eight work stoppages occurred in District 18, one of the few times that workers in other industries called more strikes—twenty nine—than the miners. Conditions in the district were so dismal that in the 1915 negotiations to replace the 1911 agreement which had given them a 10 percent wage increase after an eight-month battle, the miners were forced to come away with a new two-year agreement providing no wage increase at all.

By 1916, the cost of living had increased 16 percent from

1911 when miners had received their last wage increase. By 1916, wages of $2.47 to $3.30 a day had become grossly inadequate and with coal production climbing to fuel Canada's war machine, miners were once more in a position to make demands.

They were bound to a two-year contract that would not expire until March of 1917 but the companies that sold food and clothing and built houses were under no such contractual obligations to keep their prices down and in June of 1916, about thirty-six hundred miners walked off the job saying they wouldn't work unless the operators gave them a 10 percent wage increase. It was the first major strike in the fields in five years.

Their summer walkout netted the miners a 7½ percent wage increase but they had fallen a long way behind and were now determined to make up. In the fall, the District 18 executive again went to the operators and demanded either a war bonus of 25 percent or the establishment of a cost of living commission with the power to grant wage increases based on changes in the cost of living. About five thousand miners went on strike to back up their executive's request but they were back digging coal a few days later when the federal government appointed a special commissioner to look at the cost of living issue. By January of 1917, the miners were getting impatient with the delay and in mid-month, almost six thousand of them again went on strike.[28]

From the beginning of the war, the question of "enemy aliens" had posed a constant problem for the federal government. Any immigrant from a country at war with Canada and Britain was considered an "enemy alien" and, under the Military Service Act, ineligible for wartime service. All were required to register monthly with the police and about eighty-five hundred, who, for whatever reason, were considered a threat to national security, were sent off to twenty-four internment camps set up across the country. The bulk of those detained were from the Austro-Hungarian Empire and most of those were Ukrainian.[29] The "alien" problem for the government was particularly perplexing in the coal mines of Alberta where relatively large numbers of the miners were immigrants. The 1911 census reported that 90 percent of Alberta mine workers were not born in Canada but no breakdown of the numbers from Britain and the U.S. was provided. The 1925 Alberta coal commission found that in the Crowsnest, 23 percent of the miners were "Slovak" and similar percentages of "Slovaks, Austrians and Ukrainians" were employed in other fields in the province. With their participation in the war prohibited and many of their Anglo-Saxon comrades overseas, those percentages were probably higher during the war. During the January 1917 strike, the Mounties made special efforts to keep stores of explosives belonging to the coal companies from falling into "alien" hands. A police report from Blairmore on January 29 said the "foreign quarters" had been visited three times in one day. In Hillcrest, inspection was made of the immigrant sections of town "with a view of ascertaining if there were any signs of agitation or discontent among this particular class. Found everything quiet and orderly."

A report January 29 from Frank found that "word was circulating about town this afternoon that a special meeting would take place tonight in a pool room with the district officials in attendance."[30] The purpose of the meeting in Frank could very well have been to report to the striking miners that the federal labour minister had intervened in the strike and that they would be getting a raise of $1.75 a week, far short of their demand for a 25 percent bonus.

The miners went into negotiations in the spring of 1917 in a militant mood. In less than a year, they had fought three strikes and still felt inflation was running ahead of them. They agreed to accept a 15 percent wage increase but the operators insisted that a penalty clause they had succeeded in getting in the 1915 agreement when the miners were bargaining with a depression at their backs would have to stay in any new agreement. The clause allowed the companies to fire any miner who went on strike during the term of the contract. Considering that the workers had just been involved in three such strikes, there was little chance they would agree to the operators' demand. This was not 1915 and the miners knew it. Coal production was vital; it wasn't often they had the advantage over their employers and they weren't about to let the opportunity slip.

The strike began April 2 and before long, the entire district was shut down with about seventy-five hundred men on strike. The walkout lasted three months and brought the miners into confrontation not only with the government and the employers, but with their own union as well. The official position of the American Federation of Labour and its affiliates, including the United Mine Workers, was one of all-out support for the war effort; strikes were, if at all possible, to be avoided. The UMW's international president in Indianapolis sent the District 18 miners two orders to return to work; both were ignored but would not be forgotten.

The government feared that, with feeling in the West running high over conscription, the coal strike could turn into a general strike. The government's apprehension of a general strike arose from police reports and news reaching Ottawa that the Alberta Federation of Labour was polling its affiliates asking if they would support a general strike to oppose conscription. On June 20, Borden and his cabinet approved an order-in-council appointing a director of coal operations for the district "with authority to supervise and

Ukrainian miners in the Edson area in 1918.

direct the operations of the mines, including the rate of wages and generally the conditions of labour, also to fix prices of coal to consumers so as to reimburse operators for any increased cost of operation."[31] The person given the task of putting the miners back to work was a Vancouver businessman, W.H. Armstrong, who had made his money as a public works contractor after working for the CPR. Armstrong ordered a settlement generous enough to forestall any serious district-wide labour troubles for the duration of the war. The miners got rid of the penalty clause in the 1915 agreement and were given a 7½ percent increase on top of the 15 percent they had already secured in negotiations with the operators. In addition, a cost of living clause was written into the new agreement that would add another ninety-two cents a day by the time the contract expired March 31, 1919.[32]

The 1917 coal dispute brought a new face to the leadership of District 18, a former Cornwall tin miner and socialist, Phillip Martin Christophers, who in that year became a district vice-president. With the first possibility of government interference in the strike, Christophers was reported to have told a special convention of District 18 that: "I defy the Canadian government or any soldier to make me work. They can put me into the cage and put me down in the mine and they can make me stay there eight hours but I will be damned if they can make me dig coal."[33] Because of his activities during the 1917 strikes, Christophers was blacklisted but the operators wouldn't be able to get rid of the self-confident, stocky former tin miner that easily. And two years later, when he was at the head of the miners' revolt as a leading figure in the One Big Union, the

government might have wished they had taken him up on his defiant offer to put him in a cage and send him underground.

Christophers was just one of a new generation of leaders thrown up in the turbulence that marked Canada's participation in the First World War. In Calgary, R.J. Tallon and A.G. Broatch, both machinists and both socialists, moved into leadership positions while in Edmonton; Joseph Knight and his wife Satah began to play leading roles in labour affairs in the capital. They were joined by Carl Berg. In later years, Berg became one of the most conservative labour figures in the province—a staunch anti-Communist, a close supporter of the Social Credit government and a recipient of the Order of the British Empire, an honour which was always pinned conspicuously to his vest. But in the period leading to the 1919 general strikes, there was little evidence of what he would later become. In 1904, at sixteen, he emigrated from Sweden to the United States where he worked as an agricultural labourer and hardrock miner. He helped the Wobblies organize railway navvies and the unskilled and unemployed in Edmonton, where he was secretary for a time of the IWW local. When the IWW fell apart, Berg moved to the Labourers Union.[43]

The unrest generated by rising living costs was felt across the entire province, not just in the coal camps, and workers who had always believed in co-operation quth their employers and who had never before belonged to a union now found themselves on the picket line. Not all workers, however, were as successful as the miners. In 1917, a group of telephone workers, organized by the International Brotherhood of Electrical Workers, walked off the job demanding recognition of their union and a wage increase. About 110 employees of Alberta Government Telephones were on strike for about three weeks but the telephone department was adamant in its refusal to recognize the union; the workers did, however, receive a wage increase.[35]

Edmonton Local 569 of the Amalgamated Association of Street and Electric Railway Employees had been formed in 1911 and had always been able to resolve its differences with the city without strikes. In 1914, with the outbreak of war, the union voluntarily came forward and patriotically suggested to city council that, in spite of a new agreement just signed, the workers would take a 10 percent wage cut. The offer was gratefully accepted by the city administration. In August 1917, the men approached the city asking for a 20 percent wage increase in a new one-year agreement. A survey of prices charged in the city indicated that a family of five required a yearly income of about $1,900 to make ends meet. "The highest pay received by motormen and conductors based on a nine-hour day for six days a week amounts to about $1,063 a year, providing they do not lay off through sickness or any other causes, which means we receive $851.60 below the table of the cost of living as presented [to] the committee, who have admitted both to us and through the press that it was a fair table," the union said in a statement. "Our request for a 20 percent increase would bring the wages up to $1,263.60, which still leaves a deficit of $641."

After trying for a month to get a new contract, the union negotiating committee recommended to a mass meeting of the men that the union apply for conciliation under the Industrial Disputes Investigation Act. Instead, the workers passed a resolution saying that if a new contract with their 20 percent demand was not "signed, sealed and delivered" the next day, "we take a vacation on Saturday morning." The union then returned to the bargaining table and offered to accept a 10 percent increase and leave the outstanding amount to arbitration, but council thought the strike threat was a bluff and rejected yet another proposal that would give the workers only 6 percent with the rest in the hands of an arbitrator. The city then locked out the streetrailway men.

Council had offered a two and one-half cent an hour increase—the percentage ranging between 6.6 and 9—and it was that agreement that the union was eventually forced to accept after eleven days off the job. During the lockout, the city started hiring strike-breakers and the union men discovered they had few friends. The federal labour department advised them to return to work and so did their international union. As was the case during the miners' strike when their international took a similar tack, that action would have repercussions two years later. The men

had to reapply individually for their old jobs and there was no guarantee that strike-breakers would be fired to make room for the unionized employees. For the streetrailway men, it was a disaster and city council gave them no opportunity to save face. It was a defeat they would not forget.[36]

Borden's overwhelming victory in the 1917 federal election belied the growing militancy of the western Canadian labour movement. There was an air or rebellion in the West and it gave the government cause for alarm. Workers were resorting more and more to strike action to keep up with the cost of living but more ominous for Borden were the increasingly hardened tone of labour criticism and the heightened profile of socialists withing the movement.

In a belated attempt to make peace with labour, Borden appointed Gideon Robertson, a vice-president of the Order of Railroad Telegraphers, to the senate and then to the cabinet. But Robertson had to defend a government that more and more workers considered illegitimate and the move had little positive effect.[37] By the end of the summer of 1917, R.B. Bennett was saying the situation in the West was "more or less acute."[38] In 1917, the Mounted Police, military intelligence and the federal press censor began keeping tabs on radicals and radical organizations. Dossiers on hundreds of leading western opponents of the regime were compiled at Regina. At first, the opposition movement was believed to be the work of "German agents"[39] but the success of the Russian revolution late in 1917 and the response it excited in labour circles changed the focus of suspicion and increased the anxiety that a Bolshevik-style revolution was a possibility in the West. Events in Alberta and elsewhere in 1918 would only reinforce the government's fears.

On February 1, 1918, seventy-four employees of the Edmonton fire department walked off the job in a situation exactly parallel to that which caused the 1912 police strike in Lethbridge. An out-of-town man had been appointed fire chief over a city firefighter who had applied for the post. By February 23, the *Edmonton Journal* was reporting that there were rumours of a general strike to back the firemen and Alf Farmilo, secretary of the Edmonton Labour Council, was refusing to deny them. Threats of a general strike were, however, overshadowed by a more widespread revolt by citizens. More than ten thousand people signed a petition to city council demanding that the new fire chief be replaced by someone within the department. A mass meeting February 14 unanimously voted to refuse to pay taxes if council rejected the petition. The issue was put to plebiscite and the electorate, by a three to one margin, supported the firefighters. When a private citizen went to court seeking an injunction to overturn the

results, Farmilo told the *Edmonton Journal* that "If the injunction were granted . . . it would result in the calling of a general strike with the shutting down of every wheel of every industry in the city." Of twenty-six unions polled, seventeen voted to down tools. City council eventually relented and granted the firefighters' demands. Compared with the defeat of streetrailway men in 1916, it was a great victory and the general strike idea gained more credibility.[40]

If events leading to the 1919 crisis were a drama, the Edmonton firefighters strike was an audition and the Calgary freighthandlers dispute in the fall of 1918 was full dress rehearsal. The general strike weapon had been primed in Edmonton but wasn't used. In Calgary it was.

In 1903, freighthandlers employed by the CPR had tried, with little success, to negotiate through the United Brotherhood of Railway Employees. Their union in 1918 was the Western International Brotherhood of Railway Clerks, Storemen and Freighthandlers. To make sure there were no transportation tie-ups during the war, the government had established the Canadian Railway War Board, made up of representatives of all major railways, to negotiate with the railway unions. The board refused to recognize the freighthandlers union. Early in 1918, the

union affiliated with Canadian Division 4 of the Railway Employees Department of the American Federation of Labour, organized at about that time as the bargaining agency for all railway shopcraft workers; the board still wouldn't buy it. It told the workers to deal with G. Hall, the western vice-president of the CPR, who then told them to deal with their local superintendents.

In September in Calgary, where the union had few members, the local CPR brass fired a shed checker who was apparently trying to enlist new members. Local management then filled his position without considering seniority. When the workers complained, the superintendent told them to return to work or get off the premises. They chose to leave. Perhaps realizing the trouble the company was getting into, Hall invited a delegation of Calgary workers to meet him in Winnipeg. When they left Calgary, the dispute was over seniority but by the time they had talked to Hall and officials of Division 4 in Winnipeg, including R.J. Tallon, the president, their fight with the CPR became a "fight for democracy, a fight for the right to organize a union."[41]

The freighthandlers strike found the Calgary labour council in a feisty mood. Like its northern counterpart, it too had been talking about general strikes. A restaurant and hotel strike that winter had captured local labour attention and a city-wide walkout was discussed then but wasn't called as less drastic forms of support had won the strike. By October 4, about a week after the onset of the freighthandler's strike, the labour council had set up a strike committee to call out "unions as are deemed necessary to the situation." The fight, the council said, involved the right of workers to organize against "profiteering corporations."[42]

The next day, nineteen out of twenty-one unions voted to answer the general strike call and city employees, teamsters and truck drivers downed tools. The federal government moved quickly and within twenty-four hours, five strikers from the CPR Ogden shops were in jail. Their crime was of recent origin. On September 25, the Borden cabinet, believing that revolt was in the western air, had issued an order under the War Measures Act outlawing fourteen languages. "Enemy aliens" had first been told they could not fight for their adopted country, then told they couldn't vote and now were informed they couldn't use their mother tongue in public. But the government was just warming up. Three days later, the IWW, which was supposed to be stirring up all the trouble, was banned along with thirteen other organizations. Within weeks, another order-in-council was passed, this time outlawing work stoppages. When the general strike was called, the Director of Public Safety, Montreal lawyer C.H. Cahan, who had made a study of radicalism for the government

CPR employees leaving work at the car shops, Calgary, 1912. Railway employees in Edmonton and Calgary were in the forefront of general strike activity in 1919.

and discovered it was all the work of Bolsheviks, arrived in Calgary to make sure that new anti-strike law was enforced and had the Mounties arrest the five shopmen.

The labour council was willing to carry on the fight and two days after Cahan arrived it again called out the troops. But, having sized up their opposition, the troops were now less willing to do battle and the renewed strike call found the workers divided. Adding to their reluctance to take on the government and the Mounties was the fact that some locals discovered that their international headquarters were as displeased with the idea of a general strike as Borden was. Despite heavy fighting at the front and betrayal at their rear, teamsters, carpeters, streetrailway men, electrical workers, civic employees, machinists and other railway workers stayed in the fray but bricklayers, stone cutters and some other crafts announced a retreat.

The *Calgary Herald* and other leading sectors of polite Calgary society did not find the affair amusing and when streetrailway men, faithful to the strike committee, rolled their cars to the barns, the *Herald* was incensed. Honest citizens, said the papers, should take matters into their own hands and end the "volcano of class reign."[43] As a group of citizens was forming a citizens' committee to oppose labour's strike committee, the freighthandlers'

dispute was settled and the *Herald*'s "volcano of class reign" became dormant. The five arrested strikers were released by the courts without fines or jail terms.

By the time the strike ended, the war in Europe was almost over, but prices were still rising and now there was a new fear to fuel unrest—returning soldiers would flood the job market. Adding to that anxiety was the possibility that the veterans would be used, as they were in Calgary in a 1916 strike by movie projectionists, as strike-breakers. A limited general strike took place in Winnipeg in the spring of 1918 after city council told city employees they did not have the right to strike. The Winnipeg Labour Council was gearing up for another large-scale walkout in the summer but at the last minute, a settlement was reached. In Vancouver in August, longshoremen, metal tradesmen, construction workers and streetrailway men all left their jobs to protest the murder by police of Ginger Goodwin, a draft evader and former vice-president of the B.C. Federation of Labour. A mob of veterans angrily marched on the labour temple, which they ransacked, and then dragged Victory Midgely, the secretary of the Vancouver trades council, into the street where he was beaten and forced to kiss the Union Jack.[44]

In October, the possibility of a general strike across the

West loomed when employees of the post office—members of the Federated Association of Letter Carriers and the Dominion Postal Clerks Association, went on strike from coast to coast — the first national postal strike. Workers were receiving only three dollars a day, with no overtime pay, after eight years of service. Labour councils from Winnipeg to Victoria let the Borden government know they were behind the postal employees. In Calgary, Borden's labour minister, T.W. Crothers, was condemned by the labour council after he told it that the action of the postal workers was "unworthy of their brothers who were risking their lives for their country." District 18 and the Edmonton Labour Council were joined by councils in Victoria, Vancouver, Saskatoon, regina and Winnipeg in demanding that the government grant the wage demands of the post office employees or face a general strike. The government eventually caved in and met the demands of its employees, even to the point of paying them for time lost while they were on strike.[45]

For most workers, the general strike was an extension of familiar tactics. Far from being revolutionary, it was being used to win traditional trade union goals of union recognition and increased wages. But for Borden and his cabinet and Canadian business, the heightened militancy of the country's workers, due primarily to rising prices and the fear of a repeat of pre-war depression as soldiers returned from the front to bid for jobs, seemed intensely threatening and the sense of foreboding was increased by the Russian revolution and Cahan's report that unrest was due to Bolshevik propaganda. The publication of such newspapers as the *Soviet* in Edmonton, which carried long articles by Lenin, Trotsky and other Soviet leaders and gave extensive coverage to the developing revolution in Germany, contributed to Borden's fears.

In 1919, the Alberta Federation of Labour passed a resolution declaring itself to be "in full accord and sympathy with the aims and purposes of the Russian and German revolutions" and gave the executive authority to call a general strike if the actions of the Canadian and other allied governments in invading the Soviet Union to support anti-revolutionary forces there persisted.[46] Police records at the time show a campaign of active surveillance of union and socialist activists. A Mounted Police report in January 1919 said of Joe Knight that "a close watch is being kept on this man and several of his followers with a view of taking any action against him that may be necessary to curtail his agitation among the people."[47] Public meetings were usually attended by undercover police agents and mail was intercepted as police stepped up their efforts to quell what they believed was a coming revolution based on the Soviet model. One of the most celebrated Mountie "stool pigeons" was Corporal F.W. Zaneth, who

blew his cover as Harry Blask to give evidence at the trial of those charged following the Winnipeg General Strike. Blask was sent into the Drumheller coal field in 1918 to see if there were any Wobblies there and, according to the Calgary labour newspaper, the *Searchlight,* identified himself as an IWW member. The *Searchlight* also said that many activists suspected that Blask was a police agent.[48]

Most workers in the West were in favour of non-violent, non-revolutionary change. But the Borden government was listening to militant rhetoric and came down hard. In addition to the orders-in-council, the government moved to suppress socialist literature and arrested those found in possession of it. The *Searchlight* reported that two Calgary workers were convicted of possessing banned literature— in both cases, the magistrate imposed a fine of $250. The secretary of the Diamond City local of the United Mine Workers was thrown in jail for the same offence and two members of a union at Redcliffe, near Medicine Hat, were fined for having in their possession copies of newspapers the government considered subversive.

The hard-line government approach only served to intensify feelings that the government had declared war on its own citizens. The orders-in-council all came as the war in Europe was ending and the labour movement questioned the motives of the government's use of the wide powers of the War Measures Act to suppress criticism when it would not jeopardize a war almost won. The war had been fought for democracy, or so the slogan went. Workers were wondering about the growing lack of it at home.

CHAPTER FIVE

Revolt and Defeat: 1919

Unrest and the One Big Union

Early in 1919, the federal government established a royal commission to examine the causes of labour unrest. As the Mathers Commission travelled the country, holding public hearings, the reasons came through loud and clear and prime among them was inflation. In the four years of war, prices had jumped 72 percent.

A railway machinist in Edmonton, E.J. Thompson, told the commission that he had received an increase bringing his wages from sixty-eight cents to eighty-five cents but "we know since we got eighty-five cents that the cost of living will go up and offset that raise in wages. We are chasing a circle."

In Calgary, Mrs. George Corse told the commission that the ranks of the Socialist Party there were being swelled by women who:

.... find it practically impossible to dress our children and give them the education we feel they should have on the money which our husbands can earn. I, myself, if you will pardon me speaking personally, have taken my

two eldest boys from school and put them to work simply because I could not afford to keep them at school out of my husband's earnings. I have four other children to be kept out of those earnings. . . .

I can tell of hundreds of people that have not been out of the city for years. It is impossible for them to take holidays. They cannot go further than the little parks that surround Calgary and their only luxury very often is tobacco or a cup of tea. It seems to me that is where the government always starts, on the working man's commodity, his necessity and his only little luxury. . . . We find we have to take our children from grade eight — only 6 percent of the children in this city ever get to high school and why? Because we cannot afford to send them. They must be added to the wage earners of the family. . . .

I think any labour man will admit . . . although women have been kept in the background, women have been the backbone of the labour movement. There was never a strike carried out successfully but the women were back of the men, helping them on and keeping things going at home. . . .

At the present time, the housing condition in Calgary is very critical. There are almost no empty houses and all kinds of old places are being fitted up to be used for rental purposes. Rents are being advanced very rapidly. . . . . The war has ended a considerable time and things are not getting cheaper, in fact they are getting dearer. Butter in Calgary is 70 cents a pound and you cannot get some for less. Eggs 50 cents a dozen. . . . Boys' clothing and men's socks—50 cents a pair, they rapidly go into holes. In fact, they are not worth buying. . . . shoes are enormous prices and they are very poor. I had a very prominent man in Calgary tell me he knows for a fact that shoes which were marked up in the wholesale at $5.50 retailed for $12.

My husband is very fortunate in one way. He is almost always employed, he is a linotype machinist but at the same time we never have any increase in our income. My husband is earning $3 more today than he earned five years ago so with the dollar out to 43 cents I reckon I am getting about $17 a week.

Jean MacWilliams told the commission there had been a great deal of discussion about establishing a minimum wage, but added:

What is the use of a minimum wage when there is no maximum to the price of commodities? . . . I am the wife of a returned soldier. The separation allowance was raised and the landlords raised the rent. Then the diaryman put on extra on our milk and butter, the main things which our children had to live on. The soldier's wife . . . . was forced to leave her children and go into the labour market. In doing that, the soldier's wife had to take a dollar or two less a week than they dared offer to civilians. . . .

There is no chance of a working man having a home to himself anymore as most of them have to take in roomers and boarders to eke out their incomes and the result, in most cases, is disruption to their homes. The average worker here in Calgary is never sure of a job. The weather in the wintertime here is very severe and it take a lot of coal and heat to keep his children warm. There is blankets needed and shoes needed and overshoes—everything is needed and there is no way for him to get them and we are told to keep quiet. We will have to have a change somehow. I want to live to see it . . . . these last 30 years I have seen nothing but misery and poverty. From 11-years-old when my father had to borrow enough to bury my mother I saw it in the Old Country and I see it in the homes of Calgary today, the same as then and that was 30 years ago.[1]

Jean MacWilliams was not, by far, the only person looking for change in the Canada that emerged from the First World War. The question was how the change was to be wrought. Workers had tried political action in 1917 and that had failed. Increasingly, the doctrine of direct action—the general strike—gained more respectability.

For the government and a substantial segment of the non-labouring population, the unrest of the period was largely the work of phantom Wobblies. It was for that reason that the IWW had been outlawed under the War Measures Act, even though the organization had had its heyday some four years previous. Part of the Wobblie legacy was that workers could, with imagination and organization, overcome the odds and score an occasional victory. But the more important part of the IWW inheritance in the 1918—1919 period was its philosophy of syndicalism—"that politics," as one IWW pamphlet put it, "is deadly to unionism. Politics killed every promising union movement. We are justified in drawing the conclusion that whenever a union tries to operate outside its field—job regulation—it only defeats its purpose and destroys itself."

Syndicalism was not, of course, the invention of the Industrial Workers of the World. Its adherents could be found in trade union circles internationally. The IWW had been, however, the most successful North American proponent of it. Syndicalists shared with socialists the belief that capitalist society had to be overturned before workers, who created the wealth, would be able to claim that wealth. Until that day came, the bosses would take the profits that, by right belonged to the workers and would try to pay their employees as little as possible.

Where socialist and syndicalist bitterly parted company was over the question of strategy in bringing down the old order, and the manner in which the new society would be run. The syndicalists believed that politics was a trap—that the workers' weapon was self-evident. "Without our brain and muscle, not a single wheel can turn" goes a verse from the Wobblie anthem, Solidarity Forever. If workers didn't work, society could not function. The general strike was to be the means of ushering in the new and the workers themselves would then run things, not by delegating authority to bureaucrats and commisars, but through their union—One Big Union encompassing all workers.

In January 1919, delegates to the Alberta Federation of Labour convention gathered in Medicine Hat for what would be the most radical meeting the federation has ever held. General strikes were a frequent topic of discussion. Looking back on the Edmonton fire-fighters and Calgary freighthandlers disputes and the nation-wide postal strike, the president and secretary, J.A. Kinney and Walter Smitten, both moderates, said in their report to the convention that the "solid front presented was gratifying" but that an organization was necessary to direct such actions. A resolution was passed calling for the unconditional release of a Diamond City miner jailed for possession of banned literature. The convention itself proposed a general strike over the issue of government moves limiting freedom of speech. The government was given sixty days to comply. Failing that, the resolution demanded that the "Trades and Labour Congress take the necessary steps to bring about a general strike through the dominion."[2] Considering the events at the 1918 convention of the Trades and Labour Congress just months previous, it is surprising that federation delegates would make such a request of that body.

Frank Wheatley, one of the more moderate leaders of the United Mine Workers of Alberta, had been the federation's delegate to the TLC convention and reported to the federation convention that a manifesto on reconstruction to be drawn up by the TLC executive will:[3]

> . . . . if the present congress executive follow the lines of the past, contain matters more favourable to the government than to the working class. One of the most outstanding features of the convention was the extreme difference of opinion of the East and West, the East at times showing no tolerance towards the suggestions of the West . . . . with the result that the convention became quite riotous at times. It was on account of this extreme condition that the western delegates held a caucus for the purpose of overcoming this situation and, if possible, to obtain better representations and conditions for those they represent. At this caucus of western delegates, it was decided that, before the next Trades Congress convention, a conference representing organizations of the four western provinces should be held.
>
> I would strongly recommend the federation endorse the action, as it is most essential that the requirements of western labour unions have better consideration, and while it is not a secessionalist movement, it has most assuredly become a matter for serious consideration.[4]

At the TLC convention, every issue of importance to western delegates was defeated—endorsement of industrial unionism, opposition to allied intervention against the Soviet government, support for conscientious objectors. For the first time, the committee which presented the report of the congress executive to the convention split, with a minority report presented by westerners condemning the TLC executive for its co-operation with the government during the war. Feelings that the TLC had betrayed the interests of Canadian workers permitted a temporary and fragile alliance between all the leaders of the western movement. People like Farmilo, Frank Wheatley, David Rees and Bob Livett, a District 18 official, who would all play leading roles in the fight against the One

Big Union, found themselves in the same camp as Knight, Berg and Christophers. All of them believed that the TLC and the movement needed an overhaul.

But the alliance would fall apart over the question of how radical an overhaul was required. Frank Wheatley may have told the federation convention that the western conference, planned for Calgary in March, was not the first movement toward secession from international unions and the TLC but Knight, Berg, Victor Midgely and Winnipeg's R.B. Russell had other ideas. The executive of the federation fought a futile battle on the floor of the 1919 convention to stall the Calgary conference, "for we could not view with favour any sectional movement of wage workers." Instead of the meeting in Calgary, it suggested that the TLC call a special conference of delegates from across the country "with a view of determining a policy on matters now of vital importance to the workers throughout the Dominion." But Carl Berg and Joe and Sarah Knight had done their work well and had out-organized the executive at the convention. The delegates rejected the suggestion of the TLC-sponsored national meeting and ordered the president and secretary to attend the Calgary conference.

The Western Labour Conference opened in Calgary on March 13 and the first order of business was passage of a resolution declaring that "the aims of labour as represented by this convention are the abolition of the present system of production for profit and the substituting therefore [of] production for use." The initial tone of the meeting found few in opposition. People like David Rees and Alf Farmilo were socialists who would have no trouble supporting the first resolution but they were opposed to any move that would break workers from established organizations in favour of an entirely new structure and that move was high on the agenda.

The conference set the high water mark of syndicalism in Canada; the second resolution, passed unanimously, rejected lobbying "for palliatives which do not palliate" and called for reorganization of the movement "so that by virtue of their industrial strength, the workers may be better prepared to enforce any demand they consider essential to their maintenance and well-being." The syndicalists won that round, but not without opposition. The Alberta Federation of Labour had submitted a resolution supporting establishment of a political party uniting "labour and kindred organizations in a homogenous political party, believing that a united labour party is a necessary adjunct to the development of our industrial organizations and to the attainment of our national ideals." A.G. Broatch, a Calgary machinist and alderman representing the Calgary Labour Council, told the conference that by ignoring

Elmer Roper. Roper first became involved with the trade union movement in Calgary during the First World War, heading, for a time, the Calgary Labour Council. He attended the 1919 Calgary conference which established the One Big Union, was secretary in the Twenties of the AFL and edited its newspaper, Alberta Labour News. He went on to lead the CCF and in 1960 became Edmonton mayor.

political action, the movement was fighting with one hand behind its back.

> We have declared we are out for the destruction of production by profit and the competitive system. If we elect representatives on that platform and send them to the Houses of Parliament it will be their aim to destroy that system. Without doing it you are only doing half the job. I don't believe, and I am yet to be convinced, that the action you propose to take, striking alone, will ever give you that end.

Broatch's eloquence didn't convince the conference and the federation's political action proposition went down in defeat. Now it was the turn of the secessionists and a resolution was quickly passed calling on workers across the country to vote on the question of leaving their unions in favour of a new organization, to be known as the One Big Union (OBU). Final details of how the organization would work would be left to a later conference, after the referendum was completed.[5]

On the surface, the conference was a tremendous display of labour solidarity; even Farmilo, who became the OBU's chief opponent as a paid organizer of the American Federation of Labour, did not, according to convention proceedings, oppose what was happening. Elmer Roper, who attended as a delegate from the Edmonton pressmen's union, recalled that "it was a bit of a show. Really, it was a well-organized thing on the part of people mostly from B.C. and they had it well prepared so that anything you did say to question the policy that was being advocated was just shouted down. The thing was railroaded from start to finish. It was a beautiful piece of railroading organization, no doubt about that."[6] One delegate, J. Barnicutt of Calgary, questioned on the floor of the conference itself the appearance of unanimity. "We are not unanimous, there is no use going away with that idea. There is no use going away with the idea that we are going to form this great big union. . . ."

The One Big Union would be formed but it wasn't to be a smashing success. Whatever the attitude of Farmilo at the conference itself, he moved quickly afterward to ensure defeat for the idea of secession and the OBU. Supporters of the OBU within the Edmonton Labour Council were expelled at the end of April and it was in that city, which Joe Knight called an "exaggerated farm village,"[7] that the OBU suffered its greatest setback. Only five locals voted to support the OBU and, with the exception of the carpenters' and painters' locals, all were railway shopcraft lodges. In Calgary, the birthplace of the organiztion, the voting was very close. Thirteen locals voted to join the OBU, compared with eleven that voted no, but the nay-sayers had the numerical advantage—839 to 724. As in Edmonton, the railway workers were again in the forefront of support for the OBU but even the normally conservative bricklayers local, Alex Ross's home union, defeated the OBU idea by only five votes. In balloting across the province, of all locals voting, except the miners, the OBU received 1,633 votes and the support of twenty-seven locals while 1,611 in thirty-two locals voted to stay with their existing unions.

The General Strikes

It was decided at the Calgary conference that another meeting would be held to formalize the birth of the OBU and that a general strike would be called for June 1 to back demands for a six-hour day. In 1917, Joe Knight had misjudged the attitude of the rank and file and found himself too far in front of the ranks; this time, the case could be made that Knight and others in the OBU misjudged again—not as drastically—and found themselves slightly behind. On May 15, about thirty-five thousand workers, both organized and unorganized, walked off the job in Winnipeg. Restaurants, newspapers, streetcars, theatres, gas stations, barber shops, bakeries, dairies, ice companies,

the telephone and telegraph systems, the post office, rail yards and construction sites were all shut down and police and firemen indicated they too would walk out if so instructed by the strike committee. The frustrations of western workers with conscription, rising prices, a government that sided with their employers, companies that used every trick in the book to defeat trade unions, harsh working conditions, low pay and broken promises all came to a shuddering climax in the spring of 1919. Workers in practically every major centre in the West made plans to join their Winnipeg comrades on the picket lines. The "fight for democracy" in Europe had come home.

In Ottawa, a worried cabinet wired Borden, who was attending peace treaty negotiations in Europe, suggesting that a warship should be sent immediately to Vancouver. The army transferred what it considered unreliable units

from British Columbia and started an inventory of troops that could be made available to quash any uprising. Early in 1919, the chief of the general staff wrote his western commanders that "it will be well for you to bear in mind the possibility of disorder being fomented and to have your course, should this come to pass, clear in mind."[8] In Edmonton, the commanding officer of the Mounted Police detachment in the city wrote his superiors a confidential memo informing them that:

I am taking all precautions with regard to our own arms and our men and horses are being trained for emergencies. Revolvers have been fired in the stable to accustom the horses to the sound. I have also had the horses out on the range with carbine and revolver, also machine gun, which has worked admirably. I was in consultation with the premier the other day and informed him that should the province need our assistance in the event of not being able to maintain protection of life and property, they would have to requisition through the federal authorities before we could interfere.[9]

On May 27, the second day of the general strike in the city, Superintendent Wroughton, taking no chances, sent the following telegram in code to Regina: "Contain re sweetly weed reassured approves panegyrized. Offending earache overheard arrowy lathe. Swarming recommending oozing sceptical. Mechanics signatory sprat fitting oozing jet. Scheduled approves mammak dump telephones oozing Fanny. Automatic Fanny ineffable collect. Panoply carbonic oozing neutral sprat fitted." What he was really saying was that the strike was quiet and orderly; streetcars were not running but mail service was continuing; the rural and long distance phone systems were out of commission but the city's automatic system was unaffected and ordinary business was not much dislocated so far.

In both Edmonton and Calgary, between fifteen hundred and two thousand workers were off the job starting May 26 but many began drifting back or were ordered back by the strike committees within several days. In both cities, the strikes were not officially called off until late June and by that time, the railway shop crafts were the only large units still out. In Edmonton, the only issue was support for the Winnipeg walkout, where the principal demands involved union recognition and establishment of the right of free collective bargaining. The Winnipeg dispute started when workers in the city's metal shops attempted to get their employers to negotiate with a city-wide bargaining committee. In Calgary, the initial cause of the strike was again the situation in Winnipeg but after it had started, a local issue arose. Postal workers in the city had joined the walkout but were being told by the government that they had deserted their jobs and couldn't have them back. Said Prime Minister Borden in reply to a telegram from City Calgary Mayor R.C. Marshall who had asked the government to recognize the principle of collective bargaining and rehire its postal workers: "The government cannot reinstate men who have thus set their public duty at defiance unless it is prepared to abandon all effective attempts to maintain the public service. The postal employees dismissed themselves when they saw fit to engage in a sympathetic strike."[10]

The strike in Calgary was far less effective than in Edmonton. In the southern city, about one thousand railway shopmen were joined by metal workers, flour mill workers, postal workers, freighthandlers and express company employees. Of the building trades, only the painters and bricklayers and stonemasons joined the walkout and then

for only a few days. Only the metal workers and the railway employees stayed out until the strike officially ended June 25 and the strike committee, composed primarily of supporters of the One Big Union, was less than pleased with the response. When construction workers were voting on whether to endorse the walkout on June 7, a federal labour department official wrote the deputy minister saying considerable effort had been made to win them over. The *Calgary Strike Bulletin,* published by the strike committee, asked in its June 7 issue that the building trades and the streetrailway men, who had also refused to leave their posts, consider whether they would "allow the government to break the postal workers' organization."

The *Edmonton Bulletin* of May 28 told its readers of the situation in Calgary as of the 27th and the picture painted was much different than the one being sketched on Edmonton canvas.

Calgary May 27—The feeling over the strike here is very lukewarm and indications are that it will not last long. Streetcars are operating as usual and none of the civic utilities are suffering as a result of the strike. Everything is quiet and orderly in Calgary and according to visitors who returned to Edmonton from the southern city, it was scarcely obvious that a strike existed. Streetcars and all public utilities are in operation, the stores are open and doing good business. Hotels and restaurants are being conducted along the normal lines. Theatres and picture houses are as they were prior to the strike.

The *Bulletin* the day before had informed the citizens of Edmonton what most already knew:

. . . . streetcars, restaurants, a few business houses, closed down promptly at 11 o'clock, the time named by the vote of the 34 city unions. Electric power was shut off and water power decreased throughout the city and the strike in its most serious phase became effective. The city is orderly despite it all and the newness of the unique conditions seem to leave strike participants in a quandry. Cooks and waiters took off their overalls at 11 o'clock sharp, dressed up and locked the doors. A person hungry found his entrance barred from public eating houses and in some cases, an individual was left with a partially served meal. So far as the great war veterans are concerned, it has been stated officially that their attitude so far as the strike is concerned will be one of strict neutrality. They will refuse to act as strike-breakers, however. All the civic unions went out and business at the city hall is in the hands of the superintendents of departments and a few odd employees. The public library is closed but the reading room is still open. . . .

Rev. F.E. Mercer, who appeared before council on

An advertisement in the Calgary Herald, June 17, 1919, near the end of the general strike there.

Joe Clarke, Edmonton mayor during the 1919 general strike. Elected with labour support, he was sympathetic to the strikers. Said the Edmonton Bulletin: "Better to deal with the Soviet direct ... than the Soviet reinforced by the authority of the mayor's office."

Monday as a representative of the public health and safety committee of the strikers [said] they are agreeable that the domestic supply of light and water shall not be interfered with, also the police, fire department, hospital attendants and children's shelter. Arrangements have been made to carry out delivery of dairy milk, the strikers permitting this to be done, but no ice-cream or butter is to be made.

Council met at 10 o'clock to consider what steps should be taken in order to deal with the strike situation. The Mayor said that there were two things that he intended to protect. One was that he would protect the citizens' goods and chattels and the other was that he would guarantee the right to live under living conditions and he added later this meant the right to strike to achieve those conditions. The mayor said he did not think that the city should employ any who might be considered strike-breakers as the strikers had guaranteed police and fire protection and also that there should be milk delivery.

In another story the same day, the *Bulletin* reported that theatres would reopen "by permission of the general strike committee." Carl Berg, secretary of the committee, told the paper that "the first day of the strike was even more successful than anticipated." The police union voted fifty-seven to two to join the strike but was told by the strike committee to stay at work. It appears that the conciliatory attitude taken by Mayor Joe Clarke, who had warned in 1918 of the possibility of troops being turned against citizens to quell unrest, was chiefly responsible for the orderly conduct of the strike and the fact that workers in important public services returned to their jobs within a few days.

The *Bulletin,* the most anti-labour of the city's newspapers, was, however, not impressed with Clarke's performance. "Better," said the paper in its June 3 edition, "to deal with the Soviet direct and standing alone than the Soviet reinforced by the authority of the major's office." The "Soviet" theme was particularly attractive to the *Bulletin* and it was not alone. In almost every city where general strikes were in progress, and the list was a long one — Prince Rupert, Vancouver (where it nearly assumed the proportions of the Winnipeg walkout), Moose Jaw, Regina, Saskatoon, Prince Albert, Brandon, Port Arthur and Fort William (now Thunder Bay), Toronto (where it had, at best, marginal impact) and other smaller centres—citizens' committees had been formed to run services shut down by the walkouts and to pressure the various levels of government to come down hard on the strikers, who were usually viewed as foreigners in the employ of Lenin and Trotsky.

The fact that in all cases the issues in the strikes were collective bargaining and the right of workers to belong to a union—hardly revolutionary goals—was ignored by the citizens' committees. What had captured their attention was the rhetoric generated from the Calgary conference, the formation of the One Big Union and the fact that during a general strike, regardless of the reasons for it, the strike committee must, of necessity, take some responsibility for the maintenance of public order and the continuance of public services. It was one thing for groups of citizens, usually headed by prominent business leaders, to believe the wave of general strikes was the work of Bolsheviks taking their orders from the Kremlin but the federal government was convinced of the same "fact." Gideon Robertson, Borden's labour minister, told the Calgary mayor in a telegram May 26 that: "Events have proven conclusively that the motive behind the general strike was the purpose of assuming control and direction of industrial affairs, also municipal, provincial and federal activities."

In Edmonton, most municipal services, including the

streetrailway, were restored by the end of May but metal workers and foundry employees, brewery workers, teamsters, laundry workers and railway employees stayed out until the strike was called off June 25. The strike committee had more success in calling out the building trades in Edmonton than in Calgary—plumbers, carpenters, painters, bricklayers and stonemasons were all out, at least officially, but some members broke ranks with the leadership and either continued to work or quickly strayed back to their jobs. With the exception of the postal issue in Calgary, the Edmonton and Calgary disputes were centred on one thing—the situation in Winnipeg. It was the linchpin of the general strike movement across the country and if it could be broken, order would be promptly restored.

On June 6, the federal government showed how quickly Parliament could act when it had to. An amendment to the Immigration Act allowing for the deportation of naturalized citizens charged with sedition was passed by the Commons in all its stages in about twenty minutes and was given royal assent the same day. Less than two weeks later, on June 17, Mounties in Winnipeg, in an early morning raid, arrested the main strike leaders and threw them into jail. On June 21, a mass meeting to protest the arrests was attacked by men, some wearing the uniform of the RCMP, on horseback swinging baseball bats. On one charge through the crowd, the police and special constables drew their pistols; two people were killed, about thirty injured and one hundred arrested. The city was then placed under military rule, and by June 26 the Winnipeg General Strike was over, with none of the principal issues resolved in favour of the strikers. General strikes, which had proved such an attractive and painless method for working men and women to attain their goals in the latter years of the war, weren't magical after all. Workers could shut down the country but in the absence of action on the political front, the full power of the state was left in the hands of policians acting for the business community.

Canadian workers were pragmatists above all else. As long as the radical leaders with their ideas of direct action were delivering the goods they received support. The defeat of the strike and ferocity of the counter-attack by employers, the international unions and the TLC left the OBU and the idea of general strike—which were two distinct matters related only by the conditions which fathered them—reeling.

Miners and the OBU

It was in the coal mines of Alberta that the One Big Union clung tenaciously to life but even there, the full force of an alliance between the employers, the United Mine Workers, and the federal government acting through the director of the coal operations, would eventually bring the miners to heel.

In the referendum on the OBU, Alberta's miners had voted overwhelmingly in favour of leaving the UMW for the new organization. Only 5 percent of the miners voted to stay with the UMW. The reasoning was simple—the United Mine Workers had let them down. The war that Indianapolis (UMW headquarters) was fighting was completely different from the war being waged in the mines of Alberta and southeastern B.C. There, miners were still living in their dreary little shacks or bunkhouses within sight of the tipple, were still dying or being injured in the mines and were still scrambling to keep their budgets in line with rising living costs. A good percentage of them were considered by their own government to be "enemy aliens" and were stripped of their civil rights. And all the while Indianapolis was telling them there was a war to win and that what was happening in Europe was more important than what was going on in Blairmore. A local in Canmore that switched allegiance to the OBU said it all, in capital letters. The Canmore miners said that during their battle against the operators, the director of coal operations and the UMW they would, if necessary, return to work without any union at all "BUT NEVER AGAIN SHALL WE BELONG TO THAT ROTTEN INTERNATIONAL."[11]

At about the same time taxi drivers in Edmonton and machinists in Calgary were preparing for general strikes, almost sixty-five hundred coal miners in District 18 walked off the job, supporting their executive in a dispute over wages and the cost of living allowance established in their old contract. The agreement had expired but was extended by coal commissioner Armstrong until a declaration of peace had been signed, formally ending the war in Europe. All conditions and wages of the old contract, except the cost of living increases, were continued.

What complicated the dispute was the miners' switch to the One Big Union. One operator told his employees if they voted for the OBU, he would shut the mine down.[12] Armstrong refused to have anything to do with District 18 officials until they received a clean bill of health from the International. Given that the District 18 executive board had endorsed the OBU March 29 and that it was common knowledge throughout the fields that the miners were giving their blessing to the OBU in the referendum, it was unlikely that Indianapolis would be so obliging. John L. Lewis, then a vice-president of the international, wrote Armstrong telling him the dispute had not been sanctioned by the UMW. Armstrong was also informed that the union would probably suspend District 18's charter and send in a number of officials from the UMW to reorganize the district.

Early in July, Christophers, the leader of the revolt

Delegates attending the 1920 convention of the Alberta Federation of Labour in Calgary. Alf Farmilo is second from left in the front row; Fred White is fourth from left. Elmer Roper is second from right in the back row.

Delegates attending the 1920 convention of the Alberta Federation of Labour in Calgary. Alf Farmilo is second from left in the front row; Fred White is fourth from left. Elmer Roper is second from right in the back row.

against the international, told Armstrong the miners would return to work only if they were promised there would be no discrimination against the strikers. Armstrong rejected the offer, saying he would deal only with the UMW. On July 28, the international suspended District 18's charter and appointed a three-member commission of American officials to handle affairs in the region. On July 31, with only Frank Wheatley in opposition, the District 18 executive officially established itself as District 1, Mining Department, One Big Union.

Throughout most of the district, the strike had been without incident even though, in an attempt to bring all the pressure it could to bear on the operators, the union had called out the pump men with the other miners. But in Lethbridge and Drumheller, things did get a little ugly. On June 10, Lethbridge Mounted Police telegraphed their superiors informing them that a house in Coalhurst had been blown up the day before and that five people had been arrested.[13] Problems arose in both localities because operators attempted to keep mines operating despite the strike. About a hundred strike-breaking miners at the CPR mines in the Lethbridge district were taken every day to their places by a special train. According to the 1919 annual report of the Alberta Provincial Police, "a number of women, wives of striking miners, broke the windows of this train with stones and they [the strike-breakers] were also interfered with by the striking miners and breaches of the peace took place. On the 29th of May, this same train was attacked and considerable damage was done by both men and women."

In Drumheller, Frank Moodie, owner of the Rosedade mine and one of the most vehement anti-labour employers in the area, used returned soldiers to keep his mine operating. The Mounted Police were ordered to protect the mines and were assisted by the Alberta Provincial Police which made regular patrols of the district to preserve the peace. It was apparent, however, that the police were more interested in keeping the mines open and the OBU out than in stopping any violence. On August 9, vigilante squads began keeping their own version of the peace in the Drumheller area and were evidently given free rein by the Mounties and APP officers in the valley of the Red Deer River. John Sullivan, a leader of the OBU in the area, who, like many other OBU activists, would later become a leading member of the Communist Party, was attacked in his bed by five men who thought Drumheller would would be better off without him. The OBU leader escaped only with the help of a neighbour who had a rifle handy.

There were no more incidents over the weekend but Monday morning a squad of vigilantes arrived in one of the

When Drumheller miners belonging to the One Big Union went on strike in 1919, they were attacked in their homes (below) by squads of vigilantes.

valley's shantytowns, jumped from their cars and began to rush the strikers' shacks. The miners retreated to the brush behind their cabins and then began a counter-attack, which ended as reinforcements arrived to help the attackers, and the sound of gunfire began to echo across the valley. Miners who took to the hills were hunted down by vigilantes and beaten up. Meanwhile, the mine operators and an organization of returned veterans were saying that unless the strike ended, the strikers would be driven out of the valley. The only arrest made was of a striker who was charged with illegal possession of arms. The war in Europe had been over almost a year but the man was labelled an "enemy alien." Christophers and two other OBU leaders attending a meeting in the town of Wayne, near Drumheller, were grabbed from the podium by several carloads of special constables sworn in by the operators to protect their property, taken by force to a kangaroo court in Drumheller and then run out of town.

The 1919 annual report of the provincial police said only this about the terror visited in those several days on the strikers by vigilantes looking after the interests of the coal operators: "On the nights of August 11th and 12th, the citizens and returned soldiers' organizations expelled the agitators of the OBU from the valley and a few days later all the mines in the district were working again." The *Calgary Herald*, which in 1918 had warned citizens of the "volcano of class reign" allowed as how the veterans had acted in "an unorthodox way" but added that their actions, were, under the circumstances, "excusable."[14] The government and the operators were steadfast in their opposition to the OBU. Gideon Robertson was satisfied, he said in Calgary,

"with the way in which the [international] conduct their business" and the operators' association promised the UMW commission now running the shell of District 18 its "moral and solid support to organize District 18 for the international."

With the strike broken in the Drumheller valley and miners in other areas hurting after about three months without pay cheques or strike-pay and faced with the intractable opposition of the operators and the coal operations office, the miners returned to their jobs as members of the UMW, as advised by the OBU leadership. But the One Big Union wasn't giving up on the miners, it was just taking a rest. Said Christophers: "By God, there is another day coming."[15]

In December, despite the fact that most miners in the district belonged to the OBU (the OBU then claimed the allegiance of about eight thousand miners in the area), a temporary agreement was reached between the UMW and the director of coal operations providing a 14 percent wage increase. The main item in the contract was the long-sought-after closed shop. If miners wanted to work in District 18, they would have to belong to the UMW and sign a check-off allowing the operators to deduct UMW dues from their pay. The agreement was consecrated by Armstrong in Order 141. Said the *Searchlight* of the contract and resultant order:

Capital has declared that the miners of the district are not to be allowed self-determination in regard to the union to which they are to belong. The minister of labour and the director of coal operations have placed

the power of government on the side of capital. The coal operators have agreed with the government and with the Indianapolis machine, which has taken upon itself the control of the destiny of Canadian miners, that no miner is to be given employment unless he signs away all his rights to the UMW of A."[16]

Throughout the district early in 1920 there were several strikes and lockouts as some operators attempted to enforce the closed shop and check-off but most preferred to keep their mines working. The check-off was not universally applied until March when Armstrong, who had been refusing to meet with the OBU which had been trying to get a contract negotiated, told all the operators to make all the miners sign the check-off. Almost two thousand miners were either on strike or locked out for several weeks at the end of March but not all operators desired a confrontation with their employees. A few mines in the Lethbridge region and a mine at Nordegg in the Coal Branch continued operations. Even when miners went back, agreeing to sign what they called the "choke-off," they went back under protest. Employees of the McGillivray mine in the Crowsnest wrote the minister of labour, saying:

I am instructed to inform you that our members who

have been locked out for a period of one week because they refused to sign the compulsory check-off of the United Mine Workers of America are returning to work vigorously protesting against what we consider to be an illegal act on the part of those responsible for its enforcement. I am further instructed to appeal to you to take immediate proceedings to cause to be withdrawn this compulsory check-off that takes away our liberty. Whilst we are forced to become members of the above organization (the UMW of A), we shall not consider ourselves members and will as soon as possible again sever our connection which we hope to do without further trouble.[17]

In June, a new contract was finalized between the UMW and the coal operators through the coal operations office. It replaced the temporary December agreement and provided a 27 percent wage hike and retained the closed shop and check-off.

The final gasp of the OBU in Alberta's coal fields came in October, 1920 when thirty-four hundred miners stayed off the job for several weeks in a final attempt to break the check-off and gain recognition of the One Big Union. By this time, resolve was wearing thin. Miners had been on and off strike since the spring of 1919 and all the while the alliance between the federal government and their employers had remained strong. Even at the peak of the strike, which was centred in the Drumheller field, a full third of the miners stayed in the pits. A supreme court injuction ordering the OBU to cease its activities was the final blow.[18]

In June of 1921, the UMW commission called a convention of District 18 locals and a new constitution, much more moderate in tone than the old one, was approved. On August 1, the international granted a petition from the district returning full autonomy. John L. Lewis, by that time UMW president, told delegates attending the union's September, 1921 convention that "the long struggle against the false philosophy of the proponents of the One Big Union idea" was finally over. "I feel assured," said Lewis, "that the experience which has been gained in this struggle will be a lasting lesson to the mine workers of northwest Canada and will result in a greater degree of loyalty and appreciation of the organization's accomplishments."[19]

Lewis couldn't have been more wrong. The miners had given up on the OBU not because they loved the United Mine Workers but because they were hungry and beaten. Secession and conflict would continue to dog the UMW in District 18 until the late thirties.

Women's Work: The Great Western Garment workroom in Edmonton, 1918. The plant was one of many organized during the war.

Women's Work: The Great Western Garment workroom in Edmonton, 1918. The plant was one of many organized during the war.

CHAPTER SIX

Growth and Decline: THE TWENTIES

Growth of Union Membership

The intense activity and militancy of the period leading up to the 1919 general strikes was a hard act to follow. There has always been a marked ebb and flow of working class militancy and in the Twenties, the tide was most definitely out.

In general, workers in the Canadian West, whether miners, machinists or barbers, had suffered a major defeat in 1919. The principles of union recognition and collective bargaining had still not been accepted by either government or employers and the secession movement of the One Big Union had left many unions, the UMW in particular, in ruins that would require painstaking time and effort to rebuild. Spurred by inflation, the labour movement had expanded greatly in the late years of the war in an organizing drive that brought the idea of trade unionism to many groups of workers previously outside union ranks. By 1919, there were almost twice as many union members in

Canada as in 1914. That high of almost four hundred thousand was not to be attained again until 1937.

Alberta reflected the national trend. In 1913, 171 locals represented eleven thousand five hundred workers. Depression took its toll and by the following year, union membership dropped by four thousand. But by 1920, it had climbed to more than fifteen thousand.[1] A considerable amount of the organizing during the war was done by public sector workers. Edmonton city labourers were among the first general municipal workers to join the rapidly-expanding labour movement. They had tried out a union—the Wobblies—in 1912 but it hadn't worked out. In 1916 they tried again, and after negotiating a contract, were issued a charter by the Trades and Labour Congress on May Day, 1917. Their lead was soon followed by city inside workers in Calgary and municipal employees in Lethbridge and Medicine Hat. By 1919, a municipal federation had been formed in Calgary to negotiate with city council. It included, in addition to city hall staff and labourers, police and fire fighters, teamsters, electricians and streetrailway workers. In 1919, the first local of hospital workers in the province, Local 8, City Hospital Employees, was organized to represent workers at the Calgary municipal hospital.

In 1919, employees of the provincial government organized the Civil Service Association of Alberta, as a direct result of conditions during the war. W.T. Aiken, one of the founders of the association, said government workers faced:

.... quite a lot of hardship and the government took it on hand to cut salaries—mostly in the low paid employees. So much was taken off because the government was hard up for money at the time. . . . There was a clause in the Civil Service Act at that time—they said that anyone that asked for an increase in salary, it could be taken as tantamount to a resignation. The thing was ridiculous and actually, it was carried out in one or two cases when somebody went and asked for an increase in salary.

Another complaint of the civil servants, and one that would eventually lead to the merit system in the public service, was that chances of promotion were constantly blocked by the appointment of political cronies of the government.

When it saw that organization was inevitable, even in the face of dismissal for people who joined, the government changed tactics. Instead of fighting, it decided to try to control the association—a move that met with some success. The association was not officially recognized until four years after its founding and for many years after that was more of an advisory body to the provincial government than a trade union. Late in 1927, the association decided to affiliate with the Trades and Labour Congress and the Alberta Federation of Labour. It had, at the time, 661 members. A year later, it made another move to establish its credentials as a full-fledged union by appointing Alf Farmilo executive secretary.[2]

The year 1919 saw not only the formation of the Civil Service Association but the province's first teachers' strike. The Alberta Teachers Alliance had been formed two years earlier "to place the teachers in their proper social and economic position." Its goal was a minimum yearly salary of $1,200.[3] Early in January of 1919, the alliance began negotiating with the Edmonton school board but by the time classes resumed after the summer break, teachers were still without a contract. On October 9, they went on strike and stayed out until the 15th, when they returned with a small wage increase. Two years later, they were out again, this time for four days, in an effort to persuade the board to recognize the alliance. "The settlement obtained," said the *Alberta Labour News* of April 30, 1921,

"means that the teachers' alliance is officially recognized for the first time."

Civil servants, municipal and hospital workers, even bank workers were talking about unions. One Calgary bank clerk wrote a letter in February 1920 to the *Searchlight* and passed on the "secret" that:

. . . .quietly, we are going to build up an organization of the workers in the banks in Calgary with the idea of demanding a 100 percent increase over salaries paid in 1914. . . . My own salary now comes to $100 a month and the time and overtime that I work is over 50 hours a week. . . . I am single and pay $3.50 for my room. My meals I get at restaurants and find that I have to scrimp along very carefully to get enough to eat for $1 a day. As a bank clerk, I feel I have to wear decent clothes and laundered shirts and collars. . . . I seldom go to the Grand but once in a while I cannot resist taking in a picture show and as I was brought up in a good Christian home, I always try to go to church on Sundays and hate to have the plate passed under my nose without putting in at least two bits.

The *Searchlight* tried to set up a bank workers' organizing drive but it would be more than fifty years before Canadian banks would have to worry about unions.

In 1922, the Edmonton local of the Hotel and Restaurant Employees Union called a strike against four city cafés which were demanding a wage cut of 27.5 percent. The union was offering to accept a cut of 10 percent and the waitresses stayed out thirty-nine days to win their point. Three of the café proprietors then compromised and cut wages only 12.5 percent. The fourth restaurant owner was more stubborn and, five months later, it was still strike-bound.

Between 1916 and 1922, Edmonton waitresses had succeeded in cutting their work week to forty-eight hours over six days and bringing wages to about twenty-five dollars a week but their gains had not come easily. The first significant restaurant strike in Alberta took place in 1916. William Peebles, the union business agent, said the fifty-three men and women employed in four city cafés were "fighting to establish working conditions whereby our members, who work seven days a week, 365 days in a year, with no holidays, have a little time for recreation and a living wage."[4] The 1916 strikers asked for a one dollar a week increase for female dishwashers to bring them to eight dollars a week and a fifty cent increase for waitresses, giving them ten dollars a week. Modest enough demands but only two of the four restaurants settled with the union after a two-month strike. The other two ignored the walkout, hired strike-breakers and continued operations on their own terms.[5]

Hotel and restaurant employees, Edmonton, 1940. Organization of restaurant workers was aided during the Depression by unemployed workers on relief. Waitresses were often paid less than the minimum wage. During the First World War, it was reported that some employees rented sleeping accommodations in restaurant basements.

Conditions endured by the women who worked in the restaurants of the cities were as poor as can be imagined, as members of the 1919 Mathers commission discovered at their Calgary hearings. Jean MacWilliams testified:

> I was put on a committee to investigate conditions in the hotels and restaurants around the city here. Girls were living with sleeping accommodation down in the basement. Here were the men's quarters and here were the girls' quarters, down the basement, side by side. One little girl got into trouble and her baby was born three months after she was married. The baby was only four pounds in weight because the girl was almost starved to death. That little girl's baby died on the 14th of this month of malnutrition and starvation. The child had only started to build her home, death has entered her family, who is responsible?

Mrs. George Corse also talked to the commission in Cal-

gary about the problems of restaurant employees and other groups of women workers. F.E. Harrison, the federal government's fair wage officer, admitted, said Mrs. Corse:

> ....that it was impossible to his mind that any girl could live and remain decent on $9 a week, which is the minimum allowed by the Alberta Factory Act. . . . Girls are working in basements [under] artificial light, all day long. Other girls are working in places which has no sanitary accommodation all day long. Only recently in the daily paper, a notice appeared asking for someone to adopt a child yet to be born. This woman already has four children and she could not face the world with the fifth one. . . . Birth control is a crime to the poor women but the well-to-do woman who says she can only do justice to two or three children is commended for her intelligent outlook.[6]

Restaurant workers laboured nine or ten hours a day, often

Making chocolates, Edmonton, 1906.

in split shifts, seven days a week, all year, for as small a pay packet as the proprietor could get away with. Some café owners, afraid of getting caught in one of the far too infrequent visits by a Factory Act inspector, would pay their help with a cheque for the minimum wage and then demand that it be cashed at the till so they could take some back.[7]

In some cases, café owners doled out wages a dollar or two at a time. Rent for a cot in the basement could cost as much as five dollars a week.

Anna MacLaren, of Lethbridge, recalling her work in a restaurant before she helped organize a union, said the employers made the waitresses literally run.[8]

Restaurant workers and others like them were the forgotten underclass of western Canada. True, there were women who were fighting for women's rights but the predominantly middle-class suffragists were fighting for

things that meant little to women sleeping in café basements. The right to vote, the right to access to the professions, the right to smoke cigarettes in public—what could these things mean to women who were working every day of the year for less than the minimum wage? Theirs were more pressing concerns but if anything was to be done, they would have to do it themselves.

Individually, workers were powerless; when they acted together they could sometimes make things happen. It was this message that union organizers took into the lumber camps of Alberta in 1919. They found a ready and warm reception as bush and mill workers began their first rebellion against living conditions not unlike those found in the railway construction camps some years earlier. But as was the case in practically every industry, employer retaliation with police assistance brought a quick end to unionization of Alberta's lumber workers.

The established trade unions weren't too interested in

taking in groups of workers such as loggers and sawmill workers. In some places, the carpenters union did so but they usually organized the skilled workers in the sawmills and left the rest to catch as catch can. The Wobblies, however, were interested and in the American Pacific northwest scored some of their most impressive victories and staged some of their fiercest battles against the logging contractors. IWW organizers travelled through the lumber camps of Alberta in the early Twenties, leaving behind them no organization but some descriptions of conditions faced by Alberta loggers.

A report by a Wobblie organizer in the September 1, 1922 *Lumber Workers Bulletin* said of accommodation in the Crowsnest-area camps that the bedsprings were "rather hard as they are made of lumber." In the Coal Branch area, a Wobblie reported in the December 15, 1923 issue of the *Bulletin* that "at the [saw] mill, the conditions are not so bad but the camps [in the bush] are so bad that the dry-land homesteaders can no longer endure the filth . . . ."[9] Carl Berg's IWW heritage left him a special interest in the plight of the loggers and after the One Big Union had been formed in Calgary in the spring of 1919, Berg began organizing loggers into an OBU component known as the Lumber Workers Industrial Union and in December of 1919, pulled two strikes in the northern part of the province, one at Hylo, near Lac La Biche, and the other at Grande Prairie. The strike at Hylo attracted the most attention, especially from the Mounties.

Ever on the watch for subversion, the Mounties at first suspected the strike had been the work of OBU agitators who had somehow duped the men into leaving their jobs. The OBU and Carl Berg had been the subject of some interest by the Mounties and the commanding officer of the Edmonton-area division "instructed that secret agents numbers 16 and 61 should meet the train [from the strike area] on its arrival and mix with the men and ascertain what really was the trouble."[10] After receiving reports from his secret agents, T.A. Wroughton was forced to admit that "this is a dispute between a particular company and their employees over local conditions. From the reports submitted by the two special agents, I am convinced that the men quit because they had real grievances. It is evident that the wages were reduced and also that there were other conditions such as bad water." Secret Agent 61 said he:

. . . . met Berg and Clark, who arrived this morning from Hylo, in the Royal Palace Café and we had breakfast together and, after treating them as well with a smoke, we all proceeded to Berg's office. After asking me about my welfare (just to show you how I stand with the boys) Clark told me that the whole bunch was striking because the company reduced their wages to $49.50 a month,

unsanitary conditions of camp, stinking water and general unsatisfactory conditions.

Police concern with labour agitation and efforts to keep order were appreciated by employers who shared the police view that labour agitation would serve no useful purpose. One lumber camp operation wrote the Alberta attorney general expressing his gratitude for Alberta Provincial Police action.

We are operating a sawmill at Smoky and a logging camp eight miles up the river and are employing about 35 to 40 men. We have had considerable trouble keeping our men going because of IWW trouble and liquor. Since Bruce Murray stationed at McClennan came on the job, this situation has been thoroughly cleaned up and we want to express our appreciation.

One organizing drive met with a little more success. The packing plants of Edmonton and Calgary were hardly in the same league as those in Chicago, described by Upton Sinclair in his 1906 novel, *The Jungle,* but it was a difference more in scale than in the way the companies treated their workers. Alex Goruk said, referring to *The Jungle:*

I've read that book twice over, and as I keep reading I keep comparing it to the situation in this plant as I knew it and I'll tell you, he's right on.

The tank house is the department where we cook all the bones, the guts, the hoofs, all the inedible products [for fertilizer]. . . .

We used to hate a particular job called drying blood. The fluid blood is dumped into a great big vat and then the steam is turned on and the vat put into a circular motion. Once it's dry, we take this powder out of a roaster.

The next process was to sack it, so you would have one man holding a gunny sack and the other fellow with the scoop shovel, scooping out the blood and putting it in. After about 10 minutes of this operation, you couldn't see the fellow that's holding the bag and he's only standing about two feet away. The whole air, the whole room, would be just thick with fine dust, blood dust, and sometimes you would do this for four hours non-stop. All the time you're breathing this. For two days after that, you're spitting and choking and coughing blood our of your lungs.

The other condition that I found bad, and I worked there as well, was our feed division, where we mixed certain chemicals and alfalfa and different other materials, put them in a mixer and mixed them all together and that produced an awful lot of dust. Almost as bad as the blood and here again you breathe that eight hours a

day. And after two or three weeks, unless you were very healthy, your lungs were very healthy, you begin to lose appetite and you felt weak and all that.

Edmonton packing plant workers organized first, receiving a charter from the Amalgamated Meat Cutters Union in October 4, 1918 but it would be in Calgary, the headquarters of the Pat Burns' operation, where the packing-house workers would run into the most trouble. Local 68 in Calgary was chartered June 14, 1920[11] but didn't last the year. The Edmonton local fell apart at about the same time.

At 10:00 A.M. on 14 July 1920, 220 men and 30 women employed at Burns and two other Calgary packing plants walked off the job asking for increased wages and improvements in working conditions, and complaining that Burns had stalled in negotiations. The main issue,

however, quickly became recognition of the union. The *Calgary Herald* of July 26 reported that local labour leaders, including Alex Ross, a former head of the Calgary Labour Council elected as an MLA in 1917, believed that Burns and the other companies were making "a most determined effort to break the strike." Three days later, the strike was over with the *Herald* reporting that about eighty strikers had returned to work at Burns and that the union had asked the company to take back all those who walked out, numbering about one hundred eighty. As in countless other disputes, Burns said it would rehire the strikers as vacancies opened up but that it would reserve the right to choose who it would take back. The company, said the *Herald,* "acknowledged the inherent right of the men to organize but refused to enter into any agreement with such organization."

Calgary home of Pat Burns — owner of Burns Packing Plant. Workers at the Burns plant tried to organize a union in 1920 but the union was broken the same year. At the time, Burns was paying children 27¼ cents per hour.

Burns did agree, however, to meet with a committee of workers to discuss wages. By mid-August, most of the strikers had been rehired but the company was refusing to take back nine workers and had still not met with the committee. Trouble continued at the Calgary plant as the workers maintained their efforts to have Burns recognize their union. In September, there were reports that union sympathizers were being fired and finally, on November 3, 1920, frustrated Burns' employees walked off the job again. The *Herald* reported on November 4:

Between 70 and 80 employees struck work at noon on Thursday. The men affected are principally the men of the killing floor department and the reason for their going out on strike is the attitude officials of the company have taken over an agreement which has been under negotiation since the strike at the plant in July. The men state that one of the obstacles they have had to contend with is that the company will not recognize the meat cutters' union but deal through a committee of employees. ... They have tried to persuade the department of labour to grant an arbitration board and it is stated the department has appealed to P. Burns Co. to grant this but the firm has consistently refused to accept the advances of the employees.

The western organizer of the union, W.H. Nicholson, said there was a possibility that all its members across the country might be called out to help win the fight at Burns. If there was a general strike of packing plant workers, he said, it would probably start at Edmonton where the union was experiencing some trouble in getting a new contract. The Edmonton Board of Trade had intervened, but Mr. Bradley, manager of Swift's Edmonton plant, "informed the board that until the men could show that they were strong enough to enforce their demands, he would not sign any agreement," said a story in the November 5 *Albertan*. The plan to involve other locals of the union fell through when the international informed the men that they would not sanction even the Calgary strike.

The faltering strike received a temporary boost in mid-November when the union convinced some of the non-union men at work on the killing floor to join the walkout, but it wasn't enough. The *Albertan* of November 23 told its readers that the strike had ended and that the men had agreed to return "without any qualification whatever." Nicholson wrote the federal labour department that the strikers had returned to work "on the same condition as they were working under prior to the strike—no agreement. Men working under the rate and hours fixed by the company."[12]

After the failure of the 1920 strikes, the men, women and children—twenty-six girls and fifteen boys, some of whom worked for as little as twenty-seven and one-quarter cents an hour—found themselves outmatched in a contest judged not by justice but by power. For another twenty years, they would continue to work at Pat Burns' plant and it would take the militancy generated by yet another depression and world war to finally alter the relationship of power between Burns and his employees.

Decline

Unemployment in Alberta and the traditional hostility of employers to union organization dogged the efforts of workers to improve working conditions and wages throughout the Twenties. With the occasional exception of the miners, Alberta workers became unwilling to challenge their employers, even when faced with wage cuts. In the five years between 1923 and 1927, workers in industries other than mining were involved in only seven strikes. In 1926, only three strikes were reported and all three were called by the miners.

By the end of the war, Alberta miners had boldly used the power given them by the nation's insatiable wartime appetite for coal to make themselves among the highest paid workers in the country. During the Twenties, however, the advantage shifted back to the operators. Coal production was falling and new fuels, such as natural gas, were competing for markets. Coal from the closer American fields had taken over the Ontario markets. Miners were still receiving high daily wages but soft markets meant they went many days without work. The 1925 coal commission estimated that the full workforce in mines in Crowsnest and Coal Branch fields was employed for only ninety-five days in 1921 and eighty-nine days in 1922. In 1923, Drumheller miners worked only seventy-five days. The drop in production after the war was matched by a drop in the prices the operators received for the coal they were able to market and as they saw their profits decline, they attempted to shore them up by cutting wages.

District 18 was shut down by a strike of five months in 1922 as operators tired to strip the miners of wartime cost of living bonuses. The miners were able to hold out, but increasingly, they were spending considerable effort fighting each other at a time when unity was needed. An American railway magnate, Jay Gould, once said he had no reason to worry about the working class as long as he could hire one half to kill the other; that became the theme in Alberta's coal fields. In District 18, restoration of autonomy by the international did not mean the wounds of the OBU period had healed. Fighting among the factions continued, highlighted by the defeat in 1922 of Bob Livett, an anti-

OBU stalwart, at the hands of Rod McDonald, a former OBU organizer who received the backing of Christophers, by then an MLA, in the election campaign for international board member.

Miners entered negotiations in 1924 at a considerable disadvantage. For many, the arguments of the operators that a wage cut would win back markets and restore full production were attractive after several years of working only a few days a week. Still the miners were able to stick together for a seven-month strike but were unsuccessful in preventing their employers from finally securing a wage cut of $1.17 a day. It would be the last example of district-wide solidarity in Alberta's coal communities for more than a decade.

In the long strikes of 1922 and 1924, many of the miners were dissatisfied with the amount of strike relief given by the international. In one case in the Drumheller field, Slim Evans, a former OBU supporter who had since joined the newly-formed Communist Party of Canada, withheld membership dues payable to Indianapolis and instead returned them to his striking membership. He was charged with theft and given a term in penitentiary. Complaints that the union wasn't behind them, severe economic pressure and fighting between militants and moderates within the district made the miners easy picking for the operators. The 1924 agreement allowed the operators to cancel it on six months notice any time after March 31, 1925, but the mine owners were not content to wait even that long.

What would turn out to be a stampede from the UMW began at several mines in the B.C. section of the Crowsnest field when one large operator declared he could not make any money paying even the reduced rates set in the 1924 contract and shut down his mines. He then posted a new schedule of wages and informed his former employees that if they wanted to work, it would have to be on his terms. The men withdrew from the UMW, set up their own local association and returned to work. As the B.C. mines in the area competed for the same buyers as mines on the Alberta side, competitive pressure soon spread the lockout and secession movement across the border.

Blairmore, Bellevue and Coleman were the first to go. On March 21, 1925, Hillcrest Collieries posted a notice at the mine office informing its employees that while "you may hold out for high wages, you get little or no work, as evidenced by the fact that during the past 12 months, you have only averaged a total of about 43 full days pay." The mine company then rubbed a little salt into the wound of dissatisfaction with the lack of strike support from the international: "The men in our camp during the past 10 years have paid $64,584 in the union fund. How much of this fund are your officials advancing to you today?" The notice said a revised scale of wages was posted at the

timekeeper's office and "our mine manager will be at his office ready to sign on any man willing to work on this basis. As soon as a sufficient number of men are signed on, we will again open our mines."13

For a time, the miners, mounting a picket of between two hundred and three hundred men, were able to keep the mine closed and prevent employees from undercutting the negotiated wage rates but hunger eventually forced them to accept the company demand for a wage cut. Financially, they were not prepared to maintain themselves during a protracted shutdown: one miner told the Alberta coal commission he had worked only 16 or 18 shifts in more than a year. When work resumed, the miners discovered that the company was refusing to take some of the men back, even though new men from outside the Crowsnest were being given jobs. In all, twenty-three men found

themselves blacklisted at mines throughout the Pass. John Maddison, a Hillcrest miner with a family of four children, told the 1925 coal commission at a hearing in Blairmore that he had tried to get work at mines in Michel, Coleman and Blairmore.

"You find it impossible to work?"

"It is impossible to get work when I come from Hillcrest."

"What condition is your family in?"

"Very bad condition. I have only worked about 25 days this last 13 months, living on borrowed money, in debt about $600 now."

"What future have you? What do you propose to do?"

"Well, since I have tried all these camps, I figure I will have to do away someplace, go east or west. I have tried all these camps, no use hanging around anymore."

The coal-mining community of Wayne, in the Drumheller valley, in the early Twenties.

"It would mean leaving your family?"

That is what I'd have to do; I'd have to leave them if I go, yes, because I am broke."[14]

With Hillcrest broken, the flood toward company associations at reduced wages continued. In a vain attempt to stave off complete disorganization of the district, the UMW negotiated a new agreement with operators in the Drumheller field which established the lower wage scale being enforced in the Crowsnest. But Drumheller miners were given no say in the new agreement and the UMW found itself in a very uncomfortable position as Drumheller miners in the valley walked off the job to protest the wage cut their leaders had just negotiated for them. The UMW couldn't win. When it had refused to negotiate wage cuts, miners in the Crowsnest and in some mines in the Coal Branch left and set up company associations. When it negotiated wage cuts in Drumheller, miners there broke away and set up a new organization, the Red Deer Valley Miners Union.

The new organization called a strike in late June to prevent the wage reduction but the demoralization of the miners was evident from the fact that about half stayed on the job. Strong picket lines were established as the miners tried to stop others from working and after a fight on the line at the ABC mine the provincial police were called in. On the night of June 26, as picketers maintained their vigil near the mine, two provincial policemen fired into a group of men gathered around a camp fire, claiming they had been pelted with rocks. A young striker was seriously wounded and then dragged off to jail. A.E. Smith, leader of the Communist-inspired Canadian Labour Defence League, formed, in part, to defend workers arrested during the 1925 Drumheller dispute, suggested that the police had missed their real target: "It had remained a secret until now that the man standing beside the fire beside Louis was Tim Buck. The police had hoped that Tim was the man who dropped to earth at the crack of their rifle shot."[15]

Buck was one of the founders of the Communist Party of Canada (CP) in 1921 and would become, in the Thirties and Forties, the most widely respected leader the CP has ever had. Like many other Communist leaders, he had been active in the One Big Union in 1919 but later turned his back on it after witnessing the disastrous effects of break-away unionism. The official position of the CP, following the line established by the Communist International, was that progressive trade unionists should work within their own unions to move them to the left. Leaving unions and establishing left-wing organizations allowed right-wing leadership to carry on without challenge. The Communists had also noticed during the OBU fight that, in most instances, workers were reluctant to break with their own unions; left-wing break-aways meant that Communists within the trade union movement isolated themselves from the great majority of the class they were supposed to lead. That policy had been firmly entrenched and was one of the final and fatal blows delivered against the OBU, which had been pushing to become the trade union arm of the new party of the Canadian left.

But here was Buck in the Drumheller valley, participating in a strike which had as its object the formation of yet another break-away from the UMW. The reason was essentially pragmatic. Communist opposition to break-away unionism, or dual unionism, arose from the objective of maintaining the broadest possible contact with working people. In District 18, the miners were fed up with the UMW and wanted out. The Communists, who had taken over from the Socialist Party of Canada (which had disintegrated after 1919 with a good percentage of its membership moving to the new party) as the leading left-wing force in Alberta's coal fields, had built up a substantial following in the Crowsnest Pass and Drumheller and if it was to maintain it, a temporary lapse in its opposition to secession was required.

A long letter to Communist Party headquarters from Coleman in May of 1925 regarding "our future policy in District 18," which, although unsigned, was most probably written by Buck, argued that opposition to the formation of a new union was "ridiculous."

> Because we are opposed to secession, it does not follow that we must stand aside and see the workers of a whole industry (and our most militant supporters at that) completely smashed and demoralized. . . . The defeatist tactics of the UMW of A officialdom during the recent struggle, added to the bitterness which has existed against this union since the 1919 secession movement has produced a peculiar sentiment which may be summed up in the phrase so often heard: 'Well, we got it in the neck but by God we have something to be thankful for, this has rid us of the UMW of A.'[16]

What Buck suggested was that in a company union where the party had some influence, a call would be sent out for a conference of all miners in the Pass to form a new organization which could then reorganize the district without the substantial handicap of being part of the United Mine Workers.

The call came from the Blairmore company association and on June 1, Buck's plan received the endorsement of delegates from company associations or home locals in Blairmore, Coleman, Bellevue and Corbin, just inside the

B.C. border. Delegates also attended from Hillcrest and Michel associations but did not affiliate.

The Mine Workers Union of Canada (MWUC) had been born. During the first half of the Thirties, it would prove its mettle as the toughest organization the miners of Alberta ever had, but Buck's hopes for rapid reorganization under its banner were dashed in the Drumheller area where he had underestimated the UMW. With the support of the mine owners, the international clung tenaciously to life. By mid-September, Drumheller operators and the UMW had won out, aided in part by a court injunction against picketing by thirty-six strikers. Most miners in the area returned to work as unwilling UMW members but in a few mines, the operators refused to deal with any union at all and established open shops.[17] Drumheller was to remain the main membership base of the once-powerful UMW, which had seen its Alberta membership decline from about eight thousand to fifteen hundred in less than a year. The union was placed under international administration and affairs were placed in the hands of Bob Livett, who would rule without election for eleven years. So low had UMW stock dropped that Livett allegedly travelled the coal fields of the province with a handgun at his side.

By September, 1926, the Mine Workers Union of Canada was the largest union in the fields with almost four thousand members in fifteen camps.[18] In that year, it gained some respectability when Frank Wheatley, president of the Alberta Federation of Labour from 1922 and a member of the 1925 Alberta coal commission, was elected president. The following year, it moved, to a limited degree, into the mainstream of the labour movement when it affiliated with the newly-formed All-Canadian Congress of Labour (ACCL), headed by Aaron Mosher, president of the Canadian Brotherhood of Railway Employees, the ACCL's largest affiliate. The new congress was a grouping of industrial and nationalist unions and the newest in a long line of nationalist central bodies established since the 1902 meeting of the Trades and Labour Congress when the internationals had decreed that any Canadian union laying claim to any group of workers eligible to join a union belonging to the American Federation of Labour could not affiliate with the TLC. A mark of the MWUC's prestige in the new body was that Wheatley became its vice-president.

But its new-found respectability didn't help the MWUC gain access to the Drumheller field or negotiate a much-wanted district-wide agreement to replace the company-by-company contracts that came with the disintegration of the United Mine Workers. In many ways it was a paper organization, a federation of company associations, even as it tried to break out of that mould. Unfortunately for it and the miners of Alberta, the operators still had all the cards and were playing them against the miners, who had almost lost the will to win. Lewis McDonald, alias Kid Burns, a CP member jailed for his activities in the 1925 Drumheller strike, said on his return to the valley after release from prison that: "I never seen Drumheller so goddamn dead in my life."[19]

But the old fighting spirit could still be triggered, as it was in Coal Branch in 1925 when a Brazeau Collieries employee was killed after management had started a new work practice the men considered unsafe. The report of the MWUC president to the union's 1926 convention stated that:

> When this brother was killed, the men demanded that the new system of work be stopped. The company refused and . . . a strike was called. The men further demanded that representation by the coroner's jury be given to the mine workers. This was also refused. Nordegg is a mining camp with only the mining industry and no other occupation. They have a crew of 800 men working when things are going full blast but we find the coroner appointed as jury one baker, one boarding-house boss, one coal inspector, one grocer, one butcher and one bank manager. The coroner himself is a boarding-house boss.[20]

Miners in the Wayne field were shaken from their three-year lethargy in 1928 when six companies in the area changed the basis of payment, instituting what was, in effect, a speed-up—something that was happening more and more during the Twenties. The Wayne miners organized a local of the MWUC and in conciliation compromised on their objection to the new method of payment but added a demand that the companies recognize their new union. The companies refused and the miners walked off the job in mid-August. Two of the Wayne operators signed agreements with the Mine workers Union but the other four attempted to keep their mines operating and, as is usual when companies in a labour dispute use strikebreakers, violence resulted. The Alberta Provincial Police reported that there were several demonstrations and cases of assault and "considerable friction" but that generally "there has been no trouble at all." One striker was clubbed to death[21] by a company watchman on Christmas Day and "this rather tended at the time to excite the men on strike but nothing resulted," said the provincial police.[22]

One of the reasons that "nothing resulted" was that Frank Wheatley and the moderate leadership of the MWUC were intent on keeping things quiet, preferring to lobby government in an attempt to end the dispute. The lobbying efforts were directed at stopping the influx of British coal miners who had been recruited by the federal government for harvest work. "A most interesting feature of the announcement that 10,000 men are to be assisted to emigrate from this country to Canada for harvest work in September and October," said a story in the *South Wales News* of August 2, 1928, "is that the dominion government has expressed a special wish that recruiting for this work should be made in mining areas." Whatever the motives of the federal government in its "special wish," operators in the Wayne field weren't shy about using the immigrant miners against their own employees. Lewis McDonald wrote a letter to the Communist newspaper, the *Worker*, suggesting that, "Pleading with government officials will not win a strike. Action by the workers is the only means to stop wage cuts and save our union."[23] The strike finally ended in February 1929 in partial victory for the miners but McDonald would have to wait a few more years before the miners of District 18 would turn to fighting instead of pleading.

Political Action

The Twenties, when trade union fortunes were as low as they would ever sink in Canada, were not a time of fighting, at least on the pickets lines. During that period, working men and women took their battles with their employers to the more genteel battleground of the ballot box. Phillip Christophers was elected to the legislature representing the Crowsnest Pass in 1921 and Chris Pattinson went to Edmonton after the 1925 provincial election to look after the interests of miners in the Coal Branch.

Politics was an arena where Alberta's workers could score some unaccustomed points that took some of the sting out of defeats inflicted at practically every turn on the industrial front. Under the banner of the Canadian Labour Party (CLP), formed in Alberta in 1922 during the Alberta Federation of Labour convention in Lethbridge, working people found themselves on school boards and municipal councils, in the legislature and in various boards and agencies, including the Workers' Compensation Board where J.A. Kinney, a former president of the Edmonton carpenters and a labour alderman, was appointed chairman. They even had a representative in the cabinet when the United Farmers government, elected in 1921, appointed Alex Ross, first to the public works portfolio and then to the labour ministry.

The Canadian Labour Party was the belated outcome of the decision by the TLC in 1917 to establish a broadly-based labour party to unite communists, reform-minded socialists and other groups that held political opinions current in the labour movement, under one umbrella organization. During the Twenties, socialists and communists entered into a shaky alliance which provided labour with impressive legislative gains. In 1923,

A CPR poster for harvesting help. There were complaints during the 1928 Wayne coal strike that British immigrants brought over for harvesting help were strike-breaking.

CANADIAN PACIFIC RAILWAY

ORDER YOUR FARM HELP NOW

FOR 1927

To be of help to **WESTERN CANADIAN FARMERS** and assist in meeting their needs in securing competent farm help, the **CANADIAN PACIFIC RAILWAY** will continue its farm help service during 1927, and will include in this service, as last year, the securing of women domestics and boys.

Through experience in securing this farm help during the past few years, the Company is now in touch, through its widespread European organization, with good farm laborers in Great Britain, Norway, Sweden, Denmark, France, Holland, Switzerland, as well as in Poland, Czecho-Slovakia, Hungary, Jugo-Slavia, Roumania and Germany, and can promptly fill applications from Canadian farmers for farm help.

In order to have this help reach Canada in ample time for spring farming operations, farmers must get their applications in early to enable us to get the help needed.

Blank application forms and full information may be obtained from any C.P.R. agent or from any of the officials listed below.

THE SERVICE IS ENTIRELY FREE OF CHARGE

THE CANADIAN PACIFIC RAILWAY COMPANY
DEPARTMENT OF COLONIZATION AND DEVELOPMENT

WINNIPEG	- - -	C. A. VanSCOY, Supt. of Colonization
		THOS. S. ACHESON, General Agricultural Agent
		CANADA COLONIZATION ASSOCIATION
SASKATOON	- -	W. J. GEROW, Land Agent
		JNO. A. WILLIAMS, Asst. Supt. of Colonization
REGINA	- - -	G. D. BROPHY, District Passenger Agent
CALGARY	- -	JAMES COLLEY, Asst. Supt. of Colonization
EDMONTON	- -	J. MILLER, Asst. Supt. of Colonization
VANCOUVER	- -	H. J. LOUGHRAN, Land Agent
MONTREAL	- -	J. DOUGALL, General Agricultural Agent

J. N. K. MACALISTER,
Asst. Commissioner

J. S. DENNIS,
Chief Commissioner

Delegates at a 1924 labour convention outside the old Calgary labour temple.

labour in Calgary could count six representative on city council while in 1928, a majority of Edmonton aldermen were labour party members. In both communities, candidates of the Canadian Labour Party contested and won seats on local school boards. The party had more trouble getting its nominees into the mayors' offices. After the defeat of Joe Clarke (who was not a labour party member but depended on labour support) in Edmonton in 1920, business interests kept a firm grip on the mayorality offices. That situation lasted until the early Thirties when two typographers, Dan Knott in Edmonton and Andy Davison in Calgary, were elected to the posts.

In 1921, the United Farmers of Alberta (UFA) ended Liberal rule in the province and appointed labourite Alex Ross of Calgary first as minister without portfolio and then as labour minister. J.A. Kinney, an Edmonton carpenter and the city's first labour alderman, was given a post on the compensation board while Walter Smitten, a former secretary of the federation of labour, was placed in charge of the labour bureau. In the early period of farmer government in Edmonton, the alliance between the labour movement and the UFA paid some lasting dividends. In constituencies with both working class and rural areas, the two groups usually met to decide whether the UFA or the labour party would nominate a candidate and then agreed to support that person.

Labour's most successful year in politics was 1926 when a record number of labour candidates—six—were elected to the legislature, an achievement which to this date has never been equalled. All were members of the Canadian

Labour Party except Bob Parkyn who ran and won as an independent labour candidate. Parkyn and Calgary typographer Fred White, the labour house leader, gave Calgary labour two representatives while a teacher provided Edmonton with one. A Lethbridge member of the steam engineers, Andrew Smeaton, was elected in that city while the miners sent Christophers and Chris Pattinson to the capital. In the federal election of that year, Calgary workers elected H.B. Adshead as their representative while Bill Irvine, a former labour MP from Calgary, won a seat in central Alberta as a UFA candidate. Jan Lakeman, a labour party member and a leader of the Communist party, received more than two thousand votes in Edmonton East but failed to capture the riding from the Liberals.

In November 1929, the alliance between social democrats and communists in the Alberta branch of the labour party came to an end and when Lakeman and others were kicked out for being communists. Such expulsions from the CLP, which were happening, in other provinces as well, came in part from a decision of the CP that, as the country headed into the financial crisis of the Depression, social democrats were less attractive allies.

Except in the political field, the decade after the First World War was a dark one for workers across the country. The response to the recession had been essentially spiritless and the old craft unions were increasingly unable to deal with mass production industries. The Thirties were even darker but the tide of working class militancy came back in.

A family photographed by an Edmonton Journal *photographer in 1934. The family hadn't eaten for more than twenty-six hours and hadn't had a regular meal in months. The mother was too weak to nurse her three-month-old child. The family, said the* Edmonton Journal, *"was a pitiful spectacle of depression dereliction."*

CHAPTER SEVEN

The Depression

Conditions

"You know, we couldn't get nothing in those days, no jobs, no nothing. I even went to police station and asked to deport me back to Poland. I says you've got a lovely, beautiful country but I guess I cannot make a living here."[1]

It took a long time for Canada to show her promise to the likes of John Dec, who came to Canada in 1926. One farm went under and a second one in the Peace River country didn't produce enough to feed the family. "I went travelling through Canada on the freights. I was in the soup kitchens for five years."

In 1933, about eleven thousand five hundred Edmonton residents were on relief—almost 15 percent of the population. Both Calgary and Lethbridge were marginally better off: relief recipients numbered 10,725 in Calgary or 13 percent while in Lethbridge, nearly two thousand, or 14 percent were on the rolls. Out of a school enrolment of 1,788 in that city, 488 children were underweight—27 percent. The same 1933 provincial health department study showed that the families of 31 percent of Edmonton children were accepting relief. Even by May 1938, about seventy thousand Albertans were on the dole.[2]

Not all families took the meagre charity offered by municipal and provincial governments. Bob Atkin, a railway worker in Edmonton, said that despite five years of unemployment during the Thirties, "my dad and mother were too proud to go on the dole. Mother had to work very hard, baking bread, and dad was going delivering this bread to people he would know that would buy it."[3] Statistics don't describe the dilemma of men with families to support—proud men, used to hard work—who found themselves standing in bread lines. "I remember standing in line," said Alex Goruk. "I remember some elderly fellows standing in front of me who were so tired and the line was moving so slowly that they had to sit down and rest. They couldn't stand on their feet because, quite often, you'd have to stand in line for an hour before you finally got to where they dished out the soup." The principle elements of the Thirties were hunger and want. A United Church minister in the once-booming Turner Valley oilfield south of Calgary described the troubles of one family.

Many scores of people here are without work and are in great need. Today a man called on me in despair. He has a wife and four children and he has only had two days work since January [the letter was written in July] and they have had nothing in the house to eat. We have been keeping them in the bare necessities for some months. Today, I called on seven families in a similar plight[4]

A letter to the provincial government outlined the living conditions of a twenty-nine-year-old man and his wife.

They have a family of seven, including twins. I have visited their home, which consists of two basement rooms, about nine by 10 each. They have a bed, a Winnipeg couch, a cheap table, kitchen cabinet and a stove. Their allowance is $15 for rent, altogether too much for these miserable rooms, and $15 for all other purposes. This couple have sold all their personal possessions of value in order to get along.[5]

Overcrowding was the province's major housing problem, as the Alberta government noted in a brief to a federal commission, In urban Alberta, said the report, housing densities in 1931 stood at 104 persons for every 100 rooms, "a state which in any English industrial community would be listed as unsatisfactory. Consider conditions that permit six and eight families to live together in a single-family, frame dwelling erected 30 years ago, with no increase in plumbing facilities since that time. This is not an isolated case." According to the 1931 census, one-quarter of Edmonton and Calgary citizens lived in one, two or three-room houses. More than 7 percent of Edmonton households lived in one-room shacks, compared with the national average of 2.5 percent.[6]

Some Edmonton residents, however, had reason to envy those living in shacks. "Edmonton's Cave Dwellers Proud of River Bank Homes," was the headline on the front page of the *Edmonton Journal* of June 13, 1931.

Along the brushy banks of the North Saskatchewan, from the Highlands on the east to the golf clubs on the west, you'll find them, living in homes they have gouged out of the clay banks and built up with wood, tin and pasteboard. Some have lived there during the entire winter, some are comparative newcomers to what they themselves term "River Ave." One or two have two rooms but, for the most part, they consist of one very small room with all the wide outdoors for a front porch . . . . A few of the "River Ave." residences are without walls, consisting entirely of a roof and a bed, but they are largely covered, with doors of cardboard or linoleum. A few of the more pretentious have real wooden doors, with windows built in scraps of glass.

As late as the spring of 1940, when the Depression was supposedly over, the Calgary medical health officer reported to city council that about 30 percent of Calgary residents were improperly housed and that many empty office buildings in the city had been converted to tenements.

Many people travelled across the country looking in vain for work, riding the rails and camping in the "hobo" jungles dotting the landscape. It was a desperate time but the occasional act of kindness helped. John Dec recalled a store owner in Viking giving him bread and meat when he asked for it. Bob Basken, who rode the freights looking for work in 1930, remembered a time when he and some friends arrived in Calgary and ended up sleeping in the hay barn at Burns' packing plant. The guard told them that if they were out by seven o'clock each morning, he wouldn't report them.

But riding the rails could be dangerous and the men who covered the country coast to coast had more to worry about than railway police who often approached their job of eliminating free riders with considerable zeal. The cold, for instance, was a hazard not to be taken lightly. Basken said some trains stopped only at divisional points and if you wanted to get off in between, you had to jump while the train was moving. If you were cold and stiff, there was always the chance that you wouldn't be able to jump clear.[7] Pete Youschok, a Pass miner who travelled the country the "box car route" said that to keep warm in winter, people would often fashion a makeshift stove from the oil-soaked wheel linings. That could cause the car wheels to seize up but the real problem came if you closed the doors and lit your stove, exhausting the supply of oxygen. Bob Atkin, who worked in the railway yards in Edmonton, often saw first hand the fatal dangers of riding the freights. In winter, he said, people would "get into heated cars to keep warm and they would go to sleep in there and they would die. They would get the gas from the heaters, the carbon monoxide would kill them."

With net production in Alberta in 1932 less than half what it was in 1928, layoffs occurred in every branch of industry.[8] The Alberta committee on unemployment relief said in its 1933 report that the number of single and homeless women "had increased during the past year due to lessened demand in stores, offices, factories and institutions." Young women from the rural areas and small towns were drifting in increasing numbers to the cities. All classes of female employment were hit, said the report—

nurses, teachers, business women, waitresses. "They are cared for in various ways—in private homes, hostels, residential homes. In some cases, two women occupy one room and are allowed $10 a month for rent and $1.75 each per week for food."[9] Anna MacLaren recalled that "there was lots of girls that I know came from Saskatchewan and they turned prostitutes because they had nothing to eat. It was terrible, I'm telling you. People don't realize what it was like."[10]

Municipal and provincial governments were hard-pressed, with their limited financial resources, to meet the needs of the unemployed. After 1930, R.B. Bennett of CPR and conscription fame, was charged with leading the country out of the mess but for most of his term he maintained an inordinate faith in the free enterprise system to correct the havoc it had wrought. When governments finally did move, as often as not they moved by coming down hard on the unemployed. Most politicians, regardless of their political labels, offered little help to the needy. Dan Knott and Andy Davison, the labour mayors of Ed-

monton and Calgary, and Walter Smitten, the commissioner of labour in the UFA government and a former secretary of the Alberta Federation of Labour, could be just as unsympathetic and ham-fisted as right-wingers like Bennett.

The provincial government report showing that 27 percent of Lethbridge school children were underweight came in response to a submission from the unemployed in Lethbridge who suggested that the amount of relief they were getting was not enough to adequately feed their children. The province's deputy minister of health informed his boss that poor eating habits and physical problems were causes of malnutrition. Almost as an afterthought, the doctor added that malnutrition "may also, of course, be due to insufficient food." The 1933 report of Alberta's relief advisory committee said that a person applying for relief had to be entirely without means and had to sign an affidavit "that he is without employment, without money and destitute." Small wonder that many refused to go on the dole.

An Edmonton soup kitchen in 1933. In that year, about 15 percent of the city's population was on relief.

A common tactic of municipal administrations and the provincial government was to reduce relief payments or cut them off altogether in the summer to force people to look for jobs that didn't exist. In the cities, the unemployed were often forced to work for their relief on regular municipal projects. Because the federal and provincial governments shared with the municipalities the cost of relief, substantial savings could be made by laying off regular employees and replacing them with relief workers. A man in Cardston, a predominantly Mormon community southwest of Lethbridge, wrote the provincial director of relief in 1933 complaining of the treatment he received at the hands of local officials.

We were receiving relief last winter and spring and were cut off . . . the first of May and have nearly starved to death since we did not get enough relief during the winter to have the right and proper food for little children. They did not allow us any new milk—they found a place in town where we could get skim milk and half the time it was sour. The mayor of Cardston has made statements that they would not do anything in regards to relief without they were absolutely forced to. They simply say it is too bad for you, cannot possibly help it, you should have prepared for yourself. The town has got men who were working steady as town employees. Now they have put them on direct relief so the government has to pay their part so they [the municipalities] can get their labour at 25 cents per hour and not allow them any clothing while working. . . . When you take a bill in the town office, they telephone the store and scratch off what things they think you should not have. In the cities, they allow those on relief to do their own trading respectable. Here, they think those on relief about the lowest thing there is and insult you every time you get a bill of groceries. We got a few clothes in January and they took the clothing cost out of our relief allowance. . . . They get up in church here and make statements that it is a disgrace for anyone to be on relief. There are widows here who are going begging from door

Immigrants awaiting deportation. In 1930, the Brownlee government asked federal authorities to deport 171 immigrants who were on relief. In that year, 4,000 people were deported, 45 percent of them for being "public charges."

to door for something to eat.[11]

By writing a letter of protest to the provincial government the man was probably misdirecting his appeal. A letter in 1930 from the deputy minister of municipal affairs, the department charged with handling relief to all municipalities, stated that relief money could only be spent on:

> . . . . flour, the cheaper varieties only; beans, in bulk only; oatmeal, in bulk only; ground meal, in bulk only; sugar, four pounds per person per month; tea or coffee in limited quantities; salt bacon only (not export varieties); boiling beef or pot roasts, not to exceed fifteen cents per pound; a limited quantity of cane syrup; limited quantities of yeast cakes, soap and other necessities.

The letter also said that "Municipalities will be expected to use the greatest discretion when giving orders for supplies and if any luxuries are included, they will be deducted

from the account when presented and will not be paid for out of the dominion or provincial contribution."[12]

Late in 1930, concerned about the large number of people without work and applying for relief, the UFA government sent a list of 171 persons, mostly Germans or East Europeans, who had emigrated to Canada in 1926 or 1927, to the immigration authorities in Ottawa asking that they be deported. Premier Brownlee sent a telegram to the federal minister of immigration saying:

> We recognize difficulties your department reference such matters, but desire urge for your consideration that list cover those now applying for relief who also received relief last year, with many names applying regularly since immigration. A special registration now conducted showing approximately 40 percent total applications relief to consist those who have arrived in Canada within five years. We respectfully urge that strong move towards deportation will have a very great effect on

An unemployed drifter in the Edmonton area, 1931.

many now applying and considerably reduce our unemployment relief problem.

In 1930, the federal government deported about four thousand people, about 45 percent of them because they were "public charges." More than seven hundred were kicked out of the country because they were "very sick", "incurable", or "mentally defective."[13]

Officials in Edmonton in 1931 issued an order prohibiting transients from coming to the city. A story out of Edmonton on June 18 said: "The combined forces of the Alberta provincial police, CPR officers and city constables have plucked 66 men from incoming freight trains in the last week. Of that number, 15 of them were sent to jail, 13 given fines sufficiently stiff that only two could pay instead of going to jail and 38 were given 24 hours to get out of the city."[14]

Organizing the Unemployed

As repression and crackdowns on Depression victims mounted, the labour parties and the Alberta Federation of Labour did what they did best—sent in resolutions of protest, made speeches in the legislature and lobbied government for a change of heart.[15]

Such actions were not without effect. J.S. Woodsworth made a substantial contribution to the eventual implementation of unemployment insurance—there wasn't any during the Depression. Federation of Labour president Fred White said in his report to the 1932 convention:

Unemployment was the outstanding matter with which your federation has had to deal during the past year. Your officers are convinced that to a greater extent than ever before, the people of Canada are coming to an acceptance of the belief that has long been held by the trade union movement, namely that fundamental changes in the economic system will bring the only permanent cure for unemployment.

But as a rule, organizations like the federation which were in the mainstream of the labour movement did little to bring about those "fundamental changes." Many workers could not help but be cynical of the efforts of social democrats to come to their aid. People like Andy Davison, Dan Knott and Walter Smitten had all gained some measure of power—none of them used it to bring about the "fundamental changes" their own organizations were talking about.

In 1932, western labour parties and farm groups met in Calgary to establish a new social democratic political party—the Co-operative Commonwealth Federation. The United Farmers of Alberta, in power since 1921, was officially part of the new organization (even though the cabinet never wholly approved of the venture), and that compounded, perhaps unfairly, the growing cynicism directed against social democracy and its adherents. As the Depression wore on with the UFA presiding over the mess, the government's popularity fell sharply and the guilt of association rubbed off on the CCF. The unemployed often found their best allies were the Communists, who sent in resolutions of protest too, thousands of them, but also marshalled the forces of the jobless on the streets to demand in emphatic fashion their rights to full stomachs and freedom from repression.

Pat Lenihan, one of the founders of the Canadian Union of Public Employees and a leader of Calgary's outside municipal workers, worked in that city during the Thirties as an organizer of the Communist Party—like many others, he left the party after the Second World War. He first became interested in the party when he was in Toronto "because they were the people out in the streets trying to do something." The CCF, he said, believed in "political action—straight political action. Vote for us every five years and you could get emancipation, which is a joke."[16]

The provincial police in 1930 reported that:

. . . . we have had very little trouble with the unemployed although there are large numbers of them both in Calgary and Edmonton. . . . Continuous agitation is going on amongst them by Communists but up to the present time it has not had very much effect. Parading through the streets was stopped both at Calgary and Edmonton and this has had a good effect upon a majority of these unfortunate men who could not get work.[17]

The "continuous agitation," backed by a solid programme put forward by the party and a willingness to meet and work with the unemployed on their terms, gave the party the widest popular support it ever had.

Pete Youschok, a Crowsnest miner and never a party member, described why the Communists gained such a following in the dark days of the 1930s: "There was no other party to turn to in the hungry Thirties—where the hell were the men going? They were going Communist. Who else offered them anything? No other party offered them anything at that time that I know of."[18] Like the Wobblies before them, the Communists approached their goal with more than just determination and hard work. They used their imaginations and they organized everybody, wherever they found them—trade unions, women's auxiliaries, committees for this and that. Even the children were not forgotten. One Christmas in the Crowsnest Pass: "We served cocoa, sandwiches and Xmas fruit cake in the miners' hall. Each child received a bag containing one pound of nuts, half a pound each of grapes and candies, an apple and an orange when they left for home."[19] A report of the provincial police noted "the education of children into Communists' propaganda." In Drumheller, whenever the police moved by in formation "children would line up on the sidewalk and sing the Red Flag."[20]

Primarily under the leadership of the Communist Party and its National Unemployed Workers Association (which claimed a membership of sixteen thousand in July, 1931[21]), a new type of strike began to capture headlines—the relief strike. Social democrats like Fred White, then president of the Federation of Labour and a labour MLA, also got involved. White was always willing to put his house up as bail to get arrested protesters out of jail, said Pat Lenihan. So successful were the Communists and their allies that Premier Brownlee complained to federal officials that "with Communist activities in large centres, any policy cutting off relief . . . would certainly result in widespread disorder."[22]

In Calgary, single men receiving relief, consisting of a twenty-five cent meal ticket and a chit for a bed at night, were forced to work one day a week on various special

projects. At the end of June, 1931, the city commission board ordered that single men would have to work two days instead of one. The Calgary correspondent of the *Labour Gazette* wrote that:

> The mayor's idea in increasing the hours of labour was to make the city less attractive to drifters coming into the city via the box car route, there already being an institution established, and I understand maintained financially by local business people, known as the Mush Kitchen, where anyone can have all the porridge and fresh milk they can eat and no question are asked, thus further adding attraction for transients.[23]

Whatever the motives of Mayor Davison, the move was viewed by the single unemployed men's association—the organization of the unemployed most influenced by the Communists—as an indirect reduction in relief and they appealed to the men to oppose the action by refusing to work.

> Instead of forcing relief workers to do one day's work, they are now attempting to force us to do two days work for the same wage. . . . We are already undernourished and starving. Many of us are physically too weak to work even one day; we need more and stronger food because we cannot do a whole day's work on one meal. We demand to have relief tickets issued once a week instead of every day, and three meals and a bed per day.

The handbill issued by the strike committee noted that since senior levels of government paid 80 percent of relief costs for single men, the actual cost to the city of relief of $3.50 a week was seventy cents and that the men were therefore being asked to work for thirty-five cents a day.

The strike call was initially successful, despite threats by the mayor to cut all participants from relief rolls. At some of the projects, men continued to work, but under the gaze of city police on guard against roving squads of picketers who were able, at some sites, to convince men still working to join them. City council partially met the major demand by giving the men another meal ticket on the days they worked. What probably had most effect in bringing the strike to an abrupt halt was a brutal raid on the headquarters of the unemployed association, which doubled as Communist Party headquarters in the city, the arrest of the strike leaders and a riot downtown when police tried to break up a meeting of the strikers. During the riot, a policeman's skull was fractured and in retaliation, the unemployed association offices were raided that night. The *Labour Gazette* correspondent visited the offices in the basement of the Victoria Apartments on 8th Ave. E. after the raid and found:

> . . . . everything in disorder. All the benches used as seats

Troops arriving in Edmonton. They were called up to quell an expected riot of unemployed workers in the spring of 1931. The demonstrations, which didn't take place, were to have protested a move by the city administration cutting people off relief.

were smashed to pieces, all the windows were broken, doors were wrenched from hinges and broken, the floor was besplattered with blood and I was told by a few of the men who refused to give their names that the police entered both doors with truncheons in their hands and clubbed over the heads about 100 men and women, who, they claim, were driven into the rear of the basement where some of them were badly hurt.

City council in Edmonton was as anxious as its Calgary counterpart that year to stop drifters coming to the city amid reports that smaller municipalities were telling their relief recipients to journey to Edmonton to collect relief there. Aldermen decided that anyone unable to prove he had lived in Edmonton that winter or collected relief there would be taken off the rolls. Relief for all single men was also to be cancelled.

With the unemployed shuffled from town to town as governments at all levels attempted to shift responsibility for them, Communists in the city decided to hold protest marches in defiance of an order banning them. Premier Brownlee responded by calling out the troops. The June 18 *Edmonton Journal* reported that "61 mounted troopers of the Lord Strathcona's Horse, fully equipped with steel helmets, rifles, machine guns and sabres, arrived in Edmonton from Calgary at 4:40 A. M. Saturday." The Edmonton Labour Council condemned the call-out of troops. "The trouble," said Alf Farmilo, "is that the very people who brought these men in here to build railroads now are penalizing the poor brutes, telling them that if they don't starve quick enough, they'll help them over the barrier by blowing theim to pieces." One of the "drifters" told an *Edmonton Journal* reporter that he was going to stay in the capital, even if he didn't receive relief. "I guess we can bum meals as well here as any other place. If we stay around here we'll have more chance of getting harvesting work. We can't get relief anywhere else."[24] As it turned out, the troops, machine guns and all, weren't needed. The unemployed continued to protest but all remained orderly in the capital.

In the ferment of the Depression, however, maintenance of public order was a tenuous proposition at best. As the economic crisis deepened, the frustrations of the unemployed (and the farmers) grew in proportion and repression stiffened as the provincial government found itself unwilling to join with the radicals and attack the financial and industrial centres of power. Brownlee told the 1932 convention of the AFL: "There is a limit to the power of the provinces, city, and even the Dominion, to meet the financial burden of unemployment." Banks were refusing, he said, to lend the government more money to retire debts and meet deficits. The UFA government was being squeezed on one side by the banks and on the other by the unemployed and debt-ridden farmers and it was harder to fight the banks than the farmers.

In the fall of 1932, the Communists and allied organizations such as the Workers Unity League and Farmers Unity League made plans to bring thousands of people to Edmonton to march from Market Square to the legislative grounds to present a list of demands to the premier. The demands included unemployment insurance, cancellation of all farm debts and free medical and dental care. The premier and Edmonton May Dan Knott would have none of it. A parade permit was refused, machine guns were placed on the roof of the post office overlooking the square, and troops of Mounties were brought in. A story in the *Edmonton Bulletin* on December 21, 1932 said:

> Police batons rose and fell, skulls were cracked, men and women were trampled under foot and the hoarse roars of an angry mob echoed for two hours in downtown streets when so-called 'Hunger Marchers,' incited by known Communist leaders, came to grips with the combined force of RCMP constables and city policemen in Edmonton's first major 'Red' clash with the forces of law and order. Baton charges by a troop of 24 mounted policemen, reinforced by a hundred men on foot who mopped up behind the charge clearing the sidewalks, left several members of the mob lying on the pavement as police carried out their orders to break up the parade. About 2,000 demonstrators were involved.

At the start of the march, one orator told assembled demonstrators: "We have a constitutional right to use the King's highway to petition Parliament." When final confirmation of the order prohibiting the march from the centre of the city to the legislative grounds some fifteen blocks distant was received by the demonstrators, they decided to proceed anyway and marched off the square, taking the one path not blocked by police. Mounted police then moved to intercept them and as the crowd tried to push past the Mounties, the riot began.

Behind the mounted men, the city police and dismounted troops of RCMP constables were busy spreading across the street from sidewalk to sidewalk, sweeping everyone before them. Batons rose and fell, yells and jeers filled the air as here and there a rioter went down before the police clubs. Women among the marchers screamed imprecations at the police, charging them with being cowards who were riding down their own class, but the steady police pressure continued and the back of the parade was broken. Meanwhile, some 10,000 Edmonton citizens who had been held back in the side streets, pressed forward to see the battle and as the police swung back to retrace their steps, there was another wild rush to escape the plunging horses and swinging clubs. Riding knee to knee, the mounted men forced their way toward the post office again and as they passed the Market Building, a rain of stones and brickbats were showered on them. Several women again harangued the police and the remaining demonstrators took temporary refuge in a huge pile of Christmas trees, from which they were flushed in small groups as the troopers road through with swinging clubs.

First blood in the battle [had been] drawn . . . by police when the city force and men of the Mounted combined in a raid on the Ukrainian Labour Temple and the Ukrainian church next door. One man was arrested on a charge of assault on Sgt. Ed Watson. Red leaders' boasts that they had enough food to sustain 3,500 men for five days proved to be true as police found the headquarters packed with barrels of pork and other edibles. The 'Hunger March' label which the reds used to mask their real activity was given the lie when women at the headquarters were seen serving turkey dinners to the would-be paraders.

In all, more than forty people were arrested and the actions of Brownlee and Dan Knott gave the Communists added ammunition for their arguments that the leaders of the labour movement and the CCF were the "defenders of the capitalist class." A pamphlet published by the Hunger March committee to raise funds for the defense of those arrested said the likes of Knott and Brownlee "are even more dangerous than that capitalist class themselves because they are enemies among us."[25] Giving some support to the Communists' contention was the coverage given the Hunger March in *Alberta Labour News,* the official publication of the Federation of Labour, edited by Elmer Roper. An editorial said the authorities should have allowed the parade but added that "it must be borne in mind that both local governments are harassed by the tremendous task of making provision for the unemployed." The paper went on to say that "such abortive demonstrations of mass help-

Police and unemployed squared off in Edmonton, December, 1932. Thousands of farmers and unemployed workers from across the province came to the city to present a list of demands to the Brownlee government, but authorities refused the protesters a parade permit. When they tried to march to the legislative buildings anyway, the police moved in.

lessness can only have the effect of confusing the people who are being misled into being involved and thus has delayed any potent movement towards a real political and economic change."[26]

Throughout the Depression, more than thirty relief strikes were called in Alberta. One dispute in Edmonton in 1935 involved a large number of city restaurants where women employees were receiving less than the minimum wage. There were reports that some restaurant employees were getting as little as $1.50 a week, $8 less than the legal minimum. Most of the café proprietors eventually agreed to live up to the law, but not before large numbers of picketers were arrested and sentenced to jail terms on charges of unlawful assembly or vagrancy. In the Thirties, vagrancy was often an easy charge for police to prove — one man arrested during the dispute had two cents in his pocket.[27]

Most relief strikes were called to demand more generous treatment or to protest cuts in relief, but one group didn't have to worry about cuts in relief. The Chinese, said Pat Lenihan, who helped organize a series of demonstrations for them in Calgary in 1937, "weren't recognized as human

beings in this city. There was no relief for them, nothing." Lenihan said a group of unemployed Chinese approached the unemployed association asking for help.

We did everything—in the city council, demonstrations, nothing worked. So finally, we decided we had to do something drastic. We organized them and some others and marched them down to 8th Ave. and 1st St. W., that was the main spot, centre of the city. All the street car tracks had to come through there. There we put them down, right across the car tracks. We tied up the whole goddamn machinery and as soon as the cops had pulled some off, more were down. Well, this immediately brought the whole questions to the attention of the city people and the city council was forced to put them on relief.

On to Ottawa

Of all the various schemes to deal with the hundreds of thousands of people out of work, the most hated and troublesome was the establishment of relief camps by the federal government in 1932. The camps, administered by

A "flying squad" of picketers during a relief strike in Edmonton, May 1934. The strike patrols were a mobile picket line organized to make sure that workers on various relief projects around the city were honouring the strike.

the department of national defence, were labelled slave camps, concentration camps and the "Royal Twenty," so named because people in them received twenty cents a day in wages. The fact that the army ran them (the government's argument was that only the army had the resources to handle that many men—more than 170,248 nationally during the four years the camps were in operation) and that they were most often in isolated areas, increased feelings that the Bennett government was, at best, insensitive; at worst, trying to shuffle the single unemployed off to the boondocks where they wouldn't cause any trouble. The Women's Auxiliary of the Mine Workers Union asked Bennett to "do away with this rotten system of isolating young boys and forcing them to live unnatural lives. We are absolutely in opposition to our sons being taken away from their homes. Surely it is not their fault that there are no jobs for them."[28]

Ten camps were established in Alberta, most in the foothills and mountain areas, although several were set up near Edmonton and Calgary. Altogether, about thirteen thousand men went through the camps in the province, which were engaged primarily in highway construction.[29]

John Dec, who worked in several relief camps in the Coal Branch area, described them as very much like jails.

Bunkhouses was tents, cold like nothing. We cut wood and burn wood all night. In the front you were hot and behind you freeze. And if you had twenty people in that tent—just like sardines—you're lucky if you get to the front. In a relief camp, it's built far away from town. No recreation at all. One recreation: we come up to shave, wash, have a shower and come and play a games of cards or darts or anything—that's ourselves, we made that. Some guys sit and read books, some cards. I was playing cards—make money. Gambling, I make maybe five bucks then I quick go back to Edmonton. I can live a whole week on it, or two weeks. Sometimes you play rummy, a penny or ten cents, you can make fifty, sixty cents, you live two days on it.

At many camps, food was a constant source of friction but fortunately for Drumheller miner Art Roberts, that wasn't true of the camp he was in.

It was beautiful, you know, we had the finest of eats.

Now that didn't exist everywhere. They had proper places, bunks, for us. I remember the guy that was cooking—his brother was a Communist—we got along beautifully. CPR strawberries as they called them —prunes—a big bunch of them cooked. Nobody would touch the prunes. Everybody would take a cup of juice and old Joe would see to it that we had a piece of pie to go along with it. . . . The old major [in charge of the camp] had a couple of pigs he was fattening up to make a few bucks so the pigs used to get the prunes.

There were frequent strikes in the camps—nineteen in Alberta—and retaliation came quickly. In most cases, the organizers were thrown out of the camp. In one incident in 1935, eighty men quit work to protest the discharge of another man. Seventy-four of them were then kicked out and once that happened, it was difficult to get into another one. At Roberts' camp, the men had more subtle ways of protesting: "They had the boys working up in the hills, building a road, and the boss, he'd start kicking, [saying we weren't] putting . . . enough [into the wheelbarrow]. 'Okay,' and one would stand beside by the wheelbarrow and pat it down, pat it down and we'd keep throwing on . . . and it was up like this over the wheelbarrow. Once you'd pick it up, over she'd go. And we kept that up." Dec said there were no unions in the camps. "We are a union ourselves—stick up for each other. If the foreman catching one guy or firing him, we stick up for him, we all go. We don't make trouble, we don't fight. We tell them what we want, that's it."

But in B.C., the camp workers did have a union, an affiliate of the Communists' Workers Unity League, and on April 4, 1935, about fifteen hundred men left the camps and headed for Vancouver demanding abolition of the camps and a work-for-wages program. At the end of May, the strikers voted to continue their walkout and decided to go to Ottawa to meet the prime minister and tell him in person of their demands. The men on the On-to-Ottawa Trek had a fair amount of popular support but not everyone was pleased to hear they were on their way. Calgary Mayor Davison wired the RCMP demanding that the relief-camp strikers be stopped at the B.C. border. UFA Premier R.G. Reid (who had replaced Brownlee when he became the central figure in a sex scandal) made a similar request. Fred White complained that troops in Calgary had been alerted and asked "when has it become illegal for citizens to present their complaints to the highest tribunal, the government of Canada."[30]

The trek arrived in Calgary Friday evening, June 7 and marched from the rail yards to the exhibition grounds, under police escort, where they were greeted with hot coffee and sandwiches provided by a committee of Calgary volunteers. The men planned to stay in Calgary several days to rest and gather more recruits. But to stay they would need food, so the next morning one small group hit the streets to ask for donations in a tag day which raised thirteen hundred dollars. The bulk of the trekkers went to the provincial relief offices downtown and several of their leaders went inside to interview A.A. MacKenzie, the Alberta relief scheme director, demanding two meals a day and breakfast on Monday, when they planned to leave. Mackenzie initially refused but found himself a virtual prisoner in his own office. Outside, the trekkers and Calgary sympathizers formed a continuous picket around the building. At the end of two hours, he agreed to spend $600 to feed the trekkers until Monday.

After a mass meeting Saturday night, the trekkers were treated to a Sunday picnic, put on by local unemployment groups at St. George's Island. "Athletic events were run off, addressess of leaders heard and a basket lunch served to more than 1,000 men."[31] On Monday, the relief camp strikers, their numbers swollen by 500 Albertans, including a delegation of 150 from Edmonton, "marched from their quarters at the exhibition ground to the railway yards and boarded a freight train for a continuation of their march to Ottawa. The strikers, here since Friday evening, had a final meal . . . then they moved out in military formation, singing as they marched."[32]

Trek leaders had determined that the march on the capital was to be a peaceful one and rigid discipline was enforced. All the men were divided up into brigades and people who wanted to join had to be screened to ensure that, as far as possible, troublemakers or police agents didn't come along. A Toronto Star reporter, allowed to join the trek, wrote that:

An anxious mother walked the full length of the train scanning every face, searching for her boy. She said she wanted him to stay at home and strikers' officials gave her every assistance but without avail. At the last momen, a well-dressed young man ran down the side of the train with a sweater and a clean pair of overalls for his brother who was going along. To provide a lunch for the travellers during the night, a number of Calgary women prepared 2,400 tasty sandwiches from supplies donated by merchants. A side of beef which also came from a well-wisher was heaved aboard.

The trip to Medicine Hat was cold, wet and dirty, the reporter continued.

As the heavy rain beat down during the night, the strikers clung to the catwalk, huddling close together. Those who had blankets soon found them soaked through and many others, who had no blankets, had to take it. They were wet to the skin.

*Members of the On-to-Ottawa Trek in Medicine Hat, June 1935.
The trek was organized to pressure the federal government to
abolish work camps for single men.*

While the train was pulling out of Calgary and the residents along the side of the road and many of city dwellers cheered the boys on their way it was swell but when Engineer Hardy gave the mogul the gun, the cinders started coming down in showers. Eyes full of cinders. Ears full of cinders and cinders down the back of the neck. Then the sharp wind sweeping across the open prairie whipped up the fine coal dust in the faces of the reserved seat riders and hunks of it were whipped back off the top of the coal heap to make things more interesting.[33]

The trek was gathering momentum, public support and recruits as it moved across the country—there were reports that large numbers would join in Winnipeg—and Bennett decided that enough was enough, the trek would be stopped. He realized that breaking the trek would be a formidable task and had no wish to create a riot in his home constituency of Calgary; Winnipeg was out because large numbers were waiting there to join up. Regina was a small city with a large RCMP detachment and it was the capital of a province where the Liberal government was constantly warring with the Tories in Ottawa. As Saskatche-wan Premier Jimmy Gardiner later said in a message to Ottawa, the province "had no problem until you imported one and took steps to see that it remained here."[34]

After an acrimonious meeting between Bennett and several trek leaders, the trekkers began to understand that continuing on to Ottawa would result in bloodshed. Orders had been given to the railways not to let the trekkers continue and an order-in-council was passed declaring that anyone who assisted the trek would be prosecuted under Section 98 of the Criminal Code. The section, passed after the Winnipeg general strike, defined as unlawful associations those which proposed or defended the use of force in promoting economic or social change. The Tory government had resisted repeated attempts by the CCF in the House of Commons to have the section repealed.

The trekkers decided to call the whole thing off and planned one last mass rally in Regina's Market Square to inform the public of the decision.[35] The meeting was schedule for Dominion Day. As early as June 12, two days before the trek arrived in Regina, the RCMP were making plans. Colonel S.T. Wood, the assistant commissioner of the force, said in a memo that "at the moment there is considerable support for the strikers because the public do not realize the motive and revolutionary tactics behind the movement." He went on to say that police would not carry loaded side-arms or ammunition when they went in to break up the trek but that "revolver ammunition and gas grenades will be carried in motor trucks accompanying troops."[36] The plan was that plain clothes police would move onto the square after the meeting had started and arrest the leaders. As back-up, in cause of trouble, squads of city and mounted police were stationed in the area in furniture vans but were only to move out if trouble started.

But there was an unfortunate and fatal communications mix-up. Ronald Liversedge, a participant in the trek, described how, as the meeting got underway and the plain clothes police moved through the crowd:

> . . . . four furniture vans backed up, one to each corner of Market Square. A shrill whistle blasted out a signal, the backs of the vans were lowered and out poured the Mounties, each armed with a baseball bat (actually a specially-designed police baton). They must have been packed very tightly in those vans because there were lots of them. In their first mad, shouting, club-swinging charge, they killed Regina City Detective Millar, who had evidently come on to the square to help them. In less than minutes, the Market Square was a mass of writhing, groaning forms, like a battlefield.[37]

Police accounts of the riot, which spread from the square to much of the downtown area, were quite different. An inquiry established by the Saskatchewan government accepted the police view that Miller was killed by a group of trekkers. In the view of the government, however, the riot had been unnecessary and public opinion was generally on the side of the trekkers. A protest from the three United Mine Workers locals in Edmonton asked the government why, if they wanted to arrest the trek leaders, they didn't do it earlier and at a time when the action would have had less explosive effect. "The youth of our country," the UMW loals said, "are being driven around worse than wild animals."[38]

That fall, "Iron Heel" Bennett and his Conservative government were unceremoniously dumped from office, only managing to win forty seats. By coincidence or calculation, the Tories, as was the case during the ferment of the First World War, had been caught on the crest of unrest and fundamental social change and again proved their inability to ride with it. Instead, Bennett, like Borden and Meighen before him, had met the challenges of the Depression with the "iron heel." As J.S. Woodsworth said in the Commons after the Regina Riot:

> One of the functions of a government is to maintain law and order but a government also has another function—

to see that justice prevails within the country and that every reason for disorder is removed. When a government has removed all the reasons for disorder, then and not until then, is it justified in asking the people to support it. This government has not removed the reasons for discontent, nor has it met the just demands of the people.[39]

Miners and the Workers Unity League

For the most part, the trade union movement shied away from strike action during the Thirties. With thousands of unemployed in a huge potential strike-breaking force and with union ranks and treasuries depleted, it was not an auspicious time to fight. "The ranks of the existing unions were skeletons," said Pat Lenihan. "Here in Calgary, they had practically nothing left. It was the civic employee unions, what was left of them, that kept the Labour Temple alive. The policy of the AF of L leadership in Canada at that time was: 'There's crisis, we've got to accept wage cuts, you can't organize, you can't do anything!'"

The building trades were particularly hard hit in the Thirties. From 1931 through 1940, only five groups of construction workers dared take strike action; when they did, it most often ended in defeat. In the spring of 1931, employees of four Calgary planing mills struck to protest a proposed fifteen cent wage cut to seventy-five cents an hour. When the strike began, Local 1779 of the United Brotherhood of Carpenters and Joiners agreed to accept the recommendations of a board of conciliation. The board suggested a wage cut to eighty cents but employers were adamant that the cut would have to be deeper. After picketing for a month and a half, the men returned to work—on the employers' terms and without a contract. Plumbers ran into the same situation when they struck in Edmonton and Calgary in 1932 and in Calgary two years later, eventually accepting the wage cuts demanded by their employers. After the 1934 strike, which lasted more than two months, plumbers had seen their wages drop from $1.25 before the 1932 dispute to ninety cents an hour.[40]

As usual, the miners accounted for most of the strikes in Alberta during the Depression—76 percent of them. Many of the strikes in the fields were called by the Mine Workers Union of Canada, by then under the direct influence of the Communist Party. While the established unions were scrambling to keep their members employed, even if that meant negotiating wage cuts, the Communists and their trade union central, the Workers Unity League, fought back. In 1933, they claimed leadership in 75 percent of all the strikes in the country. In Alberta, at least, the claim was justified.[41]

Forecasting the coming Depression, the Communist

International in the late 1920s decided that the policies of the world-wide Communist movement would have to change to meet new conditions. After some resistance in the Canadian party, the new line was entrenched here. Essentially it predicted a revolutionary upsurge that would see workers flocking to the banner of the Communist parties. The social democrats were identified as the "last reserve" of capitalism and became a major enemy of the working class—it was believed they would channel the militancy of the workers into non-revolutionary activities, thereby allowing capitalists to cling to power.

The new policy toward social democracy, seen in the attitude of Edmonton Hunger Marchers toward the UFA government and Dan Knott's civic administration, was also mirrored in the party's trade union work. The establishment of the Mine Workers Union of Canada,

which the party influenced but never controlled in the 1920s, was undertaken as an admitted, but necessary, deviation from policy. After the 1928 international congress, the line of burrowing from within was scrapped. What workers needed in the coming period was a new, tough and fighting trade union centre that would not back meekly away from the tremendous obstacles to working class action. In 1930, with the formation of the Workers Unity League, that is what the workers got.

By 1930, the Communists had consolidated and strengthened their position within the MWUC, ousting the moderate leadership of Frank Wheatley and breaking with the All-Canadian Congress of Labour in favour of the Workers Unity League. They managed the coup through clever and effective organization and by offering the miners a chance to fight. "We were interested in having good men fighting for us," said Pete Youschok. One of those men was Harvey Murphy, who later became a leading official of the Mine-Mill and Smelter Workers (a new name for the Western Federation of Miners). Murphy, who died in 1977, was a life-long party member and was sent to Alberta as a Communist organizer where he spent most of his time organizing the Workers Unity League and its largest affiliate, the Mine Workers Union of Canada.

> I didn't go into the camps to talk to the guys about whether you'll get ten cents more an hour. I had to point out that you can get security and dignity by having a trade union. You had to appeal to them on a class basis in these one-industry towns. Well, hell, there's the boss where he lives up on the hill; the workers lived down below and they always looked up at that hill where all the bosses lived. How else would you organize? You can only organize on a class basis.[42]

Times were grim in the coal towns of Alberta in the Thirties. Conditions were aggravated by the isolation of the camps and the fact that they depended solely on one industry, and one that wasn't very prosperous during the Depression. Between 1929 and 1930, production of coal from the Crowsnest and the Coal Branch dropped 23 percent. From the peak production year of 1928 to the least productive year, 1933, production declined 42 percent. Similar drops in production hit the lignite fields of the Drumheller area. Miners were lucky if they could get work one day a week. Charlie Kane recalled one pay cheque of ninety cents. To supplement their almost nonexistent wages, miners turned to relief. Roberts said practically all the miners in the Drumheller area were on relief, most frequently in the summer months when the demand for domestic coal was at its lowest.

In June of 1931, the secretary-treasurer of the miners' union at Luscar, a company town near Edson, wrote Premier Brownlee asking for help for miners who had been laid off at the mine:

> Some have come into this camp with a bank account, are penniless, and receive wages below the means of sustenance of them and their dependents. Some of these are laid off now and have no means of support as the company refused them work and also refused to support them. How some of them who have been laid off managed to live is a real mystery but there is real suffering existing.
> The lack of proper nourishment is disclosing itself already. One man taken out last week . . . has already died in hospital in Edmonton. A little collection among the poor workers paid part of the expense while a total stranger paid the rest. . . . He died of galloping consumption [tuberculosis] and collection was made again to

send the rest of the family out as some of them are suspected to be similarly affected, especially a little boy of six who was sleeping with his father until the father's sudden turn for the worse. The eldest daughter (17) is also suspected and is ailing. This man has been out of work since a long time and was receiving government relief lately.

> I beg to explain this layoff system. It is unjust and inconsistent, as old-timers, decent, trustworthy and efficient in their work, have been laid off, one the father of five children, the other of three. The sad part of it is that seniority is not observed. This was given up by mutual understanding between our union and the company to meet the unemployment problem—that instead of seniority, there was to be no layoff in order to extend the work among as many as possible. But men have been laid off in spite of this. I myself profess to be a God-fearing man and write these lines with all good conscience before God and man. These poor men and their women and children have now been wronged and we have no power nor means outside of you to right it. All we can do is plead that we be avenged of our adversary.[43]

The drive to keep profit levels afloat in face of poor sales caused companies to take more chances with the lives of miners than was usually the case. On December 9, 1935, sixteen men were killed at the CPR's mine at Coalhurst, near Lethbridge. As far as Harvey Murphy was concerned, all the blame rested with the CPR. "It did economize in the mines, particularly at the expense of safety, timbering in the mine, putting up stoppings on abandoned workings, fixing the airways—the doors were broken down, etc. Only one section of the mine was working and the miners were retreating out, caving as they went." The company had announced that the mine would be closed and didn't bother to seal off its old sections, thereby allowing gas to accumulate. "They were just getting out all the cheap coal they could and turned the mine into a death trap. Sixteen of our brothers have been destroyed, 23 orphans and 11 widows remain, because the CPR wanted cheaper coal."[44]

While the response of the United Mine Workers to such conditions was to keep their membership and locals intact, even if that meant negotiating wage cuts, the Mine Workers Union of Canada threw all its resources into a series of bitter and sometimes violent counter-offensives against the operators. Not all ended in victory but the union seemed to have adopted the line put forward by Spain's leading Communist during the 1936-1939 civil war: "Better to die on your feet than to live on your knees." The miners of Mercoal, in the Coal Branch, were among the first to test the new and improved Mine Workers Union of Canada as an affiliate

of a revolutionary trade union centre. The UMW, after the 1925 dissolution, had maintained several locals in the Coal Branch and Mercoal was one of them. Early in the spring of 1930, the Mine Workers Union called a unity convention of all its locals, UMW units and company associations in the area to discuss co-operation in securing a new agreement covering the district. The UMW local in Mountain Park sent a delegate but when it was proposed at Mercoal, the meeting quickly turned into a minor riot. MWUC supporters, many of them East Europeans (who were often strong supporters of militant trade-unionism), were tossed out of the hall.

In mid-June, the Mercoal company, a subsidiary of one of the large operators in the Pass, signed a new agreement with the United Mine Workers which was not presented to the miners for ratification. Depending on the source, anywhere from thirty to seventy of the company's eighty miners were reported to have gone on strike demanding an end to the UMW check-off. To stop the miners who decided to ignore the strike call, the MWUC began to mount mass pickets and recruited men

from other unions, including the UMW Mountain Park local, to help out on the lines. In an attempt to stop the conflict before trouble broke out, Chris Pattinson, the Labour MLA for the region, proposed a referendum on which union would have bargaining rights. The UMW refused the offer, lending some credibility to the MWUC's claim that most of the miners were supporting the strike.

On July 23, according to provincial police, about twenty picketers, some carrying clubs, attacked four miners being escorted through the picket line by police. The next day Mercoal became an armed camp with the arrival by train of about a hundred regular and special APP constables. Mercoal was a company town and at about the same time, the striking miners were evicted from their homes and left to set up tents in the forestry reserve outside the town where they ran into interference from forest service patrols. Five men, including MWUC leader James Sloan, were charged and convicted with being members of an unlawful assembly—a charge used frequently during the

Depression. Sloan was found guilty of an additional charge of inciting to riot and was bound to "keep the peace" for two years.

The Communists poured everything they had into the strike, using to full advantage their various "front" organizations. The most active was Workers International Relief which issued appeals for money, food and clothing across the country. But once again, the combined forces of police, the UMW and management proved too tough for even the militants of the Mine Workers Union to handle. By late that year, the union was forced to give up the strike and the men who had held out to the last found themselves going from mine to mine looking hopelessly for work and a way around the blacklist.[45]

The strike at Mercoal and another at the Commercial colliery in the Drumheller valley in 1932, during which the mine caved in and remained closed, were baptisms of fire for the new fighting policy of the MWUC. Significant as those strikes were, however, they were nothing compared to the battle which consumed the Crowsnest Pass for the bulk of 1932. The miners of Alberta fought so many strikes that in speaking of them now, they have difficulty sorting out one from another, but no one forgot the 1932 Pass strike. Its effects were felt as late as 1974 when six residents of the area, through the efforts of their MP, Joe Clark (now the prime minister), finally, after 42 years, received Canadian citizenship papers which had been denied them because they had been involved in the strike and were suspected of Bolshevik sentiment. A provincial court judge in the area said recently that the strike should be forgotten—it was "a blight on the Pass."[46]

The strike left deep scars, many inflicted by fighting among miners themselves. Not surprisingly, a decision to oust the Wheatley leadership and affiliate with the Workers Unity League and the Red International of Labour Unions did not meet with universal favour throughout the mining areas. Support for the industrial policies of the party as reflected by the Mine Workers Union was probably based more on a desire to fight operators than a desire to fight for the kind of social change the party was advocating. Throughout the Pass, and in particular at Coleman, divisions between the party and the moderates widened to form an unbreachable chasm.

At its peak, the strike involved all the mines in the Crowsnest except Hillcrest, which had maintained its opposition to any form of trade unionism at all since the break-up in 1925. The major issue in dispute at all the mines was the demand of the miners that instead of layoffs, work should be shared equally by all employees. There were a host of other grievances as well and in

mid-winter of 1932, the whole thing finally blew up. The operators involved were International Coal and Coke and McGillivray Coal and Coke in Coleman and the two mines of West Canadian Collieries at Blairmore and Bellevue. The walkout was not caused by a pay dispute, although rumours were rife that the operators planned to force a wage cut. Pete Youschok commented:

> The wages is hardly ever even thought of in a mine. It's the little things that are happening all the time—you know, the relation between the boss and that. Maybe the bastard don't like you, he's going to dig you into the worst jobs. Maybe you're entitled to a better part of the job, you worked longer than somebody else, somebody's taken that job from you. It's things like that [which cause] disputes in the mines.

Youschok worked at the McGillivray mine and complained that management showed favouritism to certain miners, giving them the best places in the pits. It was a similar situation that brought matters to a head at the Blairmore and Bellevue mines.

> The men were buying their places from the officials. You worked a contract system and you slipped a twenty dollar bill to the pit boss, he'd shoot you into a good place, you didn't and he'd put you in a bad place—it was a rotten system like that we were fighting against. There's a certain bunch of men, they were always in a good place and they were paying for it. It was not only pit bosses. Even the fire bosses were making a little kick-back. A guy wanted a job, he came in there, he paid the boss and he got a job.

Youschok said that when assigning men to places in the mines, favouritism sometimes involved more than graft. East Europeans were often given the worst places to work. This was especially the case at West Canadian's operations where the manager promised he would eventually make Blairmore a "white man's camp."[47] First generation non-Anglo-Saxon immigrants, because of the racism they encountered and because they were generally less-skilled than British immigrants, had often shown a more marked tendency to support radical policies and such statements did nothing to change that.

For the twelve months leading up to the strike, employees of the West Canadian mines had been "tyrannized over and subjected to many indignities by certain officials," said one man. "The breaking point was reached when an attempt was made to compel a lad to abuse himself before a number of bosses because he answered back when his boss swore at him."[48] In January, miners at

Memorial Hall, March 25th 1932

one of the Coleman mines walked out to demand an equal
division of work but returned to work a day later when the
operator agreed to make changes in the way work was
distributed. On February 2, they walked out again, claiming the company had not lived up to its agreement and this
time they stayed out for a full week, joined by miners at the
other Coleman mine. Management this time refused to
budge and the men ended the strike in defeat and returned
to their places. A few weeks later accumulated grievances
at the Greenhill mine in Blairmore boiled over when a
miner was fired for alleged insubordination to one of the
firebosses. The next day, employees of the same company
at the mine in Bellevue walked off the job in sympathy. A
month later, 400 employees at the International Coal and
Coke mine in Coleman joined the 400 Bellevue and Blairmore men already on the picket line. The issue was again
sharing of work—an issue they had fought and lost two
months earlier. This time, officials of the Mine Workers
Union exerted some pressure on them to leave the pit
in order to bolster the strike at Bellevue and Blairmore.

For more than a month after the Coleman walkout, the
Pass remained quiet but all the while operators were refusing to have anything to do with the Mine Workers Union of
Canada. "We have heard nothing from our men," said the
manager of International Coal and Coke, "except from the
Red element and we'll not negotiate with them. We will
not negotiate with the Mine Workers Union of Canada."
The operators weren't shy about exploiting divisions that
existed among employees to their own advantage. There
were times during the dispute when Jay Gould's quip
about hiring one half of the working class to kill the other
came terribly close to reality as the Pass at times took on the
character of a civil war battleground. The division among
the miners came along two lines, ethnic background and
political leanings. The operators and their supporters in
the press of the Crowsnest and the small professional and
business class skilfully and with considerable effect
blended the two together. One Crowsnest newspaper
noted that less than one percent of the strikers were
English, which wasn't true, but it sounded good. Re-

miniscent of the 1919 general strike days, "citizens" committees were formed in all three strike-bound communities to "combat Communism and to promote the ideals of British citizenship among the foreign-speaking workers."[49] Coleman's Anglican minister, one of the founders of the citizens' league, said a year later that an "almost intolerable situation" with a "Russian complexion" existed in the Pass. The foreign-born, said Reverend A.S. Parkington, were uneducated and were threatening all British institutions. Bolshevik agents were active in the area and "the Crowsnest Pass has become fertile soil for the athiest movement which is seeking to overthrow Christianity."[50] Adding to the hysteria being whipped up by the likes of Reverend Parkington was a more ominous form of racism: "A fiery cross, symbol of the Ku Klux Klan, burned for about half an hour last night on the mountains that overlooked this town," said the *Lethbridge Herald* in a report from Blairmore May 18. "It was watched by hundreds.... The next morning, notices, signed by the Klan, were found painted on the union hall warning "Reds Beware" and similar messages were sent to some of the strikers.

While all this was going on, the companies in Coleman, where the strike was primarily a sympathetic one, were instrumental, after refusing to deal with the Mine Workers Union, in setting up a local committee of moderates who began working among the strikers. Their message was that the only obstacle to a return to work was the Communist-dominated union they belonged to; without it, the strike would be over. Several factors gave impetus to the move by the moderates—the Coleman miners had been the first to go out and had lost; the racial mix was somewhat different than in Blairmore and Bellevue—in Coleman, Anglo-Saxons were in the majority; churches in Coleman actively supported the anti-Communist crusade. (The priest in predominantly Catholic Blairmore remained neutral.)

After several votes supported the strike by narrowing majorities, the moderates finally took charge. Miners voted by a slim margin to withdraw from the MWUC, establish a home local and return to work under the old conditions. The meeting, in the Coleman Opera House ended in a riot. "Three men are under arrest as a result of the mêlée. Police were called to stop the fracas, chairs were thrown across the hall, the men engaged in hand-to-hand fights and almost every window in the building was broken."[51] The MWUC attempted an orderly retreat of its Coleman members, advising them to return to work. But for many, that was easier said than done as the companies again resorted to the blacklist. Said Pete Youschok:

When they broke that strike and the men went back to work, there was men, working men, standing up there

with the boss and he'd say, 'that's a Red, that's a Red,' you know, guys coming looking for their job after the strike. The boss just shook his head—'no job for you.' There was some that never did work anymore in the mines. After, during the war, when they needed men, some of them got back on but lots of them never did go back. And they couldn't get a job nowhere else because they were black-balled. Lots of people were changing their names to get a job. There was one man changed his name to MacDonald. In about two weeks they found out who the hell he was, they fired him. He was a Ukrainian but he could speak good English.

A majority of the Coleman strikers may have caved in but the workers at Bellevue and Blairmore remained solid; the blacklist at Coleman may have helped stiffen their resolve. A blacklist became an issue in negotiations between West Canadian and its employees in mid-June, a month after the Coleman miners returned to work, when the company demanded the right, in the words of the *Edmonton Bulletin,* "to virtually blacklist twenty-five men at each mine for the alleged work in spreading propaganda." The miners naturally refused the demand. An earlier attempt at negotiation had broken down when West Canadian refused to give up the right to lay off miners instead of sharing available work. While the abortive talks were going on, the company decided to open its Bellevue operations without any union at all. The *Edmonton Bulletin* reported that in Bellevue on May 5 "Royal Canadian Mounted Police officers were forced to swing their batons when picketers attempted to prevent miners returning to work. Before the crowd of picketers and demonstrators were dispersed, four men were taken into custody."[52]

After two days of rioting at the mine, the company gave up its attempt to keep the mine open but invited more trouble the next month when it demanded that fire-bosses and maintenance men, who generally stayed at work during coal disputes, start producing coal, in violation of a long-standing gentlemen's agreement in the fields that while pump men would remain at work to make sure the mines didn't flood or cave, they would not do the work of the strikers. Again the Mounties, whose numbers had been increased to about seventy-five were called on to protect the strike-breaking fire-bosses and maintenance men from the jeers and catcalls of the strikers. The action of the fire-bosses in agreeing to the company's demand that they start strike-breaking would be remembered a long eighteen years later when they went on strike, only to see the miners walk blithely through their picket lines.

The gloves were now most definitely off in the strike and for the next several months, one incident of assault followed another. In one case, an unknown assailant fired

a shot at strike leader Stokaluk, a prominent Crowsnest Communist, as he was driving in his car. As they returned from a meeting of Bellevue and Blairmore anti-communists, Emile Blas, a Crowsnest moderate, his three brothers and their step-father, were beaten up early in July by a crowd of about twenty-five people. Fifteen people were convicted of common assault. Harvey Murphy was charged with unlawful assembly following one battle at a picket line and was dragged off to jail in Lethbridge, the police hoping that his absence would weaken the strike. His bail, however, was quickly raised and he was soon back on the streets of Blairmore and Bellevue. He was later convicted and sentenced to three months hard labour.

Striking miners had their water and electricity cut off and throughout the dispute were forced to rely on donations collected by the Workers International Relief. Sympathizing farmers, many belonging to the Farmers Unity League, the agrarian equivalent of the Workers Unity League, donated food and three times a week, the union opened a storefront from which it dispensed flour, butter, tea and sugar. For meat, the miners took to the hills and caught rabbits, poached bigger game or fished. In addition to mobilizing the miners, Murphy and other organizers spent considerable effort building support among the families of the miners. A youth wing of the union held dances, picnics and other social activities for the children, who were also brought, to a certain extent, into the struggle, as a report in the July 16 *Edmonton Journal* indicates: " 'Down with the monkey-faced scabs' and 'Down with the yellow scabs' were two inscriptions on banners carried Friday by the Young Communists in their second parade at Bellevue. Youths, many of them mere tots, paraded to the homes of the moderates and were taught to boo by their adult leaders."

By mid-July, traditional strike tactics were proving ineffective and in desperation, a delegation of miners went to Edmonton to see Premier Brownlee. He responded by banning all open-air demonstrations in the Pass. It would be another month before he became actively involved, eventually working out an agreement that ended the strike by Labour Day. An official of West Canadian wrote Prime Minister Bennett late in 1932 complaining that the company had "positively declined to deal with the illegal organizations represented by the Mine Workers Union of Canada and its affiliations" but that "practically at Mr. Brownlee's dictation, I was obliged to sign an agreement with this organization and the leaders who had continuously flouted all law and order and preached open sedition and militant revolution."[53]

The strike had lasted seven months. The moderates re-

fused to be party to an agreement signed by the MWUC and
they demanded and won the right to set up their own
independent locals which also signed the contract. The
miners went back on the basis of the old agreement and
didn't win a wage increase but neither did they take a wage
cut and during the Depression, that was no mean accom-
plishment. They also won agreement from West Canadian
that there would be no general layoffs and that the company would have to rehire the "Red agitators."[54] Some
observers of the strike have attempted to judge the success
or failure of the 1932 Pass strike by looking at what was
won or lost in the contract. Such a view may well do
disservice to the miners of the Crowsnest Pass. Their greatest victory was the strike itself—as one miner's wife wrote:
"This strike is different from any other. Before, everyone
was idle. Now, everyone is busy—it is a question of the right
to live."[55]

The miners of Blairmore were able to claim a little more
dignity in the municipal elections that followed the strike.
A workers' slate was elected to council and much of its
legislation earned the town for some time thereafter the

nickname "Red Blairmore." The main street of the town
was officially renamed "Tim Buck Boulevard" and when
Buck was released from prison and visted the town, a civic
holiday was declared. A dog licensing tax was imposed,
but only on purebreds, on the grounds that only the bosses
could afford purebred dogs. The little coal mining village
got its first park under the workers' council and mine
officials, who lived in a company-owned apartment block,
found themselves in the same position as tenants in Edmonton and Calgary—they were stripped of the right to
vote, leaving the company with only one vote for its
apartment. Harvey Murphy, who became the town solicitor,
said the council "worked out a taxation system whereby
... the whole burden of taxation fell on the company.
Under law, we put up these miners' homes and shacks for
auction but nobody would bid when we told them not to
and these miners lived there and drew rent relief. They'd
give it to council; we applied it to their debts and in two or
three years they got their houses back with taxes paid
off."[56] The effect of the strike and the election of a workers'
council was described in the June 3, 1933 issue of the

Communist Party newspaper, *The Worker.*

Here it is the businessmen who walk past depressed and sullen, the scabs who won't walk boldly but slink home to grouch and plot. Even the Mounties lose their habitual arrogance when they walk the streets of Blairmore. There has been no revolution in Blairmore, as is loudly proclaimed by its enemies. All that has happened is that the miners have won the respect and fear of the exploiters.[57]

The 1932 strike marked the last major campaign of the Mine Workers Union of Canada in Alberta. In 1936, the Alberta Federation of Labour convened a meeting of representatives "from practically every mining camp in Alberta and British Columbia."[58] The rhetoric the United Mine Workers and the Mine Workers Union of Canada had hurled at one another for eleven years was now forgotten and unity was once again established in District 18. Unfortunately for the miners, all the unity and solidarity in the world would not prevent the coming crisis—the death of the industry in Alberta. The illness had taken hold after the first war, went into remission during the second and became terminal in the late Forties and early Fifties.

The decision of the Mine Workers Union of Canada to return to the fold of the United Mine Workers was motivated less by a desire to re-establish unity in the shattered district than by yet another change in party policy. The rise of fascism in Europe had persuaded Moscow to change the "class against class" line that had seen the social democrats denounced as the chief villains of the working class. Communists the world over were now encouraged to link arms with their former enemies in a "common front" against fascism. The Workers Unity League was disbanded and its members sent back into the mainstream of the labour movement. But before the league was ordered into limbo, its organizers moved into an area where few union organizers had ever bothered to go. The Wobblies had tried, but failed, to organize harvest workers in Alberta and Saskatchewan. Like the Wobblies, the Communists viewed it their mission to organize everyone everywhere and weren't inhibited by the failures of other groups. Among the grain harvest workers, they had limited success—there were reports that they led strikes in the Pincher Creek area east of the Crowsnest and in parts of Saskatchewan. It was in the sugar beet fields in the Lethbridge-Taber area where their efforts yielded results.

In contrast with the situation today, the sugar-beet workers, employed from spring to fall in planting, thinning and harvesting, were, in the 1930s, a relatively stable population, made up in the main of immigrants from the beet growing regions of Czechoslovakia and Hungary. The farmers were organized into an association of beet growers but the real power in the area was the Rogers Sugar Company, a large, B.C.-based corporation that, with only several other companies, held a virtual monopoly in the country's sugar industry. The beet workers' grievances were twofold: From 1930 they endured one pay cut after another. Their rate per acre dropped from twenty-three dollars to seventeen dollars with accompanying declines in bonuses. Enjoying the competition provided by thousands of unemployed roaming the country looking for any kind of work, the company and growers association also set up a share-cropping system which, in many cases, resulted in even lower wages per season. In 1934, the growers also started demanding that the beet workers perform other tasks, at no extra pay, such as mending fences and hauling manure. But Pete Meroniuk, an activist in the Mine Workers Union of Canada who was approached by the beet workers who wanted help in dealing with the growers, said that the "biggest grievance was living accommodation—a proper place to live in, that's all we asked. They were living in rebuilt chicken coops and they were treated very inhumanely."[59]

During the off-season of 1934, the workers decided to form a union and by the spring of 1935, the Beet Workers Industrial Union, an affiliate of the Unity League, had called its first strike, asking for $22.00 an acre instead of the proposed reduction to $16.50 from $17.00. The growers responded by refusing to deal with the union because of its Communist affiliation and threatened to evict the strikers from their shacks. Feelings were so bitter that negotiations, which ended with growers agreeing to make improvements in living conditions and raise the per acre rate to $19.00, were held under police surveillance. The productivity bonus was also raised and much of the free work was eliminated.[60]

The following year saw another walkout when eleven hundred workers left the fields in mid-May demanding a cash rate of $21.50 and recognition of their union. This time, the growers and the company (which had paid $1.00 of the per acre increase the previous season) were determined not to give in. Strikers were evicted from their chicken coop homes and the RCMP "maintained constant patrol in the beet-growing districts." The growers were also successful in persuading the new Social Credit government to help them break the union by having the provincial labour bureau recruit strike-breakers, a move that tarnished the Socred image as a progressive and peoples' government. The *Edmonton Journal* of May 21 reported that "three busloads aggregating 104 men left Edmonton in the past few days for the sugar-beet fields of Southern Alberta." When they arrived they were met by a squad of picketers. Said Meroniuk: "We went there, we de-

Japanese sugar-beet workers in the Lethbridge area during the Second World War. Workers in the industry had been organized since the mid-Thirties, but in 1942, the beet-growers association, with the encouragement of the Rogers Sugar Company, asked the B.C. Security Commission to send in Japanese families who had been stripped of their property. The union never had an easy job of it and the forced Japanese migration gave it the final push.

monstrated, we talked to the boys, says to the boys, we're on strike, and there was mostly boys there off of relief. They turned back. We didn't have to picket them at all. Some people referred to them as scabs. They weren't, they were good, honest workers, were eager to get a job and at that time, jobs were scarce."

After ten days on strike, the workers received an increase of one dollar an acre but had to settle for signing individual contracts as the growers would not budge from their refusal to recognize the union, although local grievance committees were recognized. It was the last strike in the fields, although the union, which affiliated with the Congress of Industrial Organizations (CIO) when the unity league was disbanded, continued to negotiate with the growers. In 1940, it received a substantial setback when its

secretary, William Repka, who had been an organizer for the Young Communist League during the height of the Depression but later dropped out, was arrested and thrown into an internment camp under the wartime Defence of Canada Regulations—a fate that befell many other Communists. By 1942, it was reported that the union was "only a name" and had ceased to operate.[61]

Many, but not all of the industrial disputes in Alberta during the Depression involved miners and Communist Party organizers. One of the few that didn't was called by the International Typographical Union at the *Calgary Albertan* newspaper. The strike, led by Calgary alderman and MLA Fred White, was called to prevent a wage cut, planned to take effect the day before Christmas and five months before the existing two-year contract was due to expire. Like

other groups of workers in established trade unions, Calgary printers had seen their wages steadily cut in the agreements negotiated with their employers. In 1932, they were making $1.06 an hour but after the settlement of the 1933 contract with the four major Alberta newspaper publishers, their wages dropped to 85c an hour. As well, they lost three paid holidays and improvements in working conditions won in more prosperous times.

When the *Albertan* offered to cut wages another ten cents an hour in return for a profit-sharing scheme that excluded the only profitable arms of the *Albertan's* little empire, workers rebelled. The strike, which began January 11, 1936, forced the *Albertan* to publish a much smaller edition for the first day but it quickly re-established itself, recruiting strike-breakers, including several union members who had to be escorted through the picket line by police. The union and its members tried everything they could to win the battle but the paper was able to hold out: the ITU suggested arbitration but was turned down; the Alberta Federation of Labour declared a boycott against the paper; the union itself published several editions of a strike paper; and one frustrated printer somehow got into the *Albertan*'s plant and took it out on a typesetting machine, for which he was fined fifty dollars and charged thirty-seven dollars for the damage he had caused.

The strike ended, for the company, on a bizarre note. The announcement that the dispute had ended was made, not by the management of the *Albertan*, but by E.C. Manning, provincial secretary in the Social Credit government. Under consistent attack by newspapers in the province, the Social Credit party decided one way to turn things around was to buy a paper and they entered negotiations to purchase the *Albertan*. The Social Credit government had an initial image as a pro-labour government which it didn't want to lose and resolved that any paper it owned should carry a union label. The ITU label wouldn't do as they were still refusing to accept a wage cut and still considered themselves locked out so the *Albertan* and the Socreds found a union that didn't have any qualms about coming in and organizing scabs. On February 9, Manning announced that the *Albertan* strike-breakers would be joining the Canadian Printers Union, an affiliate of the All-Canadian Congress of Labour. After the Mine Workers Union of Canada had withdrawn, the national congress, with only one major affiliate left (the Canadian Brotherhood of Railway Employees) unabashedly scrambled for whatever membership it could lay its hand on.

Social Credit

It is, perhaps, one of the intriguing paradoxes of Canadian history that the rising militancy and radicalism generated by the collapse of the capitalist economy during the Thirties gave rise to one of the most conservative political movements in the country—Social Credit.

The Social Credit sweep in the provincial election of 1935 was so extensive that only seven opposition members were elected and Social Credit destroyed forever the United Farmers of Alberta as a political movement and wiped out entirely the legislative arm of the Canadian Labour Party. Across the province, both farmers and workers rejected the appeals of their former representatives in the UFA and the labour party and gave an immense vote of confidence to a political party that only recently had been formed. The victory of Social Credit provides further evidence that the militancy and radicalism of the province's population was not based on any ideology but was, in fact, raw anger waiting to be shaped by leaders who stepped out of the wings offering a way out of the wilderness.

William Aberhart and his infant party rode the crest of a wave of support for Social Credit philosophy brought to Alberta by William Irvine, a UFA stalwart and former

labour MP, and by the UFA itself which, while it was still in office, brought over the English founder of "funny money," Major Douglas. The principle of Social Credit—that all the world's problems could be traced to the power of large financiers—found a ready audience in Alberta where farmers in particular had always identified vague eastern interests as the source of their woes. The message carried even more appeal at a time when financial institutions were repossessing farms as farmers forfeited on their mortgages. Aberhart's broadcasts from the Prophetic Bible Institute became the messianic vehicle for carrying his particular blend of Prairie populism, religion and Social Credit.

An unfortunate series of circumstances prevented the CCF from joining the bandwagon of discontent that took Aberhart to power. The UFA had decided to affiliate with the CCF when it was formed but maintained an ambivalent attitude toward it, based primarily on the hesitation of the cabinet ministers to commit themselves. Consequently,

the CCF found itself in a next-to-impossible position. The UFA decided to contest the 1935 election on its own, leaving the CCF no alternative but to sit it out. But it was common knowledge that the UFA had become part of the new party and the CCF thereafter would have to carry part of the blame that electorates everywhere dumped on the governments that had ruled them during the Depression.

Much of Social Credit's appeal to Alberta workers was due to Aberhart's promise that every adult in the province would receive a twenty-five dollar a month dividend from the government. "When they promised that twenty-five dollars a month," said Pete Youschok, "Christ, everybody voted for it. Why, my mother and father, they never heard of any such thing, that people give you twenty-five dollars a month. My father and mother, you damn rights they voted for them. Old Aberhart promised $25 a month—my mother said 'gee, I could live good on $25 a month, we never made $25 a month.'"

The *Alberta Labour News* commented after the election,

Executive of the Alberta Federation of Labour at a convention in Edmonton, January 1934. Alf Farmilo is in the front row at far left; president Fred White is third from left. Carl Berg is in the back row at right.

"In urban as well as rural constituencies, Social Credit has swept everything before it. Analysis of the vote shows that votes previously cast for UFA and labour candidates went Social Credit. That the vote was a protest against present economic conditions in the country, leaders of all parties are prepared to agree." Social Credit picked up almost 55 percent of the popular vote, leaving the UFA a poor third behind the Liberals who managed to hang on to 23 percent. An indication of support for the Communist Party in the 1930s was that nine candidates in this election received close to 6,000 votes, slightly more than the labour party which ran almost the same number of candidates—eleven and one independent labour. In Edmonton, Jan Lakeman, a Communist, did better than any of the labour candidates running in the multiple-member constituency, outpolling his nearest labour rival 1,096 to 505. Alf Farmilo and Carl Berg between them only managed slightly more than 300 votes.[62]

In its early stages, the Social Credit government gave some credence to the prediction of Elmer Roper that the party would move to the left instead of the right. Aberhart passed the first general minimum wage order in Canada which also set another first—time and one half wage for all

overtime. In 1938, the Industrial Conciliation and Arbitration Act gave labour the right to collective bargaining, a long-sought-after piece of legislation designed to prevent strikes over recognition. The Alberta Federation of Labour at its 1937 convention noted that a "certain amount of useful labour legislation" had been enacted by the new government but it was less than pleased with an act setting the hours of work in the province at fifty-four. Federation president Fred White warned the convention that labour should concentrate its efforts on building strong unions rather than depending on government action. "Recent developments have indicated that to place too great reliance on government action is not altogether sound. This does not apply to the provincial government alone."[63]

It is significant that several Social Credit moves away from its "progressive" image were made by the party's second-in-command, E.C. Manning, who, after Aberhart's death in 1943, moved into the premier's office. It was Manning who announced that the Albertan had signed a contract with a union representing the strike-breakers at its printing plant and it was Manning who vetoed a request by coal miners to have a representative on the inquiry into the 1935 Coalhurst mining disaster.[64] It would be Manning who would confirm Social Credit as a conservative political instrument and dash the early hopes of people like Elmer Roper that an agreement could be reached between the Aberhart movement and the CCF, thereby establishing socialism in Alberta. As Roper said after the election, the CCF had "missed the boat." It would be a long wait before another one happened by.

CHAPTER EIGHT

Division and Re-union: 1936-1956

Formation of CIO

The turbulence and ferment of the Depression, the tremendous expansion of Canada's manufacturing base during the Second World War and the early signs of fatal trouble in Alberta's coal industry, for forty years the radical heart of the labour movement in the province, left an indelible mark on the nature of the province and its trade union movement.

By the mid-Fifties, a railway machinist or Crowsnest coal miner suddenly transported from the period of the First World War would have had great difficulty believing he was in the same province. The 1923 convention of the Alberta Federation of Labour had given a lusty ovation to Tim Buck and had closed with a singing of the Red Flag. By the late 1940s, some delegates were suggesting that unions involved in illegal strikes should be disbanded and ovations were reserved for representatives of the Social Credit government which, by then, had its former image of a progressive and populist government securely locked in the closet. The miners found themselves replaced as the largest union in the province and technological advances on the railways and other transportation modes had left the rail unions shadows of their former selves. The CPR's Ogden shops and the militant machinists who worked there found themselves outdistanced by geologists and white-collar workers who crowded into Calgary office buildings to service the oil industry. Things had changed.

The reunion of Alberta coal miners with the rest of their brothers and sisters in the labour movement, wrought by the self-destruction of the Workers Unity League, was a short-term development. By 1939, coal miners were again on their own, not because that's what they wanted but because that's what Washington wanted.

From the beginnings of the twentieth century, a new industrial revolution had been gathering force and, given a mighty push by the first war, was remaking the face of the industrial centres of North America. As the first industrial revolution had left the old artisans' guilds out of step with the way the world worked, so too did the second leave the craft unions of the American Federation of Labour and their Canadian branches anachronisms in a new era of mass-production industries. In the early Twenties, the federation had tried to come to grips with the new reality by attempting an organization of the steel industry but its heart wasn't in it. Workers in the automobile plants, the steel industry, rubber, metal mining, all found themselves on the outside of the labour movement looking wistfully in. The Wobblies and Communists had tried to bring the benefits of union organization to these workers but generally found themselves without the resources needed to tackle the new citadels of industrial power.

By the mid-Thirties, some leaders of the American Federation began to realize that if the labour movement was not to suffer the same fate as the guilds something would have to be done. Led by John L. Lewis, the head of the United Mine Workers, one of the few industrial unions in the American Federation of Labour, a Committee on Industrial Organization was set up within the federation and, making common cause with the Communists, started an organizing drive. Lewis' committee was first tolerated reluctantly by the old-guard of the federation but as its success mushroomed the unions forming the committee were expelled and the Congress of Industrial Organizations (CIO) was founded as the most powerful rival trade union centre the American Federation of Labour had ever faced.

The Alberta Federation of Labour and other groups of Canadian workers were less than pleased with the split south of the border and moves to expel the offending unions from the Trades and Labour Congress were resisted. But, as they had in 1902, the international unions pulled rank and threatened the TLC that they would stop sending in membership dues. In 1939, by a standing vote of 231-98, the Trades and Labour Congress followed the line dictated from Washington. A year later, the CIO unions in Canada joined with the remnants of the All-Canadian Congress of Labour to form the Canadian Congress of Labour (CCL).[1]

When division came, it initially meant nothing more in Alberta but that the coal miners were once again on their own, cut off from the main body of organized labour in the province. With Alberta's limited manufacturing base, the CIO/CCL had considerable difficulty getting a toehold. But two long-neglected groups of workers in the province were to receive the attention of organizers of the new congress—lumber workers and employees in Alberta's large meat-packing industry.

Conditions in the lumber industry had changed little since the First World War when lumber and sawmill workers had last attempted to join a trade union. Dave Graham, who worked in the woods in the early Forties, said of conditions:

> They had long bunkhouses and they had double bunks and everybody carried their blankets, of course. When you wanted a mattress, you'd go to the barn and get some hay or straw and spread it over the bare floors and that was your mattress. Of course, the camps were lousy. They were double bunks but they were sort of separated by one board . . . between the two of you.[2]

There had been sporadic strikes since Carl Berg and the OBU had tried to organize lumber workers but little came of them.[3] With the formation of the CIO, however, a new union—the International Woodworkers of America (IWA)— was ready to move into the bush. In January, 1938, the union's two organizers, Syd Thompson (now a leading IWA official in B.C.) and J. Savage pulled a strike of between one hundred and two hundred men at the Etter McDougall company in the Buck Lake district southwest of Edmonton. The walkout spread to the Edson area where it involved about three hundred workers employed by three companies. The secretary of the Edson local of the IWA was none other than Carl Berg.

The Social Credit government had as much to do with the disputes as the companies. The government had set a minimum wage of thirty-three and one-third cents an hour but a delegation of industry executives was successful in having the government reduce the minimum to twenty-eight cents an hour. The companies also raised the charge for board from seventy-five cents a day to one dollar. Edward Hinton, the secretary of IWA Local 110, said in a letter to the union's B.C. district council that: "We are also out in protest of the intolerable working conditions now existing in the lumber camps."

The strikers in both districts were able to force the companies to return to the old wage and board rates but only the Edson workers went back to work with the IWA as their recognized bargaining agent. When Dave Graham went to work for Etter McDougall in 1941, he tried again to get a contract between the company and the IWA but never succeeded, even though most employees belonged to the union. From its base in central Alberta, the union pushed into the lumber camps in the Lesser Slave Lake and White-court regions (northwest of Edmonton). By 1949, it held bargaining rights with four companies and during the peak logging period in the winter could count about one thousand members,[4] but in that year, calamity fell. A bitter internal dispute in British Columbia, involving the Communists, consumed all the energies of the IWA. Dave

Sawmill workers in the Crowsnest Pass, late Forties. Conditions in Alberta's lumber industry were often primitive and employers bitterly fought union organization.

Graham, who was then the IWA's Alberta representative, was laid off and the Edmonton office was closed. Alberta locals were left in limbo, despite a determination "that we will find a solution to the problem of maintaining our organization so that we will not again slip back to the conditions prevalent in this industry prior to 1946."[5]

But slip back they did. When Mike Sekora and Bill Gray began to reorganize the IWA in 1955, Sekora found conditions in the camps "very primitive. I remember going into several camps on the Slave Lake line and there wasn't even an outdoor toilet, just a two-by-four pitched between trees." Bunkhouses were "jammed with beds" and workers carried their own blankets. Sekora said the reorganization, after various attempts spanning almost forty years, finally met with little resistance.[6]

Lumbering in Alberta has never been a major industry. It employed about one thousand workers in 1935, but much of the work was seasonal. By contrast, the meat packing

industry was, in 1935, the largest manufacturing industry in the province, employing about fifteen hundred people and accounting, by itself, for 22 percent of all manufacturing in Alberta; 38 percent when combined with the allied flour and feed industry. Almost 17 percent of all workers in manufacturing were employed in the two industries.[7] Almost all were unorganized and conditions were brutal in the extreme.

Packing plant workers had two basic grievances with the companies. The most gnawing was the shape-up. Jack Hampson worked at Canada Packers from the late Thirties until he became a representative of the United Packinghouse Workers. He described what he said was the worst thing about employment there.

We had this great huge dressing room, everybody on the payroll, seven o'clock you all came in. . . . The foreman would come along and say, 'well, I don't need all you guys today so I'll take you, you and you.' And you see some guys sitting there that worked for Canada Packers many years and some kid that come off the street yesterday would be sitting there and he'd get a day's work. But he said 'we'll see what happens at nine o'clock, maybe more hogs would come in, so you guys stick around.' And stick around you did—if you walked out of there, you're fired. So you sat there. And of course at nine o'clock, he might come down for a man or two, he might not—if he didn't need a man he wouldn't bother coming down till five o'clock that night.[8]

For the time they spent in the company dressing room, the workers received not a cent.

The other concern was health and safety. In a mass-production industry like meat packing, the company need only increase the speed of an assembly line and employees had to keep pace or be replaced. A refinement of the speed-up was the time-and-motion study. A certain task, like boning a ham, was assigned a particular time value and when the values were being set, company supervisors made sure the employees worked as fast as they could. After the time value was established, workers who couldn't keep up were liable to dismissal. Alex Goruk said being fired for falling behind was not automatic but the threat was always there. "That was the frightful thing—everybody had to carry that load and I have seen people . . . faint here on the killing room floor." There were also the dust and chemicals in the blood-drying and fertilizer operations but the most frequent accidents involved cuts, not surprisingly, with people walking around in clouds of steam on slippery floors, carrying long, sharp knives and moving as fast as they could to spare themselves a dressing-down from the foreman. Goruk said workers needed permission to go to the bathroom and were often timed. If you were sick and went several times in one day or spent too long in the toilet, the foreman demanded an explanation. Hampson recalled one Christmas Day when Canada Packers called in a crew to load a box-car on the company siding because it didn't want to pay any extra rental charges to the railway. The following day, with the work completed, the crew was laid off.

From 1920, when Pat Burns succeeded in putting his employees back in their places, until late in the Depression, the companies found their employees as easy to herd and bully as the cattle but human beings can tolerate such treatment for only so long. The explosion of grievances finally came in 1937 when the workers resorted to a tactic that was becoming the trade-mark of the CIO—the sit-down strike. Left to fend for themselves for more than a decade, packing plant workers in Edmonton and Calgary finally found a union that was interested in taking on Pat Burns, Canada Packers and Swifts. The Canadian Victuallers and Caterers Union was a branch of the All-Canadian Congress of Labour and although the spirited battles of 1937 ended in defeat, the spark of revolt had been permanently kindled.

In Calgary, the union applied late in 1936 for a conciliation board to deal with a dispute at Union Packing, where the main issues were wages, working conditions and union recognition. In February 1937 the company refused to deal with the conciliation board and fired the five employees who had signed the application for the board. The other workers then stopped work and occupied the plant—an internal picket line. The action forced the company to agree to conciliation and it promised that no action would be taken against the strikers—promises promptly broken when it refused to hire fifty employees after they called off the sit-down. Forty-eight employees also found themselves before the courts on various charges arising from the occupation of the plant. When the strike ended, the company withdrew its nominee from the conciliation board and said it would not accept any of the board's findings and that the five men fired were dismissed because of their activity in the union and would not be rehired. That ended the dispute in Calgary. The action then shifted to Edmonton where it engulfed the entire industry.[9]

Early in April, about three hundred employees of Swifts in Edmonton sat down at their posts and demanded that the company give them a half-day holiday Saturday afternoon and recognize their union. Several days later, about sixty Gainers employees and a similar number at Burns also staged sit-down strikes. At Gainers, the main issue was an end to the time and motion studies but the union also charged that Gainers had been processing meat for Swifts since the strike there had started. The sit-down developed into a minor epidemic among the unorganized in Edmonton that spring as packing plant workers were joined by employees of two laundries and a delivery service. Women working in the laundries were earning twenty-six cents an hour and one told the *People's Weekly,* the new name of *Alberta Labour News,* that:

. . . . girls have collapsed, unable to stand the extreme humidity and in all the time I have been employed there, there has only been one fan installed. At times, the steam has collected to such an extent that it is difficult to see one another. The girl's washroom is small, without ventilation. It is alive with cockroaches; the lavatories are almost constantly flooding the floor.

After several weeks on strike, the union admitted defeat and its members were advised to return to work on management's terms—if they could. Burns officials told

The lunch detail during the 1937 sit-down strike at Edmonton packing plants.

the union that the jobs of strikers had been filled "temporarily." The daughter of one of the Gainer's strikers said in an interview that her father never was re-employed and couldn't find work anywhere until the war and had to support his family on relief.[10]

Following the All-Canadian Congress of Labour into the packing plants was Carl Berg who set up a directly-chartered local—number 78—of the Trades and Labour Congress which, by 1938, had established a beachhead. By the war all the plants were organized, in spite of company opposition. The most common tactic, said Hampson, who was an officer of Local 78 before switching his allegiance to the United Packinghouse Workers of the CIO/CCL, was establishment of plant councils under management control where employees had at least a formal mechanism to express their grievances. By many, however, Local 78,

which represented all Edmonton packing plant employees, was considered little better than a company council. Hampson, who, of all the leaders of the packing plant workers, held out the longest in his support of the TLC, admitted that Local 78 did have its problems. It organized all the employees in the plants, including electricians and other maintenance workers, but that quite definitely cut across the Trades and Labour Congress grain and relations between the local and the congress were strained.

Perhaps the most important element of dissatisfaction with Local 78 was its lack of militancy. Goruk and Dec said the local often failed to take up grievances with the companies and part of the problem seemed to be Carl Berg, who was proving that he had come a long way from 1919. Hampson recalled an impromptu sit-down strike at

Canada Packers protesting the company's refusal to post a scale of wages as promised. Company officials called Carl Berg who ordered Hampson to end the strike. Hampson refused and the company, after the government applied some pressure, met the demand and the sit-down ended. But Hampson said Berg's actions lost him and Local 78 a lot of respect among packing plant employees.

Workers in Edmonton realized that if they were to sucessfully challenge industry giants like Canada Packers, Swifts and Burns, bargaining would have to be done at the national level. An isolated strike in one corner of the companies' empire could be easily defeated by supplying markets from other plants. Hampson said that, at first, the congress refused to give Local 78 a national charter so it could organize packinghouse workers across the country and by the time it did, it was too late.

During the war, the United Packinghouse Workers of America (UPWA), an affiliate of the CIO/CCL, had moved into Canada, first picking up the crucial Toronto and Vancouver plants. Although the cattle industry was centred in western Canada, the development of the packing industry followed the general Canadian pattern where raw materials from the West were shipped East for processing. Alberta plants however were responsible for a significant share of national production. In Edmonton, the UPWA made its entry in the fall of 1943 and several months later established its first local, 233, at Burns where John Lenglet, the Local 78 representative in the plant, was instrumental in swinging support to the new union. In the government-supervised vote early in December, Local 78 received only nine votes.[11]

Canada Packers proved more difficult. So clouded was the situation there that in the fall of 1944, the government issued a statement saying it wasn't quite sure who represented Canada Packers' employees.[12] In the early stages of the organizing drive, both unions had almost equal strength and unlike the case at Burns, where Lenglet had supported the UPWA, Hampson remained convinced that, in spite of its problems, Local 78 offered the best hope for his members. Confounding the matter was an Alberta law requiring a majority of all employees entitled to vote to cast ballots supporting the union before it could win bargaining rights. In most other jurisdictions, a union could be certified by receiving a majority of those voting. The law, which remained on the books a long time, was to be a constant thorn in the side of union organizers.

In the first vote at Canada Packers in January, the UPWA received a slight majority of those voting, beating out Local 78 by 291 to 276, but the 69 people who didn't vote were, in effect, counted against UPWA Local 243. That spring, the federal government moved into the plant to conduct another vote assisted by staff from the Board of Industrial Relations. The margin for the Local 243 widened but was not sufficient to claim a victory. Meanwhile, the company was honouring its agreement with Local 78. The contract had expired in the fall of 1943 but contained a clause that until it was terminated by either party it continued in effect. That summer, the UPWA was preparing for national negotiations with the companies and wanted to include the Edmonton Canada Packers plant but was stymied by a conciliation report recommending that no more votes be held in the plant until January of 1945. Local 243 then presented a petition signed by the majority of all the Canada Packers employees demanding an immediate vote and in late August began a slow-down strike to support its demand. Early in September, the provincial government responsed by sponsoring another vote, which was won in convincing fashion by Local 243. Less than one hundred people cast ballots for Local 78.

But the TLC local was still not prepared to accept the inevitable and charged that there were irregularities in the September vote and once again Canada Packers employees went to the polls set up on the lawn of the plant and again the UPWA was victorious: Local 78 received only 31 votes.[13] That fall, the UPWA entered negotiations with the companies, its major demand being an industry-wide contract. Without it, said Fred Dowling, the union's national director, packing plant employees were in a next to hopeless situation. "In the past," he said, "the companies have insisted on dealing with the union on a local plant basis and have continually played one off against another. . . . Almost any request involving hours, wages or working conditions has always been refused on the grounds that, granted in one plant, would upset the company's relations with its other plants in the country."[14]

To give backing to the demand, UPWA locals across the country began taking strike votes and in Edmonton, workers at Burns and Canada Packers voted overwhelmingly to walk off the job. The vote at Burns was unanimous while only three Canada Packers employees voted against a walkout that the union had no intention of calling. The strike votes, at a time of national emergency, with plants producing overtime to supply the troops and Britain with canned meat, incensed public opinion. Even the rest of the labour movement, in the form of the Trades and Labour Congress was outraged. Carl Berg, by then a TLC vice-president, said a strike would be a "betrayal of the nation's fighting men."

The negative public reaction was exactly what Dowling was hoping for. Up to then, the federal government had been saying it could not get involved because the packing industry was not considered a national industry under wartime controls then in effect. Faced with a national walkout, the federal government amended its position and

One of many union certification votes at Canada Packers. Edmonton, 1944.

appointed a conciliation board under the 1944 order-in-council P.C. 1003. P.C. 1003 was, in effect, a national labour code which recognized the rights of workers to organize and provided that companies could not refuse to bargain with unions representing their employees. In return, unions gave up the right to strike during the term of the agreement. It became, after the war, the model for most labour legislation in the country.

The union didn't win its major demand in 1944 but it came close. Provision was made for all local contracts to expire at about the same time and some standard wording was contained in local contracts. In addition, the union won for its members a guaranteed minimum work week of forty hours, thus ending the shape-up, and a basic national minimum wage of seventy-five cents an hour. Between 1939 and 1945, average wages in the industry had risen

almost 45 percent. The union paid particular attention to increases for female employees in the industry, who, in 1939, were making only thirty-three cents an hour, almost twenty cents an hour less than men. In 1945, the union at Burns in Edmonton threatened to strike over the issue of equal pay for equal work and made a special appeal to the Wartime Labour Board, which controlled wage rates during the war. The board dealt with the issue and the strike was not called.[15]

In 1945, the union called a national wildcat strike of all Canada Packers plants, citing what it said was a violation of the contract by the company. There is, however, some evidence to suggest that the strike was called to soften up the company prior to negotiations for a new contract. To forestall a national strike the federal government used its wartime powers to take over the plants and placed the issue before a conciliation board.

The union failed in both 1945 and 1946 to get its national contract but was finally victorious in 1947 when it called what was, outside the railway industry, the first national strike in Canadian history. Workers employed by the Big Three—Canada Packers, Swifts and Burns—were on strike from late August to the end of October.[16] This time the union was hampered by the fact that federal control of the industry had expired and jurisdiction was returned to the provinces, each of which had enacted their own labour laws, modelled loosely on P.C. 1003, but with enough differences in procedure to make it very difficult for the union to comply with all the legislation and yet call a national walkout beginning and ending at the same time—a problem which has continued to plague it to this day.

The major goals of the union were reached with the 1947 agreement and subsequent negotiations focused on improving on principles already won. In Alberta, the union moved beyond its Edmonton base and organized the Calgary plants and various feed and flour mills.

The pattern of negotiations in the packing industry after the union was established gives some indication of what was happening to the labour movement across the country and in Alberta. The bitterest disputes in the province had been fought over the right of a union to exist at all. In the United States during the Depression, the federal government and some leading employers began to realize that trade unions were a fact of life and that attitude, by no means universally held, had taken hold in Canada during the war years. In basic industry, at least, workers had, after years of bloodshed and blacklists, forced their employers to accept, however reluctantly, their right to belong to a union that would bargain and sign contracts on their behalf.

With the growth of the UPWA the United Mine Workers found itself rivalled as the largest and most politically active union in the province, although the politics of the two largest affiliates of the Canadian Congress of Labour in Alberta differed sharply at the local level. Communists had been active in the formation of the UPWA in Edmonton but the leading role had been taken by members of the CCF. The union has since been a major base of CCF/NDP support in the labour movement. The United Mine Workers continued, as it struggled for life in a dying industry, to provide the Communists with their main base.

The Second World War had put a prompt end to the Depression. Industrial and mining production was on the rise and miners found themselves in the unfamiliar position of being needed. As was the case during the First World War, they used the fact as a lever in keeping up with cost of living increases that accompanied the war. However, alarmed that coal miners, particularly the younger ones, were leaving the pits for more pleasant employment, the federal government froze all miners to their jobs in 1943 and even stipulated that former miners could be taken from other employment and put back in the mines. On October 14, 1943, the federal Liberal government passed an order-in-council outlawing all coal strikes for the duration of the war. In defiance of the order, about ten thousand District 18 miners walked out of the pits November 1, in the first district-wide strike since 1925. The miners wanted a $2.00 a day wage increase to $7.78 a day, time and one-half for the sixth day of the work week and two weeks paid vacation. District 18 chief Bob Livett said the miners were fed up with the War Labour Board, claiming that it had been "dilly-dallying" with district contract proposals. Anxious to get the mines back into production, Ottawa appointed a royal commission with war labour board powers. Livett then ordered the miners back to work.

The Alberta miners were not to be put off that easily, however. The Edmonton sub-district condemned Livett for his action and several days after miners had been told to return to work, more than fifty-five hundred were still manning picket lines. The *Vancouver Sun* reported November 10 that miners in the Crowsnest were trying to persuade those who had accepted Livett's command to rejoin the strike. But by November 13, Livett and District 18 officials had succeeded in putting down the rebellion and the strike ended. The royal commission gave the miners their two weeks paid vacation and granted one dollar of their two dollar a day wage demand. The walkout was one of the last major battles to be fought by the UMW in Alberta.[17]

As late as 1946, the coal industry was still the source of most industrial disputes in the province, but the coal industry was experiencing increasing competition from natural gas and oil. Conversion to natural gas and fuel oil for home heating sounded the death knell of the Drumheller field while the railways' change from coal to diesel spelled disaster for mines in the Crowsnest and Coal Branch, which had always relied on the railways as their primary market. The Alberta fields couldn't compete with the United States for the major Ontario market and the provincial government, involved in a love affair of considerable intensity with the oil industry, would have nothing to do with demands by the UMW that the government encourage the construction of coal by-product plants in coal mining areas. The government did set up a special emergency fund to help the miners but often it only assisted in relocating them from a dead to a dying mine. By 1953, coal production in Alberta had dropped to about 6 million tons, compared to almost 9 million in 1946. In the

Employees at Canada Packers in Edmonton, 1941. The work was dangerous and employers had all the rights. On one occasion, workers were called in Christmas Day and laid off Boxing Day.

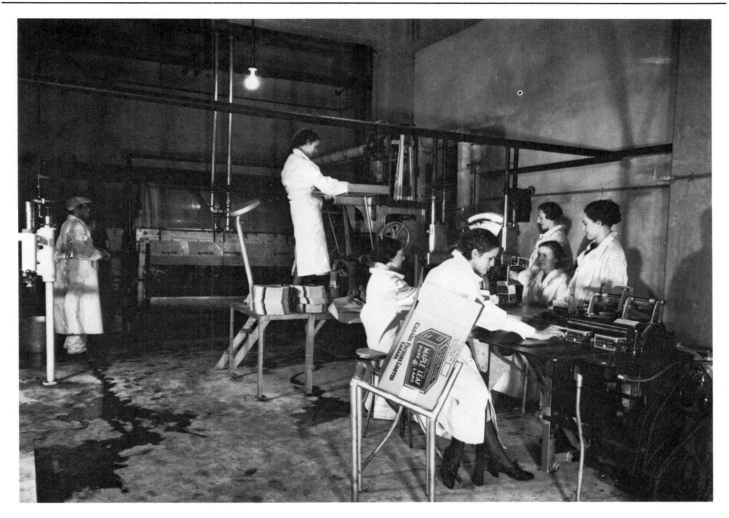

same period, employment in the mines had declined from eighty-six hundred to fifty-eight hundred. In 1955, the UMW was reporting only twenty-eight hundred members to the Industrial Federation of Labour and by the late Fifties, only one mine was operating in Alberta. Miners scrambled to find whatever jobs they could. Art Roberts said many from the Drumheller area moved to Calgary, taking their families with them and settling in districts like Bowness.[18]

Energy would, however, continue to be the province's dominant industry, in one form or another. In 1948, Imperial Oil opened the first refinery in Edmonton, hard on the heels of the discovery by the company of the Leduc field just south of the city. From 1922 to 1934, the province produced almost 8 million barrels of crude but over the next fifteen years, the figure mushroomed to more than 140 million. By 1951, the province had eleven refineries with a capacity of sixty thousand barrels a day.[19]

The labour movement had succeeded in making the coal industry its major base but in the oil industry would face an almost impossible task even gaining a toehold. Neil Reimer, the Canadian director of the Oil, Chemical and Atomic Workers (OCAW), who came to the province in the early Fifties to organize the industry, insists that the Social Credit government made a deal with the industry to the effect that if it invested heavily in the province, it would be able to operate without worrying about trade unions. Some evidence of this may be found in the fact that the industry, even today, is only partially organized in Alberta, certainly not the case in the rest of the country and in the United States. Workers in the province tended to view the oil industry as a gift from heaven and anything that interfered with it was, by definition, bad, Reimer said. "They'd found a golden egg down here and they weren't going to allow any union representative to spoil it."[20]

The first move to organize oil workers in Alberta came in 1942 in the Turner Valley field but it was a short-lived effort. On July 27, thirty-nine employees of Royalite Oil applied to the Canadian Congress of Labour for a charter.

The charter was granted and nothing was ever heard from them again.[21] In 1947, the CCL chartered another local in the Turner Valley field, this time representing employees of B.A. Oil (now Gulf) and Gas and Oil Refinery Ltd. but the congress found the temporary executive was unable to resist the pressure exerted by the companies and couldn't hold the union together. When the government-supervised vote was taken, the workers voted two to one against having Local 16 of the United Oil Workers of Canada represent them. Tom McCloy, the CCL organizer in the province, wrote that "with the decision of the workers as it is and bearing in mind the actions of the temporary executive, it was necessary for us to withdraw the charter. . . . I suggested previously it would assist greatly to have someone enter the organizational field who already had experience in the oil industry."[22]

McCloy was a former official of the UMW and certainly didn't have "experience in the oil industry," but late in

1948, he was hired by the Oil Workers International Union (OWIU), now the Oil Chemical and Atomic Workers, as its Alberta organizer. Assisted by Alex McAuslane, a congress vice-president and official of the OWIU, McCloy used his contacts in Leduc and in the spring of 1949 set up a local of oil well drillers in the field. Before the vote was taken, said Reimer, the company transferred half the drillers to the Northwest Territories, the other half to Northern B.C. and hired a new crew, which voted against a union. Some time later, McCloy was fired by the union because of his lack of success in Alberta and was rehired by the congress.[23]

When Reimer arrived in the province from Saskatchewan, he immediately began looking for any group of workers even vaguely within the union's jurisdiction just to establish a beachhead and, no doubt, prove to union headquarters that Alberta wasn't entirely a wasteland. On March 22, 1951, Local 630 was certified as the bargaining

Roughnecks on an Imperial Oil site. The Oil Workers union established a local of oil-well drillers in the Leduc area in the spring of 1949 but the company was able to prevent it from becoming certified.

agent representing about thirty employees of Liquid Carbonic in Edmonton—a chemical plant. It was the first oil workers local that lasted longer than several months.[24]

After setting up his first local, which also gave the union a voice in the Industrial Federation of Labour of Alberta, the CCL's answer to the Alberta Federation of Labour, Reimer turned his attention to B.A.'s Edmonton refinery. The drive started in the spring of 1952 and by the end of July, Local 654 had, according to union minutes on file with the Board of Industrial Relations, signed up seventy-two members, or 63 percent of the intended bargaining

unit. With that large a sign-up, the board could have automatically granted certification if there was no challenge but Reimer was not to be that lucky. He said that at the board meeting, B.A. had a large number of its board of directors who pleaded for a vote. "They knew Mr. Reimer, he wouldn't use any coercion, but maybe these people didn't understand what they were getting into," Reimer recalled. The union's request for certification was also attacked by the company union in the plant. The B.A. Employees Collective Bargaining Association was a national organization but the union had beaten it in Clarkson,

Ontario and at B.A. plants in Saskatchewan and British Columbia. Alberta was, however, much more tolerant of company unionism.[25]

The board ordered a vote taken at the plant August 21 and Reimer said that during the campaign preceding the ballot, his members were subjected to various forms of harassment and intimidation by the company. One of the tactics of company officials, Reimer said, was to find out when and where the union was having meetings and then stand outside the hall, jotting down the names of people attending. "It was illegal but who was going to stop them." When the vote was held, Reimer saw his majority in the plant cut to a minority of 34 percent.[26]

But the oil companies' most effective tool in combatting trade unions was the company unions they set up. In this, they found the provincial government more than willing to co-operate. The company unions, as was the case in the packing plants, signed contracts and even fought the occasional grievance. They gave the appearance of organization and allowed the companies to find out what their employees were thinking. As with many other aspects of Alberta labour history, the oil industry's company unions were closely connected to MacKenzie King. In 1914, King had been hired by John D. Rochefeller, who had an intense dislike of unions, to advise him how best to handle his employees at Colorado Fuel and Iron. King presented the oil baron with the concept of company unionism, which Rockefeller enthusiastically took up and applied throughout his empire, including Standard Oil (now Exxon). Other oil companies outside the Rockefeller orbit liked the idea too. So it happened that when the labour movement tried to tackle Standard Oil's arm in Alberta, Imperial Oil, who did they run up against but Mackenzie King and his company unions.

In Alberta, Reimer said, the onus was on the union to prove that a company association was dominated by the employer and therefore ineligible for certification. "That was hard to do."[27] After the failure of the drive at B.A., the company association was given bargaining rights under the labour act. (Where evidence of company domination was obvious, the government gave company unions the option of being chartered under the Societies Act, an opening taken by the company council at Texaco's Edmonton refinery.) Government acceptance of company unionism also posed another but lesser problem for the union. Under the labour act, a union moving into a situation where a company and another union have a contract must apply to replace the other union during a short and clearly-defined time period. The provincial government, even where company unions were obviously run by the employer and not recognized under the act, considered them bona fide trade unions for the purposes of that section. Said Reimer:

Manning sold Alberta on the basis of industrial peace. I think it's our union he wanted to keep out. He wasn't going to have a . . . situation like British Columbia where basic industries were organized. There appeared to be a master plan to keep unions out. Those guys that wanted the union have been just frustrated by collusion and by shenanigans between the companies and the government.

OCAW finally did break into the industry it was formed to organize in September 1952 when Local 658 was certified to negotiate for the employees of Husky Oil in Lloydminster, on the Alberta-Saskatchewan border.[28] To this day, the refinery is one of the few in the province that the union has succeeded in organizing.

By 1955, the oil workers in the province represented five hundred and fifty workers while all the CIO/CCL unions had a combined membership of just over eight thousand, hardly in the same league as the Alberta Federation of Labour which, a year earlier, reported twenty-four thousand members. One union within the AFL, the Civil Service Association, had almost as many members, five thousand, as the entire CIO/CCL in Alberta.[29]

The only two CIO unions of any size were the UPWA and the UMW, which was in decline. With the exception of the Canadian Brotherhood of Railway Employees, most CCL affiliates in the province were able to organize only small units. The United Automobile Workers, with help from the Teamsters, organized forty employees of the Ford Motor Company parts department in 1950. In 1951, the Newspaper Guild tried to organize reporters at the *Calgary Herald* but failed. One of the Guild members involved in the organizing effort was fired.[30]

In 1953, the United Steelworkers had two representatives in Alberta, Howard Mitchell and Jim Russell, surveying organizational possibilities. A year later, the union organized its first local at Westeel in Edmonton with a membership of about seventy. (A local existed in Edmonton in 1945 but went under.)

The Industrial Federation and Communist Expulsion

There was an obvious need in the industrial unions for some co-ordination of effort, both from an organizational and a political standpoint. In 1945, labour councils of CCL unions were set up in both Edmonton and Calgary and a year later a "continuation committee"—a provincial executive—was established to represent the industrial unions before the Social Credit government. Early in 1949, the provincial body was formalized as the Industrial Federation of Labour of Alberta at a meeting in Calgary with

Jack Hampson of the UPWA as president. At the time, its major affiliates were the UPWA, the UMW, the Canadian Brotherhood of Railway Employees and the Mine, Mill and Smelter Workers. Mine-Mill (the new name for the Western Federation of Miners) organized metal shops, Cominco's fertilizer plant and glass and clay products factories in Medicine Hat-Redcliffe.

There were also a number of smaller unions, including the Amalgamated Building and Construction Workers of Canada, an offshoot of a British union of carpenters which had existed in the province from the turn of the century. Under the wing of the CCL, it had taken on the rather thankless task of separating construction workers from their American craft unions and bringing them into an all-encompassing industrial union.

The Amalgamated didn't amount to much (although it did negotiate a few contracts), but it did provide a home for Jan Lakeman, one of the province's leading Communists. Lakeman had been expelled from his union and from the Canadian Labour Party in the late Twenties because of his Communist Party membership, a signal to the battle between Social Democrats and Communists during the first part of the Depression. In

those years, the Communists and their more moderate opponents were constantly at each others throats, but in the late Thirties, many moderate socialists were warily making common cause with their left-wing foes in the industrial organizing drives sweeping the continent. Conditions cooled, however, in 1939 when the Communists opposed Canada's entry into the war against Hitler. The reason had nothing to do with conditions in Canada but was dictated by the Communist International in Moscow. The Soviet Union, in the summer preceding the outbreak of war in Europe, signed a non-aggression pact with Germany which would give it time to marshall its resources for the war it knew very well was coming. Unfortunately, the Communist International decided that Communists all over the world should follow the line dictated by the treaty with Hitler. For two years, until the expected German invasion of the Soviet Union occurred, the Communists balked at even minimal support of the Canadian war effort. Then, in an abrupt about-face, with German troops advancing on Moscow, they became the most fervent patriots to be found, even to the point of pushing "no-strike" pledges in the unions they influenced. The traditional concerns

Women at work in a Calgary box plant, 1954.

of party members with the rights of workers all went by the boards as the Communists put everything they had into making a success of the war they had opposed for two years.

With the outpouring of patriotism and official government propaganda extolling the virtues of her Russian ally, Canadian Communists reached the pinnacle of their popularity and respectability, even managing to elect a member to the House of Commons. Relations with the social democrats were once again firmed up although the CCF was less than pleased with the Communist Party's support for Mackenzie King and the Liberals. The strange twist of Communist Party positions during the war would not be forgotten by CCF supporters in the labour movement when peace finally came. The gloves didn't come off immediately when the war ended, but gradually, both the Canadian Congress of Labour and the more conservative Trades and Labour Congress were swept into the wave of McCarthyism and cold-war hysteria. As was the case at the end of the first war, Bolshevism became the chief worry and witch-hunts were carried out with considerable vigour in Canada and the United States.

In Alberta, most of the Red-baiting was directed at two men: Jan Lakeman, from 1946 to 1949, the chairman of the continuation committee, and Bill Longridge, an official of Mine-Mill in Calgary. Mine-Mill was one of the major bases of Communist Party support in the labour movement, both in Alberta and nationally. The party still had a substantial following in the United Mine Workers but this element was held in close rein by Bob Livett and John L. Lewis. Membership in the party was, in fact, prohibited under the UMWA constitution.

The chief proponent of Red-baiting within the congress, or at least the person who personified it, was former Drumheller miner Pat Conroy who had risen through the ranks to become secretary-treasurer of the Congress. His chief lieutenant in Alberta was another former miner, Tom McCloy, the CCL organizer in the province, who was just as combative as his boss. At the 1948 CCL convention, when Conroy was challenged by a Drumheller miner to present his anti-Communist views to the miners in the valley, he said: "... I believe it is the job of this congress to clean Communists out of trade union business because our movement is a fighting movement and we cannot fight ... the Communists with one hand and the bosses with the other. To fight the boss, we must get rid of Communism."[31]

In Alberta, the showdown came in 1949 at the founding convention at the Industrial Federation. Conroy, McCloy and the leadership of District 18 had carefully prepared for the meeting. Conroy had dispatched Alex McAuslane, a CCL vice-president, and William Mahoney, a steelworkers

official, instrumental in beating back the Communists in their B.C. stronghold, to give McCloy a hand. The UMW leadership of Angus Morrison and Bob Livett had also done its part in ensuring that, as far as possible, only reliable delegates represented the union. The UPWA assisted by pressuring Jack Hampson, who had been the secretary of the continuation committee, to run against Lakeman for the presidency.[32] Hampson did so reluctantly as he was a personal friend of Lakeman. Hampson was most definitely not a Communist, or even a sympathizer, but he had earlier suggested to the congress that the anti-Communist "hysteria may be used to interfere with honest trade union activities."[33]

With the anti-Communist forces carefully marshalled by the congress, there was essentially no contest. "They cleaned house," Hampson said. First blood at the January convention was drawn over whether the federation should follow the national policy set by the CCL and endorse the CCF, a familiar battleground for the CPers and the social democrats almost from the time the congress was founded. The debate over the form of political action the industrial unions should follow moved in 1949 from the national to the Alberta stage and, at times, the Communists came up with some ingenious arguments. They couldn't very well come out and say they wanted the federation to support them so they cloaked their real position by saying that the movement should steer clear of supporting any political party. Their official stand was that labour should line up behind all "progressive forces," but at times, the Communists sounded more like the Wobblies and Sam Gompers. A resolution from one local said that "the individual member's right to his beliefs, be they religious or political, must at all times be respected."[34] The Communists had a head start on the issue because the resolutions committee was made up of Art Roberts, as chairman and Mine-Mill delegate Frank Rogess, as secretary. They proposed to the convention a substitute resolution which was basically an outline of party policy. Debate on the issue lasted three hours and culminated with Roberts leading his supporters from the hall, threatening, rather wistfully, in view of the hold Livett held on District 18, that the UMW would disaffiliate over the issue. The walkout came after CCF supporters had succeeded in defeating the substitute resolution, directing the resolutions committee to bring in a motion that reflected national congress policy—support for the CCF.

The margin of defeat for the Communists was only one vote but from then on, matters went from bad to worse. Hampson trounced Lakeman forty-five to twenty-two. The former CCL provincial president contested almost every other position for the executive and lost by the same margins; Longridge, however, managed to hold an executive council seat. The rout was complete. After the convention, McCloy wrote Conroy saying that "as promised, a complete job has been done in the removal of those who antagonized the acceptance of the national policy. It was certainly a great victory for one who has watched the score in this province for the last few years to see Lakeman and his colleagues defeated in each position they attempted to take by a 2 to 1 vote."[35]

McCloy, Mahoney and the UPWA had broken the back of the Communist Party in the Alberta section of the CCL and it would be given no opportunity to convalesce. The same year, Mine-Mill was expelled from the congress and however much the congress tried to dress up the reasons for it, the union was dumped solely because of the presence of Communists in leadership positions. Immediately after the expulsion, McCloy went about the province trying to woo Mine-Mill members back into other congress unions.

Following the 1950 convention of the federation, McCloy wrote Conroy, telling him that the meeting had been the quietest one he had witnessed in several years, "no doubt by consequence of absence of our red-tainted brothers."[36] McCloy and Conroy didn't take on the Communists by themselves, of course. They were aided by the press, the provincial government and the employers, all as interested as the CCL establishment in weeding out the "Commies" wherever they were found. The *Albertan* editorialized after the 1949 convention that "An important step has been taken toward clearing Communist influence from the whole labour movement in Alberta."[37] After the expulsion of Mine-Mill, the beleaguered union managed to keep its members at Cominco's fertilizer plant in Calgary, despite a raid by an American Federation of Labour affiliate which congratulated itself on its "firm anti-Communist policies." The *Calgary Herald* was not impressed with the Mine-Mill members' loyalty to their union and told them in an editorial that loyalty to their country was more important: "The national interest requires that a body under Communist influence should not be allowed to dominate a plant whose operations in wartime would be vital."[38]

In 1951, Alberta's Social Credit minister, responsible for civil defence, claimed there were between five hundred and six hundred Communist spies and potential saboteurs working in Alberta industry and urged employers to study carefully records of persons applying for jobs. In a speech to the Edmonton branch of the Canadian Manufacturers Association, he suggested that employees should be fingerprinted and tagged and that "off-colour" activities should be reported to the RCMP.[39] The same year, the labour minister revealed to the legislature that some employers had requested a change in the province's labour code prohibiting Communists from taking part in negotiations. The job of the Communists, J.L. Robinson said, was "to mislead, rather than lead, the workers. Their purpose is to use and seduce their fellow-travellers in the CCF and their purpose is finally to confuse and befuddle everyone."

Relations With Social Credit

It is traditional at labour conventions to give the labour minister a chance to speak but unwritten rules require that he limit his remarks to defending the government's record. At the 1950 convention of the Industrial Federation, J.L. Robinson, replying to criticism of the government, told delegates to "keep out of politics because it will destroy your effectiveness as a trade union movement and you will slowly become a political organization." (Perhaps the minister wouldn't have minded if the federation had endorsed Social Credit.) He was taken to task for interfering in the "internal affairs of the Canadian Congress of Labour."[40] Robinson, though, received a far different reception at the Alberta Federation of Labour convention when he told them the same thing two years earlier, even adding that politics shouldn't be discussed at all "at a convention of this kind." Instead of attacking the minister for not minding his own business, the president and secretary told delegates that during the 1948 election, no one could accuse the federation of "being the kite of any political organization."

For the Alberta Federation of Labour, the late Forties were a time of retreat from militancy and radicalism. So taken was the federation with Social Credit, free enterprise and labour peace that it even failed at times to defend trade union principles. Its rivals in the Industrial Federation believed their craft union colleagues had become the unofficial arm of the Social Credit party. Anna MacLaren, a vice-president of the AFL in that period, said the craft unions were very close to the government but that during the Fifties, the relationship began to sour. In 1954, the convention was moved to condemn the government for ignoring "practically all the requests which have emanated from our conventions in the past three years."[41]

The tone of the condemnation was muted but the AFL had come a long way from 1948 when it had endorsed an amendment to the labour act which set severe penalties for unions involved in illegal strikes. The most draconian measure provided that, in the event of an illegal strike, the contract between the union and the employer was automatically declared void. The act, Bill 91, came as a result of a strike by Mine-Mill at Medalta Potteries in Medicine Hat, the constituency of the labour minister. Amid some controversy, the strike was declared illegal and the company then tried to recruit strike-breakers who had to be escorted through picket lines by police. A supreme court injunction was granted, prohibiting union leaders from picketing, and several members were thrown in jail after a fight broke out on the line. The walkout had originally been called to back wage demands but as it wore on, the issue became the refusal of the company to take all the strikers back. After several months, strikers returned to work without a contract and Mine-Mill was defeated. Social Credit was determined that such a situation would not again arise in a province that prided itself on maintaining industrial peace.[42]

The CCL declared war in 1948 against Bill 91, calling a special conference of all its Alberta unions and taking the fight to the floor of the legislative chamber during committee debate. One mark of how seriously the Social Credit government took the labour movement was that the legislation was handled by the house agricultural committee. Some sectors of the AFL supported the industrial unions in the Bill 91 battle, notably the teamsters and civic employees, two groups who were to play an important role in moving the federation from its pro-Socred stance. The CCL's special conference was told by Lakeman and Hampson that the bill received:

> . . . . endorsation [by] two leading union officials, one the secretary of the Alberta Federation of Labour, the other a vice-president of the Trades and Labour Congress of Canada, Mr. Berg and Mr. Cushing. It was indeed a sordid picture to those of us present at the hearings to see the secretary of the Alberta Federation of Labour assume the entire responsibility for the defence of the reactionary piece of legislation.[43]

Berg later denied that he had defended the measure but said he had refrained from "taking a dogmatic position of opposing something that we knew was to be implemented."[44]

In 1950 Harry Boyse, then AFL president, said that for labour movement, "the day of strong-arm methods is past. Labour is a big boy now. Our dealings must be ever on a high and business-like level. Labour and government must work together." But the right-wing leadership of the federation, personified by Berg, Farmilo, Boyse and Sam Sligo, a street railway official from Calgary, came under pressure in the mid-Fifties from those who wanted to see the federation take more militant positions and reach an agreement with the industrial unions. Pat Lenihan said he led a move to replace the old leadership with Rob Rintoul,

another Calgary transit union official and a man of moderate political disposition, but, said Lenihan, better than the old guard. Lenihan was joined in the move by Bob Scott, a Calgary teamster who had been involved in the OBU, the 1920 Calgary packing-plant strike and the 1937 sit-down at Union Packers.[45] In 1950, Scott had taken issue on the floor with the remarks made by Boyse about the need for government and labour to work closely together. "If we hope to make greater achievements in the near future, my opinion is that we will have to get a bit firmer and start demanding action instead of requesting and also stop patting the government on the back."

Various factors combined to give the young turks in the AFL a boost into leadership positions. Unemployment had been increasing in the early Fifties and the Korean war was pushing up the cost of living, motivating both congresses to make a joint submission to the federal government calling for the introduction of price controls. As well, the Socred government was refusing to act on many of labour's concerns. One persistent bone of contention was the government's insistence on maintaining a forty-four-hour work week, even though the forty-hour week had been adopted in other provinces. Socred acceptance of company unionism rankled many, as did various decisions of the Board of Industrial Relations.

If any event can be seen as a turning point in the AFL's subservient attitude, it would be the provincial strike in 1954 by beer parlour workers. Up to that time, the Hotel and Restaurant Employees Union had succeeded in organizing most of the hotel workers in Alberta under a Rand formula union membership agreement where all employees, whether members of the union or not, are required to pay membership dues, on the grounds that all benefited from the gains made by the union. Early in 1954, a conciliation board recommended that hours in the industry be reduced from forty-four to forty without a reduction in take-home pay. But the Alberta Hotel Association was determined to keep its employees working a forty-four-hour week and break the union. It did. At its peak, the strike involved about eight hundred workers at fifty-five hotels in Edmonton, Calgary, Medicine Hat and Lethbridge. The *Calgary Herald* of June 3 reported that members of the hotel association were refusing to negotiate because they desired an open shop. Several days previous, the hotelmen reopened their beverage rooms with non-union help and shortly afterward six picketers were charged with assaulting strike-breakers. By mid-August, Edmonton strikers, who held out the longest, tried to return to work on the owners' terms but found themselves in the same position as tavern workers in other centres—the hotel operators were keeping strike-breakers on the pay-

Striking bartenders in Edmonton, 1954. The strike was broken by the hotel owners. The union never fully recovered from the setback but the strike did manage to heal wounds between the two federations of labour.

roll; many of the strikers found themselves blacklisted.[46]

The strike ended in complete defeat from which the union has never been able to recover, but there was a silver lining. The walkout was of such magnitude and over such an important principle to the labour movement—the open shop—that it forced both the AFL and the industrial federation to forget past differences. At both the municipal and provincial levels, joint action committees were set up to help the strikers. Increasingly, the two federations came to recognize that unity between the two bitterly-divided factions of the movement would be required if workers were to successfuly challenge both hostile employers and an unsympathetic government, a sentiment shared throughout the continent. In 1955, when the American Federation of Labour and the CIO merged, the two Alberta federations signed a no-raiding pact which ended the internecine rivalry that often left employers as prime beneficiaries. In 1956, the two Canadian congresses and all their subsidiary bodies, including the Alberta Federation of Labour and Industrial Federation of Labour, agreed to set aside differences and reunite the "House of Labour."

Two of the Alberta Federation of Labour's young turks took the two top positions in the newly-merged federation, Scott becoming secretary-treasurer and Charlie Gilbert, an Edmonton typographer, president. Within the pre-merger AFL, Scott had supported both the CCF and industrial unionism—unpopular causes in that body. Jack Hampson of the packinghouse workers became first vice-president and would head the federation after Gilbert's appointment to the compensation board.

The 1956 merger convention marked the end of an era for Alberta labour. It had been seventy years since the first trade unions were formed and the nature of the movement had undergone a radical change, reflecting the change that had transformed a frontier into a modern, urban, industrial society. In the early years of the movement, the railway workers and coal miners had been its heart, replaced in 1956 by packing plant employees and public employees. The only constant was the influence of construction unions, representing an industry that has continued in importance from the beginnings to the present.

Gone were two men who had represented the movement almost from the start. Alf Familo had died and Carl Berg was to die shortly thereafter. Gone also were the Communists, who had played such an integral part in the movement, both through the CP and before that, through the Socialist Party of Canada. Tom McCloy, Pat Conroy and shifts in the line of the party itself had ensured its role as an inconsequential sect within the new Alberta Federation of Labour.

Many of the major battles had been fought and won, but it would be a mistake to think the war was over. Employers would continue to view every victory by the labour movement as temporary.

Epilogue

Social Credit came to Alberta as a populist movement propelled to power by the economic crisis of the Depression. With the death of Aberhart and the passage of several years in office, Social Credit began to lose its patina of progressivism. And then came oil. Alberta has never been the same.

Social Credit and oil draped a heavy cloak of conservatism over politics in a province once known as a centre of radical thought (the CCF was first formed in Calgary; the Communist Party was well established). The labour movement was much affected by conservative orthodoxy and has taken a long time to shake it off.

The Alberta Federation of Labour began to move to less-conservative positions in the late Fifties, under the pressure of economic events such as inflation and depression and the growing strength of industrial unions. But as late as the mid-Sixties, the executive secretary of the federation could still propose that the labour movement cooperate with the Manning government in bringing in Billy Graham as a centennial project.

The major change in the movement since the merger of 1956 has been the growing power and influence of public sector unions. Civic employee unions had been formed in the ferment of the First World War but existed as independent and unconnected locals chartered by the Trades and Labour Congress. The Civil Service Association was organized at about the same time but could never gather enough strength to challenge a succession of governments determined to deny collective bargaining to their employees. In October, 1950, municipal employees established an Alberta joint council which, by 1954, under the leadership of Pat Lenihan, represented about 3,000 members. In that year, the council changed its name to the Alberta Federation of Public Employees.[1]

The merger of the two federations in 1956, for the first time placed unions of the old TLC federation in the position of being affiliated with a labour movement which endorsed a political party — the CCF. That caused particular problems for the Civil Service Association (CSA), which withdrew in 1958. A report to the 1958 CSA convention on the goings-on at the AFL meeting earlier showed the sentiment of government employees at the time: "Throughout the convention, the provincial government, especially the department of industries and labour, constantly came under fire. Attacks were made against the person of the Honourable R. Reirson (the minister) and Mr. Kenneth Pugh (the BIR chairman) and were more vitriolic than usual."[2] The disaffiliation of the CSA meant an immediate membership drop for the Alberta Federation of Labour from 35,000 to 30,000.

The labour movement had, in varying forms, been supporting the CCF for some years but outside of Saskatchewan, the party had met with little success. That was even more the case in Socred Alberta, where only Elmer Roper and a few others ever managed to win seats in the legislature. In the late Fifties, following the party's disastrous showing in the 1958 Diefenbaker sweep, the CLC called for the formation of a "new party" to grow out of the CCF and replace it. In 1961, the New Democratic Party was born with the labour movement as one of the parents. In Alberta, Neil Reimer became the provincial leader but had even less success than Elmer Roper had as head of the old CCF. Reimer couldn't even get into legislature.

In 1963, moves toward centralization by municipal and school-board employees reached the national level with the formation of the Canadian Union of Public Employees (CUPE). Several years later, the federal government gave its public employees collective bargaining rights. The rapid expansion of the service and government sectors of the economy reshaped the labour movement. As the growth of mass-production industry and its organization had swelled the ranks of labour with new members, so too did the growth of the white-collar sector. The significance and impact of this trend is yet to be felt.

Government employees had never been noted labour militants (although they played leading roles in the general strikes of 1919), but by the Sixties this was no longer the case. The change reached even the recesses of the Social Credit bureaucracy. In the early Seventies, although prohibited from doing so by law, liquor board and hospital workers, represented by the Civil Service Association, went on strike. The association reaffiliated with the federation of labour and changed its name to the Alberta Union of Provincial Employees. It is now the largest union in the province and with CUPE represents more than 40 percent of federation membership.

Outside of government service, where much of the growth has been in existing units, the labour movement in Alberta continued to have an uphill fight organizing industrial workers. OCAW in particular has been stymied in organizing in its principal area of jurisdiction. The beginning of oil sands exploitation by Sun Oil's Great Canadian Oil Sands (GCOS) at Fort McMurray in the mid-Sixties gave the union a large potential membership base but one it hasn't been able to enfold. The organizing attempts at GCOS lasted for several years but victory was finally claimed by a company union — the McMurry Independent Oil Workers. Gene Mitchell, now the executive secretary of the federation, was one of the organizers OCAW sent to the northeastern boom town and tells stories of being barred from company property and trailer camps where the workers were living. The union made several applications for certification to the Board of Industrial Relations but all were unsuccessful.

In the late Sixties, OCAW finally was able to organize a refinery belonging to the majors — the Imperial Oil plant in Calgary — but the plant was later shut down as part of a company reorganization plan. The workers and the union offered to purchase it but Esso turned the offer down.

Edmonton's Texaco refinery is today the only refinery operated by one of the huge multinational oil companies in which the employees belong to OCAW. There are several hundred gas plants in Alberta but only a tiny fraction of them are organized.

The opening of the Japanese market and the energy crisis has meant a slight revitalization of the province's coal industry but the coal fields are still divided territory for trade unionism. Miners at Grande Cache, north of Edson, belong not to the United Mine Workers but to the Steelworkers. The UMW has a local in the Crowsnest Pass and one in the Coal Branch while workers at a large strip mine east of Edmonton belong to a directly-chartered local of the Canadian Labour Congress.

The labour movement in Alberta is today a far different creature than it was either in the heady days of 1919 or the darkness of the post-Second World War period. No longer are the workers of Alberta among the most militant and politically radical in the country, but they have also come a long way from the time when Social Credit was their unofficial political party.

Some of what was lost during the Second World War and late Forties and early Fifties has been regained. The death of the coal industry and technological change on the railways took away two of the most militant groups of workers in the province — the miners and machinists— but that is only a partial answer to the question of what happened to one of the most militant and radical movements in the country.

The bitterest battles in Alberta — the 1906 Lethbridge coal strike, the 1908 and 1918 shopcraft and freight-handlers dispute, the miners' strikes in support of the OBU, the 1932 Crowsnest Pass strike and the 1937 sit-downs in the packing plants — were all fought over one principle — the right of working men and women to have a union to bargain on their behalf. In the organized sector (still very small — just over 30 percent) of the province, those battles have, by and large, been won. Trade unions that have established those rights are no longer fighting just to exist — their role today is defending what has been won and making advances along lines already established.

Working class militancy does not exist by and of itself. It is a response to conditions of work and life. The 1919 general strikes were not the work of paid Bolshevik agents but occurred because of rising prices, employer resistance to trade unionism and collective bargaining, the fear of unemployment and government repression. Any such combinations of circumstances could again build the kind of movement that existed in Alberta before the Second World War. Cost of living increases in the Seventies, combined with federal government controls on wages led the Canadian Labour Congress in 1976 to call the first national general strike in Canadian history. Even though it was only a one-day stoppage and was not called a general strike, it showed that working men and women and their leaders are still capable of putting up a fight. In Alberta, almost 50,000 workers participated in the October 14 Day of Protest.

The solidly-entrenched construction unions in Alberta are now being shaken from complacency by a growing move toward "right-to-work" legislation by major contractors. "Right-to-work" has little to do with providing full-time employment and much more to do with breaking the trade unions by denying workers, once they have established a union, the right to say that only union members can work for that employer. Such legislation harkens back to the days of Mackenzie King as the one-man federal labour department with his "non-discrimination" clauses — putting membership in a union in the same category as belonging to the Kiwanis Club. In American states where "right-to-work" legislation has been enacted, average wages are generally far below the national average.

The federal government has been rethinking the wisdom of the collective bargaining rights granted to its employees in the Sixties, and provincial and municipal workers are faced with budget-imposed wage increases that fail to match cost of living rises. Workers will fight when they feel their rights and interests are under attack. That is the history of labour, in Alberta as elsewhere. And employers, who still have most of the power in the working world, are loathe to give up even a little of that power without a battle.

But the real fight is still in the unorganized sector, where workers are denied even the basic rights won over the years by the labour movement. For unorganized workers wishing to join unions, the basis issue is still at stake— the very right to belong to a union.

In the spring of 1976, employees at CJOC Television in Lethbridge went on strike. Before they were organized— as a local of the National Association of Broadcast Employees and Technicians — many were receiving only the minimum wage and although wages were certainly high on their list of bargaining priorities, the main issue was their right to have a union at all. Television and radio stations, like modern refineries, don't require a large and well-trained staff to operate. Supervisory staff can handle the vital functions and the operation can limp along while strike-breakers receive on-the-job training. That is what happened at CJOC. The station, controlled by the Southam interests that have the media in Alberta pretty well wrapped up, was able to find people willing to cross picket lines, and the strike, more than three years later, is still on and will probably never end. The union was undeniably beaten.

In March of 1977, more than sixty employees of Parkland Nursing Home, most of them women, walked off the job in their first dispute with their employer. The group had recently been organized by CUPE and wanted a raise from the minimum wage most had been receiving to the $4.32 an hour that workers employed by other Parkland homes in Alberta were receiving. But as the strike dragged on, a more basic issue prevented a settlement. The company said it would settle with the union but that a number of employees would not be taken back. The company's proposal received the backing of the province's labour minister. The workers have faced the same alliance of foes that often faced workers in Alberta many years ago. The employer stood firm in its position that only a blacklist would settle the dispute, picketers complained of harassment by police and the courts became involved.

Early in the dispute, when picketing was making recruitment of strike-breakers difficult, the Alberta Supreme Court granted Parkland an injunction which prohibited workers on the line from singing, placed tight limits on the number of people who could be on the line and then went one step further — forcing the much-reduced picket line to form across the street from the nursing home, in front of a row of apartments. The provincial government has funnelled several thoughsand dollars a day in subsidies to the privately-owned home and suggested that the workers agree to a blacklist, all the while claiming neutrality.

Some things never change. A feature of strikes by CPR employees and miners at the turn of the century was the involvement of government agencies in the side of employers, determined to keep workers in their company-appointed places. Eighty years later, the same combination of forces is at work to deny workers the right to belong to a union.

Alex Goruk, looking back on the gains won since packing plant employees organized, thinks about the bottles of whiskey purchased for foremen, sexual harassment of female employees, the shape-up and crews brought into work Christmas Day and laid off the next. "Them days are gone forever. Nobody buys the boss any booze, nobody is going to date the boss to keep their jobs. You're humanized today, you can walk in there, lift your head up and you can tell the foreman, o.k., I'm working too hard, or whatever. You can stand toe-to-toe to him and talk to him without fear of getting fired. And this is what unions have done. We have created an atmosphere where everybody is proud to be a human being and is, in most cases, treated like a human being."

For Alex Goruk, Harvey Murphy and others, the labour movement in Alberta was built, not just to increase wages, but to win respect for workers. In 1978, almost a hundred years after the first local was established in the province, many are still waiting.

1. CLC Papers, Vol. 8, mg. 28 I103, Public Archives of Canada.
2. Report of delegates to 1958 AFL convention, Farmilo Papers, Alberta Archives.

Notes

Notes, CHAPTER ONE

1. Vernon C. Fowke, *The National Policy and The Wheat Economy* (Toronto: University of Toronto Press, 1973), pp. 1-69, 76-77.
2. R.C. MacLeod, "Canadianizing the West: The Northwest Mounted Police as Agents of the N.P., 1873-1905," in *Essays in Western History*, L.H. Thomas, ed. (Edmonton: University of Alberta Press, 1976), p. 104.
3. L.G. Thomas, ed., *The Prairie West to 1905: A Canadian Sourcebook* (Toronto: Oxford University Press, 1975), p. 208.
4. Gustavus Myers, *A History of Canadian Wealth* (Toronto: James Lorimer & Co., 1972), pp. 159-160.
5. John Peter Turner, *The Northwest Mounted Police, 1873-1893* (Ottawa: King's Printer, 1950), 2:7; RCMP Papers, vol. 2947, Public Archives of Canada.
6. Turner, p. 16.
7. *Calgary Herald,* Dec. 12, 19, 1883.
8. Turner, p. 31.
9. Ibid., pp. 149-153.
10. Ibid., pp. 27, 273.
11. Martin Robin, *Rush for the Spoils* (Toronto: McClelland & Stewart, 1972), pp. 63-71; Fowke, pp. 53-54.
12. Thomas, p. 208.
13. Ibid.
14. Canada, Sessional Papers, "Commission to Inquire into Complaints Respecting the Treatment of Labourers in the Crowsnest Pass Railway," 1898, 90A, pp. 7-8, National Library of Canada.
15. Ibid., p. 12.
16. Ibid., p. 8.
17. Canada, "Commission to Inquire into the Deaths of McDonald and Fraser on the Crowsnest Pass Railway," 1899, pp. 40-42, Department of Labour Library.
18. Ibid., p. 2.
19. Ibid., p. 18-19.
20. Ibid., pp. 13-15.
21. Ibid., pp. 15-16.
22. Ibid., p. 18.
23. Ibid., pp. 18-19.
24. Jack Williams, *The Story of Unions in Canada* (Toronto: J.M. Dent & Sons, 1975), pp. 43-51; Charles Lipton, *The Trade Union Movement of Canada, 1827-1959* (Toronto: NC Press, 1973), pp. 68-72; Sidney Lens, *The Labour Wars* (Garden City: Anchor Press/Doubleday, 1974), pp. 64-67; Douglas R. Kennedy, *The Knights of Labour in Canada* (London: University of Western Ontario, 1956), p. 35.
25. CLC Papers, mfm. M2214, vols. 248, 255, Public Archives of Canada. (Most of the information on the organization of the early trade unions comes from this source.)
26. CLC Papers, vol. 255, Public Archives of Canada.
27. Robert H. Babcock, *Gompers in Canada: A Study in American Continentalism Before the First World War* (Toronto: University of Toronto Press, 1974), passim.

Notes, CHAPTER TWO

1. *Calgary Herald,* June 21, 1901.
2. Ibid., Aug. 31, 1901.
3. Lipton, p. 100.
4. Ibid., p. 101.
5. Martin Robin, *Radical Politics and Canadian Labour* (Kingston: Industrial Relations Centre, 1968), p. 71 fn., pp. 72-73.
6. Paul Phillips, *No Power Greater—A Century of Labour in B.C.* (Vancouver: B.C. Federation of Labour, 1967), p. 40.
7. Lipton, p. 102.
8. Stuart Jamieson, *Times of Trouble: Labour Unrest and Industrial Conflict in Canada, 1900-66,* Task Force on Industrial Relations, Study 22 (Ottawa: Information Canada, 1968), p. 116; Bernard Ostry and Henry Ferns, *The Age of Mackenzie King* (Toronto: James Lorimer, 1976), pp. 59-63; Phillips, pp. 38-41; Robin, pp. 71-73.
9. Ostry & Ferns, p. 61.
10. Records of the Department of Labour, vol. 40, Public Archives of Canada.
11. *Calgary Herald,* Aug. 6, 1908; Elizabeth Taraska, "The Calgary Craft Union Movement, 1900-1920," M.A. Thesis, 1975, pp. 16-24, University of Calgary: Department of History.
12. Records of the Department of Labour, vol. 68, Public Archives of Canada.
13. *Calgary Herald,* Oct. 6, 1908.
14. John Blue, *Alberta Past and Present* (Chicago: Pioneer Historical Publishing, 1924), vol. 1, pp. 369-370; UMW Papers, Glenbow Archives, Calgary.
15. Warren Caragata, Interview with Art Roberts, 1978, Alberta Archives.
16. Alberta, Report of the "Royal Commission on the Coal Mining Industry in the Province of Alberta," 1907, Alberta Archives.
17. United Mine Workers, early agreements, in possession of author.
18. Alberta, 1907 Coal Commission, Alberta Archives.
19. Alberta Federation of Labour, Proceedings of the 1930 Convention, Department of Labour Library; *Wedge,* Edmonton, Sept. 3, 1921, Farmilo Papers, Alberta Archives.
20. Alberta, 1907 Coal Commission, Alberta Archives.
21. Blue, vol. 1, pp. 366-368.
22. MacInnis Collection, box 33, file 4, University of British Columbia; CLC Papers, M2214, vol. 255, Public Archives of Canada.
23. RCMP Papers, vol. 141, file 580, Public Archives of Canada.
24. Ibid., file 577.
25. Lorne Thompson, "The Rise of Labour Unionism in Alberta," typescript, 1965, p. 19, Alberta Archives.
26. Ibid., p. 23.
27. Ibid., p. 28.
28. Williams, p. 187.
29. Ibid., p. 189.
30. *Lethbridge Herald,* Dec. 29, 1976.
31. Ibid.
32. *Labour Gazette,* Ottawa, 1906-1907, 7:647, 660.
33. *King Papers,* vol. 16, Public Archives of Canada.
34. Ibid., p. 5440.
35. Ibid., pp. 5441, 5442.
36. Ibid., p. 4371.
37. Ibid., pp. 149-153.
38. *Labour Gazette,* Ottawa, 1906-1907, 7:647, 660.
39. Sources for formation dates of various locals from: Thompson; Taraska; CLC Papers, mfm. M2214, vols. 248, 255, Public Archives of Canada. Material on 1903 strike from: Thompson, pp. 56-59; Taraska, pp. 3-4.
40. Alberta Federation of Labour, Proceedings of the 1931 Convention, Department of Labour Library.
41. *Bond of Brotherhood,* June 5, 1903; Records of the Department of Labour, vols. 40, 41, Public Archives of Canada.
42. Meagher Papers, Alberta Archives.
43. Calgary Trades and Labour Council, "Souvenir of the Twenty-Seventh Annual Convention of the Trades and Labour Congress of Canada," 1911, p. 93, Alberta Archives; Records of the Department of Labour, vol. 300, file 3537, Public Archives of Canada; CLC Papers, vol. 255, Public Archives of Canada; Thompson, pp. 95, 96; Edmonton Trades and Labour Council, *Labour Day Annual,* 1958, p. 30; Taraska, p. 5; Thompson, p. 82.
44. *Bond of Brotherhood,* Dec. 19, 1903; Taraska, p. 5.

Notes, CHAPTER THREE

1. Accounts of the disaster are taken from: *District Ledger,* June 19, 20, 27, 1914; Warren Caragata, Interview with Charles Kane, 1978, Alberta Archives; Warren Caragata, Interview with Emile Blas, 1978, Alberta Archives.
2. See also: *Edmonton Capital,* Jan. 14, 1911.
3. United Mine Workers, List of Fatalities, 1904-1963, Glenbow Archives, Calgary.
4. Alberta, 1907 Coal Commission, Alberta Archives.
5. Caragata, Interview with Art Roberts, 1978, Alberta Archives.
6. Warren Caragata, Interview with Pete Youschok, 1978, Alberta Archives.
7. Warren Caragata, Interview with Harry Gate, 1978, Alberta Archives.
8. Alberta, Report of the "Alberta Coal Commission," 1926, pp. 283-284, Alberta Archives.
9. Alberta, 1907 Coal Commission, Alberta Archives.
10. Ibid.
11. Alberta, Workmen's Compensation Act, 1908.
12. Alberta, 1907 Coal Commission, Alberta Archives.
13. Andrew Ross McCormack, *The Origins and Extent of Western Labour Radicalism, 1896-1919,* Ph.D. thesis, 1973, pp. 197-198, University of Western Ontario: Department of History. Later published as *Rebels, Reformers and Revolutionaries.*
14. Alberta Federation of Labour, Proceedings of the 1912 (Founding) Convention, Department of Labour Library.
15. Alberta Federation of Labour, Proceedings of the 1913 Convention, Department of Labour Library.
16. Martin Robin, *Radical Politics and Canadian Labour* (Kingston: Industrial Relations Centre, Queen's University, 1968), p. 108; Alberta Federation of Labour, Proceedings of the 1913 Convention, Department of Labour Library.
17. Alberta Federation of Labour, Proceedings of the 1914 Convention, Department of Labour Library.
18. King Papers, vol. 7, p. 6638, Public Archives of Canada.
19. Bradley Rudin, "Mackenzie King and the Writing of Canada's Anti-Labour Laws," *Canadian Dimension,* Winnipeg, Jan. 1972, vol. 8, nos. 4-5.
20. Jamieson, pp. 128, 129.
21. King Papers, mfm. C1910, p. 11081; mfm. C1911, pp. 11939, 11940, Public Archives of Canada.
22. Jamieson, p. 132; UMW, early agreements, in possession of author, Records of the Department of Labour, vol. 298, file 3330, Public Archives of Canada.
23. Jamieson, p. 77.
24. *Edmonton Capital,* July 6, 1912.
25. Irving Abella and David Millar, *The Canadian Worker in the Twentieth Century* (Toronto: Oxford University Press), pp. 65-66.
26. O.T. Martynowych, "Early Ukrainian-Canadian Socialists," Toronto, 1976, vol. 1, no. 1.
27. Blue, vol. 1, p. 218.
28. Abella & Millar, p. 61.
29. RCMP Papers, vol. 430, file 513, Public Archives of Canada.
30. Martynowych, p. 29.
31. Abella & Millar, pp. 65-66.
32. RCMP Papers, vol. 430, file 513, Public Archives of Canada.
33. Abella & Millar, pp. 62-63.
34. Blue, p. 217.
35. Alberta, "The Case for Alberta," 1938, p. 27, Farmilo Papers, Alberta Archives.
36. James G. MacGregor, *A History of Alberta* (Edmonton: Hurtig Publishers, 1972), p. 193.
37. Calgary Trades and Labour Council, "Souvenir of the Twenty-Seventh Annual Convention of the Trades and Labour Congress of Canada," 1911, p. 93, Alberta Archives.
38. Henry C. Klassen, "Life in Frontier Calgary," A.W. Rasporich, ed., *Western Canada Past and Present* (Calgary: McClelland and Stewart West, 1975), pp. 47-48.
39. Taraska, p. 35.
40. *Edmonton Capital,* Oct. 9, 1912.
41. MacGregor, pp. 238-239; *Searchlight,* Calgary, Oct. 22, 1920.
42. Alberta Provincial Police, 1918 Annual Report, Alberta Archives.
43. Canada, Report of the "Royal Commission on Industrial Relations," (Mathers Commission), 1919, p. 908, National Library of Canada.
44. Blue, vol. 1, p. 391; CLC Papers, vol. 255, Public Archives of Canada.
45. Taraska, p. 35.
46. *Edmonton Capital,* Jan. 30, 1914.
47. Lens, p. 179.
48. Ibid., p. 175.
49. Joyce Maupin, *Labour Heroines, Ten Women Who Led the Struggle* (Berkeley: Union WAGE Educational Committee, 1974), p. 21.
50. MG 31, B8, p. 21, Public Archives of Canada.
51. Records of the Department of Labour, vol. 300, file 3604, Public Archives of Canada.

Notes, CHAPTER FOUR

1. Records of the Department of Labour, vol. 3009, file 151, Department of Labour Library.
2. Ibid.
3. Laurier Papers, pp. 190620-190623, Public Archives of Canada; *Toronto Globe,* Feb. 17, 1914.
4. Industrial Workers of the World Records, Proceedings of the 8th Annual Convention, 1913, p. 2, University of British Columbia.
5. MacGregor, p. 220; McCormack, p. 328.
6. Laurier Papers, pp. 190622, 190623.
7. Records of the Department of Labour, vol. 3009, file 151, Department of Labour Library.
8. McCormack, p. 324.
9. Edgar McInnis, *Canada, a Political and Social History* (Toronto: Rinehart and Co., 1947), p.406.
10. Ibid., pp. 409-410.
11. Report of Unemployment Conference, Calgary, 1914, Department of Labour Library.
12. CLC Papers, vol. 112, Public Archives of Canada; McCormack, p. 347; Minutes of Edmonton Trades and Labour Council, Aug. 3, 1914, Alberta Archives.
13. Report of the 1915 Convention of the United Mine Workers, District 18, Farmilo Papers, Alberta Archives.
14. Taraska, pp. 47-48.
15. Records of the Department of Labour, vol. 307, Public Archives of Canada.
16. McInnis, p. 413.
17. McCormack, pp. 350-351, 363; Taraska, p. 52.
18. Robin, pp. 120-122.
19. McCormack, p. 364.
20. Alberta Federation of Labour, Proceedings of the 1917 Convention, Department of Labour Library.
21. Alberta Federation of Labour, Proceedings of the 1918 Annual Convention, Department of Labour Library.
22. J.M. Beck, *Pendulum of Power: Canada's Federal Elections* (ScarboroughL Prentice-Hall of Canada, 1968), p. 136; McCormack, pp. 379-391; Parliamentary Guide, 1918, pp. 235-237.
23. McInnis, p. 411; Lipton, p. 167.
24. Michael Bliss, *Sir Joseph Flavelle, Bart* (Toronto: MacMillan, 1978), p. 298.
25. McCormack, p. 40; McInnis, p. 408.
26. Lipton, p. 167; Bliss, p. 356.
27. Records of the Department of Labour, Strikes and Lockouts Finding Aid, Public Archives of Canada; Canada, Mathers Commission, pp. xxvii, xxx, xxxi, National Library of Canada; Jamieson, p. 159.
28. Jamieson, p. 162.
29. Martynowych, p. 33.
30. Borden Papers, vol. 213, pp. 120234A, 120263-120266, Public Archives of Canada.
31. Ibid., p. 120340.
32. Jamieson, p. 165; David J. Bercuson, *Fools and Wise Men, the Rise and Fall of the One Big Union* (Toronto: McGraw-Hill Ryerson, 1978), pp. 196-197.
33. Bercuson, p. 68; Warren Caragata, Interview with Nicholas Christophers, 1977, Alberta Archives.
34. Bercuson, p. 51.
35. Records of the Department of Labour, vol. 307, Public Archives of Canada.
36. Ibid.
37. McCormack, p. 374.
38. Ibid.
39. Ibid., p. 375.
40. Records of the Department of Labour, vol. 309, file 168, Public Archives of Canada.
41. Taraska, pp. 66-72.
42. Ibid., p. 69.
43. Ibid., p. 70.
44. McCormack, p. 423.
45. Ibid., pp. 422-423; *CUPW* (Canadian Union of Postal Workers), Ottawa, Oct.-Nov. 1977.
46. Alberta Federation of Labour, Proceedings of the 1919 Convention, Department of Labour Library.
47. RCMP Papers, vol. 1931, Public Archives of Canada.
48. *Searchlight,* Calgary, Dec. 19, 1919.

Notes, CHAPTER FIVE

1. Canada, Mathers Commission, Testimony of Mrs. George Corse, p. 635, Department of Labour Library.
2. Alberta Federation of Labour, Proceedings of the 1919 Convention, Department of Labour Library.
3. Ibid.
4. Ibid.
5. Proceedings of the Western Canada Labour Conference, 1919, Farmilo Papers, Alberta Archives.
6. Warren Caragata, Interview with Elmer Roper, 1977, Alberta Archives.
7. Bercuson, p. 132.
8. McCormack, p. 464.
9. Records of the Department of Labour, vol. 313, file 153, Public Archives of Canada.
10. Borden Papers, vol. 113, file OC 564 (1) (B), pp. 61764, 61766, Public Archives of Canada.
11. Williams, pp. 249-250.
12. RCMP Papers, vol. 1931, file 2.2, Public Archives of Canada.
13. Ibid., vol. 580, file 438.
14. Bercuson, pp. 198-200; *Searchlight,* Calgary, Nov. 14, 1919.
15. Bercuson, p. 201.
16. *Searchlight,* Calgary, Dec. 6, 1919.
17. Ibid., Apr. 9, 1920.
18. Records of the Department of Labour, vol. 323, file 357, Public Archives of Canada.
19. Williams, p. 251.

Notes, CHAPTER SIX

1. *Labour Organizations in Canada, 1974-1975* (Ottawa: Information Canada, 1975), p. xviii; Blue, pp. 381, 391, 392.
2. George Brandak, Interview with W.T. Aiken, 1968, Oral History Collection, Alberta Archives; S.J. Frankel, *Staff Relations in the Civil Service: The Canadian Experience* (Montreal: McGill University Press, 1962), pp. 236, 238; *Alberta Labour News,* Dec. 3, 1927.
3. Blue, vol. 1, pp. 391-392; Thompson, pp. 104-105.
4. *Edmonton Bulletin,* July 10, 1916.
5. Records of the Department of Labour, vol. 305, file 67, Public Archives of Canada.
6. Canada, Mathers Commission, Testimony of Mrs. George Corse, p. 635, Department of Labour Library.
7. Records of the Department of Labour, vol. 371, file 180, Public Archives of Canada.
8. Warren Caragata, Interview with Anna MacLaren, 1978, Alberta Archives.
9. IWW Records, University of British Columbia.
10. Records of the Department of Labour, vol. 318, file 426, Public Archives of Canada.
11. Patrick Gorman to Warren Caragata, Apr. 10, 1978, Alberta, Archives.
12. Records of the Department of Labour, vol. 322, file 290; vol. 323, file 376, Public Archives of Canada.
13. Alberta, 1926 Coal Commission, acc. 64.11, boxes 2, 3, exhibit 30, file 52, Alberta Archives; Sources for district negotiations of 1922 and 1924: Jamieson, pp. 204-205; Alberta, 1926 Coal Commission, pp. 198-201, Alberta Archives; Allen Seager, "A History of the Mine Workers Union of Canada, 1925-1936, "M.A. thesis, 1977, McGill University, pp. 21-32.
14. Alberta, 1926 Coal Commission, Testimony of John Maddison, p. 1115, Alberta Archives.
15. Seager, p. 44.
16. Communist Party Papers, pp. 10 C 2155-2157, Ontario Archives.
17. Seager, pp. 38-48.
18. Mine Workers Union of Canada, Proceedings of the 1926 Convention, Department of Labour Library.
19. Communist Party Papers, p. 6B 1012, Ontario Archives.
20. Mine Workers Union of Canada, Proceeding of the 1926 Convention, Department of Labour Library.
21. Seager, p. 74.
22. Alberta Provincial Police, 1928 Annual Report, Alberta Archives.
23. Communist Party Papers, p. 6B 1044, Ontario Archives.

Notes, CHAPTER SEVEN

1. Warren Caragata, Interview with John Dec, 1977, Alberta Archives.
2. Premiers Papers, files 512, 1011, Alberta Archives.
3. Warren Caragata, Interview with Bob Atkin, 1978, Alberta Archives.
4. Premiers Papers, file 518, Alberta Archives.
5. Ibid.
6. "The Case for Alberta," pp. 325, 328, 329.
7. Warren Caragata, Interview with Bob Basken, 1977, Alberta Archives.
8. The Case for Alberta, p. 109.
9. Alberta, "Advisory Committee on Unemployment Relief," 1930, HD 5730, A21, p. 5, Department of Labour Library.
10. Interview with Anna MacLaren.
11. Smith Papers, Glenbow Archives, Calgary.
12. Premiers Papers, file 520, Alberta Archives.
13. Ibid., file 492; *The Canadian Labour Defender* (Canadian Labour Defence League), Toronto, June 1931.
14. *Medicine Hat News,* June 18, 1931.
15. Premiers Papers, files 509, 214, Alberta Archives.
16. Warren Caragata, Interview with Pat Lenihan, 1978, Alberta Archives.
17. Alberta Provincial Police, 1930 Annual Report, Alberta Archives.
18. Interview with Pete Youschok.
19. *Unity* (Workers Unity League), Jan.-Feb. 1936.
20. Alberta Provincial Police, 1925 Annual Report, Alberta Archives.
21. Communist Party Papers, p. 3A 2310, Ontario Archives.
22. Premier Papers, file 512, Alberta Archives.
23. Records of the Department of Labour, vol. 348, file 51, Public Archives of Canada.
24. *Edmonton Journal,* June 15, 1931.
25. "Down with the Brownlee Government," Political Pamphlet Collection, Glenbow Archives, Calgary.
26. *Alberta Labour News,* Dec. 24, 1932.
27. Records of the Department of Labour, vol. 368, file 61; vol. 374, file 32. Public Archives of Canada.
28. Bennett Papers, mfm. M1454, p. 494972, Public Archives of Canada.
29. Canada, Final Report of the "Unemployment Relief Scheme for the Care of Single, Homeless Men," vol. 1, p. 20; vol. 1, app. 10, Department of Labour Library.
30. Ibid.
31. *Ottawa Citizen,* June 10, 1935.
32. *Toronto Mail and Empire,* June 11, 1935.
33. *Toronto Star,* June 11, 1935.
34. Ronald Liversedge, *Recollection of the On To Ottawa Trek* (Toronto: McClelland and Stewart, 1973), p. x.
35. Ibid., pp. 111-112.
36. Regina Riot Commission, mfm. M1186-1188, pp. 113-122, Public Archives of Canada.
37. Bennett Papers, mfm. M1455, pp. 496209, 497246, Public Archives of Canada.
38. Ibid.
39. Liversedge, p. 253.
40. Records of the Department of Labour, vol. 347, file 36; vol. 351, files 58, 60; vol. 365, file 246, Public Archives of Canada.
41. Ivan Avakumovic, *The Communist Party of Canada, A History* (Toronto: McClelland and Stewart, 1975), p. 70.
42. Interview with Harvey Murphy, David Millar Collection, Public Archives of Canada.
43. Premiers Papers, file 518, Alberta Archives.
44. *Unity* (Workers Unity League), Jan.-Feb. 1936.
45. Alberta Provincial Police, 1930 Annual Report, Alberta Archives; Communist Party Papers, pp. 1A 8653, 21H 1046, Ontario Archives; Seager, pp. 97-105.
46. *Lethbridge Herald,* June 15, 1974.
47. Seager, p. 134.
48. Ibid.
49. *Calgary Albertan,* June 11, 1932.
50. *Edmonton Journal,* May 18, 1932.
51. Ibid.
52. *Edmonton Bulletin,* May 8, 1932.
53. Bennett Papers, mfm. M989, pp. 94846-94861, Public Archives of Canada.
54. *Edmonton Journal,* Aug. 20, 1932.
55. Seager, p. 160.
56. Interview with Harvey Murphy, David Millar Collection, Public Archives of Canada.
57. Seager, p. 168.
58. Alberta Federation of Labour, Proceedings of the 1937 Convention, Department of Labour Library.
59. Allen Seager, Interview with Pete Meroniuk, 1977, Glenbow Archives.
60. Records of the Department of Labour, vol. 386, file 54, Public Archives of Canada; CLC Papers, vol. 45, Public Archives of Canada.
61. CLC Papers, vol. 49, Public Archives of Canada; Records of the Department of Labour, vol. 376, file 51, Public Archives of Canada.
62. Parliamentary Guide, 1936, pp. 395-401.
63. Alberta, *These are the Facts: An Authentic Record of Alberta's Progress, 1935-48* (Edmonton: Alberta Publicity Office), Political Pamphlet Collection, Glenbow Archives, Calgary; Alberta Federation of Labour, Proceedings of the 1937 Convention, Department of Labour Library.
64. Premiers Papers, file 805, Alberta Archives.

Notes, CHAPTER EIGHT

1. Williams, pp. 159-163.
2. Warren Caragata, Interview with Dave Graham, 1978, Alberta Archives.
3. Records of the Department of Labour, vol. 394, file 367, Public Archives of Canada.
4. CLC Papers, vol. 132, Public Archives of Canada.
5. *Edmonton Bulletin,* Aug. 31, 1949.
6. Warren Caragata, Interview with Mike Sekora, 1977, Alberta Archives.
7. "The Case for Alberta," p. 28.
8. Warren Caragata, Interview with Jack Hampson, 1978, Alberta Archives.
9. Records of the Department of Labour, vol. 3006, file 125, Department of Labour Library; Premiers Papers, file 929, Alberta Archives.
10. Records of the Department of Labour, vol. 385, files 69, 70, Public Archives of Canada; Warren Caragata, Interview with Kathleen Brooks, 1977, Alberta Archives.
11. File LR 999, Alberta Board of Industrial Relations, Edmonton.
12. Premiers Papers, file 929, Alberta Archives; Records of the Department of Labour, vol. 436, file 80, Public Archives of Canada.
13. Records of the Department of Labour, vol. 436, file 80, Public Archives of Canada.
14. CFAW (Canadian Food and Allied Workers) Papers, vol. 7, Public Archives of Canada.
15. Ibid.; *Edmonton Bulletin,* Oct. 3, 1944; Proceedings of UPWA District 10 conference, June, 1946; *Montreal Star,* July 9, 1945.
16. Jamieson, p. 280.
17. Records of the Department of Labour, vol. 433, file 408, Public Archives of Canada.
18. Industrial Federation of Labour of Alberta, Proceedings of the 1954 and 1955 Conventions, Alberta Archives.
19. Alberta, *The Alberta Story* (Edmonton: Department of Economic Affairs, 1952), p. 50, Political Pamphlet Collection, Glenbow Archives, Calgary.
20. Warren Caragata, Interview with Neil Reimer, 1977, Alberta Archives.
21. CLC Papers, vol. 93, Public Archives of Canada.
22. Ibid., vol. 73, 132.
23. Ibid., vol. 32.
24. OCAW (Oil, Chemical and Atomic Workers), Certifications File, Local 630, OCAW National Office, Edmonton.
25. Harvey O'Connor, *History of Oil Workers International Union (CIO)* (Denver: Oil Workers International Union, 1950), p. 151.
26. File LR 807, Alberta Board of Industrial Relations, Edmonton.
27. Warren Caragata, Interview with Neil Reimer, 1978, Alberta Archives.
28. OCAW, Certifications File, Husky Oil, Excelsior Oil, North Star Oil, Wainwright Producers and Refiners, OCAW National Office, Edmonton.
29. Industrial Federation of Labour of Alberta, Proceedings of the 1955 Convention, Alberta Archives; Alberta Federation of Labour, Proceedings of the 1954 Convention, Department of Labour Library.
30. CLC Papers, vol. 132, Public Archives of Canada.
31. Ibid.
32. Ibid.
33. Ibid., vol. 154.
34. Industrial Federation of Labour of Alberta, Proceedings of the 1949 (1st Annual) Convention, Alberta Archives.
35. *Calgary Herald,* Jan. 11, 1949.
36. CLC Papers, vol. 154, Public Archives of Canada.
37. *Calgary Albertan,* Jan. 12, 1949.
38. CLC Papers, vol. 132, Public Archives of Canada; *Calgary Herald,* July 14, 1951.
39. *Calgary Herald,* Feb. 17, 1951, Mar. 3, 1951.
40. CLC Papers, vol. 154, Public Archives of Canada.
41. Alberta Federation of Labour, Proceedings of the 1954 Convention, Department of Labour Library.
42. Records of the Department of Labour, vols. 456, 457, files 154, 157, Public Archives of Canada.
43. CLC Papers, vol. 154, Public Archives of Canada.
44. Alberta Federation of Labour, Proceedings of the 1948 Convention, Department of Labour Library.
45. Alberta Federation of Labour-Industrial Federation of Labour of Alberta, Programme of Merger Convention, 1956, Alberta Archives.
46. Records of the Department of Labour, vol. 505, Public Archives of Canada.

Index

War Labour Board, 132
War Measures Act, 66, 68
Wartime Elections Act, 60
Watson, Sgt. Ed., 105
Western Canada Coal Operators
    Association, 36, 37
Western Federation of Miners, 14, 18,
    19, 112, 137. *See also* Mine-Mill
Western International Brotherhood of
    Railway Clerks, Storemen and
    Freighthandlers, 66
Western Labour Conference, Calgary,
    1919, 71, 72
Western Labour Union, 18
Wheatley, Frank, 71, 78, 92, 111, 114
White collar workers, 144
White, Fred, 26, 102, 108, 120, 123
Winnipeg Labour Council, 13, 67
Wobblies. *See* Industrial Workers of the
    World
Wood, S.T., 109, 110
Woodsworth, J.S., 102, 110
Worker, The, 93
Worker's Compensation Board, 93
Workers International Relief, 114, 117
Workers Unity League, 110–112, 117,
    119, 125
Working class, 82
Working conditions, 3, 5–9, 15–18, 22,
    23, 31, 32, 37–41, 77, 84, 85, 88, 112,
    126–128, 141, 145. *See also* Cost of
    living; Living conditions; Navvies;
    Wages
Working condition, Inspection, 32
Wroughton, T.A., 86

Yellow-dog contracts, 37
Youschok, Pete, 18, 32, 97, 102, 111,
    112, 114, 122
Yugoslavs, 39

Zaneth, F.W., 68